# ALTERNATIVE COMEDY

CULTURAL HISTORIES OF THEATRE AND PERFORMANCE

The Bloomsbury series of *Cultural Histories of Theatre and Performance* recognizes that historical knowledge has always been contested and revised. Since the turn of the twenty-first century, the transformation of conventional understandings of culture created through new political realities and communication technologies, together with paradigm shifts in anthropology, psychology and other cognate fields, has challenged established methodologies and ways of thinking about how we do history. The series embraces volumes that take on those challenges, while enlarging notions of theatre and performance through the representation of the lived experience of past performance makers and spectators. The series' aim is to be both inclusive and expansive, including studies on topics that range temporally and spatially, from the locally specific to the intercultural and transnational.

*Series editors*:
Claire Cochrane (University of Worcester, UK)
Bruce McConachie (University of Pittsburgh, USA)

GEORGE FARQUHAR: A MIGRANT LIFE REVERSED
*David Roberts*

THE POLISH THEATRE OF THE HOLOCAUST
*Grzegorz Niziołek*

A CENTURY OF SOUTH AFRICAN THEATRE
*Loren Kruger*

SOVIET THEATRE DURING THE THAW: RETURN OF THE AVANT-GARDE
*Jesse Gardiner*

# ALTERNATIVE COMEDY

## 1979 AND THE REINVENTION OF BRITISH STAND-UP

*Oliver Double*

*methuen* | drama
LONDON · NEW YORK · OXFORD · NEW DELHI · SYDNEY

METHUEN DRAMA
Bloomsbury Publishing Plc
50 Bedford Square, London, WC1B 3DP, UK
1385 Broadway, New York, NY 10018, USA
29 Earlsfort Terrace, Dublin 2, Ireland

BLOOMSBURY, METHUEN DRAMA and the Methuen Drama logo are trademarks of Bloomsbury Publishing Plc

First published in Great Britain 2020
This paperback edition published in 2021

Copyright © Oliver Double, 2020

Oliver Double has asserted his right under the Copyright, Designs and Patents Act, 1988, to be identified as the author of this work.

For legal purposes the Acknowledgements on pp. viii–ix constitute an extension of this copyright page.

Series design by Adriana Brioso
Cover images © British Stand-Up Comedy Archive

All rights reserved. No part of this publication may be reproduced or transmitted in any form or by any means, electronic or mechanical, including photocopying, recording, or any information storage or retrieval system, without prior permission in writing from the publishers.

Bloomsbury Publishing Plc does not have any control over, or responsibility for, any third-party websites referred to or in this book. All internet addresses given in this book were correct at the time of going to press. The author and publisher regret any inconvenience caused if addresses have changed or sites have ceased to exist, but can accept no responsibility for any such changes.

A catalogue record for this book is available from the British Library.

A catalog record for this book is available from the Library of Congress.

ISBN: HB: 978-1-3500-5280-2
PB: 978-1-3502-3948-7
ePDF: 978-1-3500-5282-6
eBook: 978-1-3500-5281-9

Series: Cultural Histories of Theatre and Performance

Typeset by RefineCatch Limited, Bungay, Suffolk

To find out more about our authors and books visit www.bloomsbury.com and sign up for our newsletters.

*For Jeremy Hardy and Linda Smith*

# CONTENTS

| | |
|---|---|
| Acknowledgements | viii |
| Introduction | 1 |
| UK 1979 | 9 |

## Part One  History of Early Alternative Comedy

| | | |
|---|---|---|
| 1 | Prehistory: Influences and Origins | 15 |
| 2 | The Beginnings of Alternative Comedy | 37 |
| 3 | The Spread of the Circuit | 62 |

## Part Two  Alternative Comedy Performance

| | | |
|---|---|---|
| 4 | 'Bits of Me Haven't Been Finished Yet': Reinventing Stand-Up from Scratch | 85 |
| 5 | 'Anti-Matter Comedy': Stylistic Innovation | 95 |
| 6 | 'Advanced Social Thinkers': Persona and Perspective | 118 |
| 7 | 'Comedy of Direct Confrontation': Relating to Audiences | 140 |
| 8 | 'I Tell Jokes Which Precipitate the Downfall of Capitalist Society': Politics | 163 |

## Part Three  Legacy of Alternative Comedy

| | | |
|---|---|---|
| 9 | Alternative Comedy Now | 191 |

| | |
|---|---|
| Notes | 204 |
| References | 207 |
| Index | 218 |

# ACKNOWLEDGEMENTS

The author and publishers wish to thank the following for permission to use the images used on the cover illustration:

- Alternative Cabaret flyer: Alexei Sayle (designer) and Andy de la Tour (donator).
- Pentameters poster: Nigel Planer (designer) and Arnold Brown (donator).
- Meccano Club poster: Lucinda Denning (designer) and Monika Bobinska (donator).
- CAST New Variety poster: Roland and Claire Muldoon (for CAST) and Warren Lakin (donator).

I'd like to thank everybody who has helped me in putting this book together – and there are a lot of them to thank. I'll start with Monika Bobinska and Andy de la Tour, whose donations of material to the British Stand-Up Comedy Archive (BSUCA) inspired the whole project, as well as other key donators whose material has been invaluable to my research: Tony Allen, Jim Barclay, Arnold Brown, Ivor Dembina, and JJ Waller. I would also like to thank Elspeth Millar, Karen Brayshaw, Jo Baines and everybody in the Special Collections and Archives team at the University of Kent, who have been so helpful in helping me to access material held in BSUCA.

Many thanks to those veterans of the 1980s alternative cabaret scene who were kind enough to let me interview them: Tony Allen; Andrew Bailey; Jim Barclay; Monika Bobinska; Arnold Brown; Olly Crick; Kevin Day; Andy de la Tour; Ivor Dembina; Lucinda Denning; John Dowie; Jenny Eclair; Ben Elton; Ellie Gibson; Peter Grahame; Steve Gribbin; Jeremy Hardy; John Hegley; Charlie Holland; Mark Hurst (AKA Mark Miwurdz); Jenny Lecoat; Norman Lovett; Maria McErlane (AKA Maria Callous); Pauline Melville; Paul Merton; Roland Muldoon; Joe Norris; Bernard Padden; Nigel Planer and Roberta Green; Nick Revell; Peter Rosengard; Ian Saville; Alexei and Linda Sayle; Maggie Steed; Mark Steel; Mark Thomas; JJ Waller; and Don Ward. I should also thank people who helped me set some of these interviews:

## Acknowledgements

Dave Thompson (for Ben Elton); Arnold Brown (for Peter Rosengard and Norman Lovett); Tracy Bohan (for Pauline Melville); Mandy Ward (for Paul Merton); and Belzy Day (for Maggie Steed).

Thanks are due to my old friend Sian Roderick for Welsh translation. I'm very grateful to the University of Kent for giving me study leave so that I had time to write the book. I would also like to thank all at Methuen Drama, particularly Mark Dudgeon, Lara Bateman, Claire Cochrane and Bruce McConachie.

Finally, thanks to my wife Jacqui and my sons Joe and Tom for general excellence and hilarity.

# INTRODUCTION

I should start by declaring an interest. I've been interested in alternative comedy since I was at school. A friend told me about a programme he'd seen which turned out to have been *Boom Boom Out Go the Lights*, the first TV showcase for this new type of comedy. Later, I became a fan of *The Young Ones* when its first series was broadcast in late 1982. I enjoyed watching Ben Elton's stand-up routines on a BBC2 youth programme called *Oxford Road Show*, and pored over a *Sunday Times* interview with Rik Mayall, which gave me the first hint that Mayall and *The Young Ones* were part of something bigger. The new breed of performers even had a name, the article referring to them as 'alternative comedians' (Pile 1983: 32).

At university, my interest grew with the second series of *The Young Ones* and the first of Channel 4's *Saturday Live*. An anarcho-feminist friend told me about a Tony Allen stand-up gig she'd seen at the Guild of students, and shortly after graduating I had my first live encounter with alternative comedy when I saw Ben Elton at the University of Exeter's Great Hall on 24 November 1986, a date on his first solo tour. As a student I also started moving from fan to performer, taking my first steps onstage as a comedian in a termly event called Chaotic Cabaret, before moving on to non-student venues like Barts Tavern and the newly-opened Exeter Arts Centre. This continued in Sheffield as a postgraduate, where I started a collective of performers called Red Grape Cabaret.

After I finished my PhD, like many others on the alternative cabaret circuit, I started out as a professional comedian on the Enterprise Allowance Scheme, a government initiative which gave a small weekly income to new businesses. Shortly after I finished on this, I helped to set up the Last Laugh, a weekly comedy club based in a pub in the Hunters Bar area of Sheffield, which I compèred and co-ran for five years. By this point I was getting regular work as both a solo comic and a member of Red Grape Cabaret.

In 1993, we were successful enough for *The Guardian* to review us at Hemel Hempstead: 'Whoever it was that wrote off Alternative Comedy, they forgot to tell Red Grape Cabaret … Their anarchic performance style disrupts the normal patterns of joke telling – not pretty, but always invigorating. If only more comics were as concerned with challenging conventional formats, rather than duplicating winning formulae.' I was described as 'the most unusual for the trio', and the review concluded by quoting one of my 'subtler observations': 'We're never going to fuck the system ... unless we all work together' (Cook 1993).

We were being praised for upholding the values of alternative comedy, and what the reviewer picks out are the qualities that have often been claimed for it: disrupting normal joke patterns, challenging conventional formats, and jokily threatening to fuck the system. In short, it was supposed to subvert the status quo both artistically and politically.

Having declared an interest, I'll admit that my aim here is to celebrate alternative comedy and argue that it did both of those things. In my view, it represented a radical reinvention of the form of stand-up in the UK, and the roots of the current British comedy scene can be traced back to the 1980s when it first rose up to challenge what had come before. Other views are, of course, available.

## 'Alternative and unfunny'

Recent scholarship has often been far more critical, questioning the achievements of alternative comedy. In 2016, Gavin Schaffer wrote an article in which he challenges 'the idea of 1979 as a new dawn for British comedy' (397), arguing that 'the impacts of radical alternative material were limited and ambiguous' (374) and that alternative comedy could even be seen as 'a manifestation of Thatcherite hegemony' (376). In 2013, Lloyd Peters – who had been in an early incarnation of Rik Mayall and Ade Edmondson's 20th Century Coyote – contended that 'most performers' in the early scene 'were quite conservative (small "c") in content and form' (6).

Going further back, in his influential 2007 book *A National Joke*, Andy Medhurst confessed that in choosing his examples, 'I spared myself the masochistic chore of grappling with comedy that makes no substantial inroads into my own laughter ... Thus you will look in vain for extended considerations of ... the "alternative comedy" of the 1980s' (7). A decade earlier, Howard Jacobson was similarly sniffy: 'It wasn't many years ago that comedians calling themselves "alternative" would turn up on chat-show sofas fulminating against mother-in-law jokes. There must be no sexism, grated Ben Elton, the first of the anti-comedic red-brick ranters' (1997: 173–4).

## Introduction

Such attitudes have been around almost as long as alternative comedy itself. In November 1981, Andy de la Tour launched Comedy Cabaret, filling the vacuum left by the recently departed Comic Strip in the Raymond Revuebar's Boulevard Theatre. De la Tour was the compère, and resident acts Ben Elton and Combo Passé were joined by guests like Keith Allen and Skirted Issue for twice nightly shows on Fridays and Saturdays. Peter Hepple's review was titled 'Alternative and unfunny' and scathingly suggested that '"alternative" on this occasion merely means not as polished, not as funny and not as good as an evening in an ordinary social club' (1981). By December, Comedy Cabaret had closed after playing to only 45 per cent capacity. According to *The Stage*, it was 'defeated by a combination of bad weather and rising overheads' (Petty 1981b).

Even though the venture failed due to a specific set of circumstances, that didn't stop the same newspaper publishing an editorial entitled 'Only an alternative to the real thing', which begins, 'The apparent collapse of "alternative" comedy in the West End is another example of the dangers of sticking an elitist label on something and converting what should be a spontaneous art form – for want of a better word – into a passing fashion ... Our experience of alternative cabaret has been that it is neither as good nor as professional as the mainstream variety' (*Stage* 1981a).

De la Tour's vigorous response was published in the letters page a fortnight later. The full text of the letter is angrier, arguing that, 'One might expect a straight newspaper or magazine to elevate a single closure to the status of a portentious [*sic*] catastrophe if it makes better copy. For a trade journal to do so is simply irresponsible.' He gives five examples of alternative cabaret venues with 'regular packed houses' and claims there are a 'dozen or so' more. He argues that the 'professionals' with whom comedians like him have been unfavourably compared are 'simply joke-tellers who attempt neither to stretch the different forms of comedy nor to expand into subject matter beyond the myopia and prejudice of nagging wives, ugly mother in law and thick Irishmen.' He complains that, 'the very term "alternative" is most avidly perpetuated by journalists themselves more often than not as a useful stick with which to beat anyone who tries to break with convention' (BSUCA [British Stand-Up Comedy Archive]).

What this incident reveals is that opinions on alternative comedy have always been sharply divided. To supporters, it was a necessary reaction to the prejudice and lack of imagination of the comedy that immediately preceded it, explicitly aiming to expand the creative possibilities of form and content.

To detractors, it was conservative, unprofessional, unfunny, elitist, and its radical ambitions remained unfulfilled.

*The Stage*'s editorial was not an isolated example, but a symptom of a cultural divide between a showbusiness establishment feeling under threat and the alternatives who hoped to challenge it. Certainly, comedians with more traditional career paths were often scathing. Bobby Davro declared, 'I'll never laugh at Alexei Sayle in a million years. Most new comedy stars seem to be emerging in the Mayall and Co mould. Comedy today has gone a bit strange.' In the same article, Bob Monkhouse argued, 'There is a considerable puritan backlash in 1985 comedy ... Today a kind of humourlessness has crept into bureaucracy which says you can't do racial or sexist gags' (Barrow 1985). The comic actor Bill Pertwee was more scathing: 'I think much of it is filth. The new breed are frightened and lack confidence, and believe if they shock the audience they will get laughs ... I think the audience should walk out and those artists never employed again' (Green 1988).

There were even critical voices among those connected with alternative comedy. Eccentric musical comic Bob Flag, who appeared on the first night of the Comedy Store, recalled that after his initial involvement, 'I gave "Alternative Comedy" ... as wide a berth, as I had "decjays" and hypnotists' (2015: 66). Keith Allen – a pivotal figure in the scene for a short period – proclaimed, 'I was a founder member of Alternative Cabaret. Hated the name, thought it was rubbish. Their content, virtually all the time, is not "alternative" to me. The performance is exactly the same, the structure of the jokes is exactly the same' (Kohn 1981: 45).

Onstage, Pauline Melville joked, 'This is the Alternative Cabaret, which is the alternative to having a really good time somewhere else. [laughter]' (Alternative Cabaret 1981). On one level it's a simple self-deprecating joke, but it also wryly comments on the sniping aimed at the new comedians and sends up the term 'alternative' itself.

## '*Alternative* comedy, though?'

When I interviewed Comedy Store co-founder Peter Rosengard in 2017, he told me, 'I never invented the word "alternative comedy". I never even heard the word "alternative comedy". I mean I think the media did that.' This highlights the distaste for the term that exists on both sides of the cultural divide, and expresses the widespread belief that it was spawned by journalists. The truth of its origins are complicated, not least because this strand of

## Introduction

comedy is terminologically tangled. For example, Nick Revell recalls, 'We always used to call ourselves "alternative comedians" and talk about "alternative comedy" in conversation, but . . . it was often "alternative cabaret" for listings and so on' (2017).

The terms 'alternative comedy' and 'alternative cabaret' sprung into existence around the same time, and have often been used interchangeably. In this book, I'll treat them as synonymous, because being able to choose between the two will help me to avoid the grind of repetition. I'll also use the shortened form 'altcom' for reasons of both variety and brevity.

Alternative Cabaret was the first-coined term, being chosen as the name for a group of performers who had met at the Comedy Store and decided to start putting on their own shows. It probably first appeared in print on an iconic flyer (see front cover), which shows a stark black-and-white image of a crowd of people wearing gasmasks. At the bottom, in tiny letters, is a signature which reads 'A.S. 1979', revealing that it was designed by Alexei Sayle. It's not dated any more precisely than that, but the name appeared in listings as early as November 1979, when the group's fortnightly show at the Elgin pub appeared in *Time Out*'s 'Theatre: Fringe Shows & Events' section (1979a). Intriguingly, an even earlier show had been listed in September when the group appeared at the Pindar of Wakefield under the variant name 'Alternative Kabaret' (*Time Out* 1979b). Soon afterwards, the phrase started to appear in lower case to refer to the genre rather than the specific group, a review of Threepenny Theatre in March 1980 noting, 'Alexei Sayle and Bill Monks have put together a unique form of "alternative cabaret" for fringe venues' (*Stage* 1980a).

The first usage of 'alternative comedian' followed a few months later in August 1980, when a columnist mentioned Alexei Sayle and Tony Allen's appearance at the Edinburgh Fringe, referring to 'two alternative comedians [who] harangued the audience on drugs and allied matters' (Pile 1980). The following month, September 1980, saw 'alternative comedy' appear in print in a broadly positive review of the Comic Strip that complained about the re-use of familiar material: 'Alternative comedy is fine, but how about some alternative material?' (Petty 1981a).

The actual origin of the word 'alternative' being used in this way is less than straightforward. It's often been attributed to Tony Allen (Absalom 1981; Cook 2001: 16). Allen himself has written, 'Just for the record, and so that nobody has to ask me again, I can't ever remember coining the phrase "Alternative Comedian" or "Alternative Comedy"' (2002: 116). On the other hand, Martin Soan and Malcolm Hardee from comedy troupe the Greatest

Show on Legs have staked their claim on the term. In Soan's account, 'There's a very good-natured dispute between us and Tony Allen about the phrase Alternative Comedy ... He says that he coined it, and Malcolm and I insist that we coined it with the help of a landlord in Salcombe' (Cook 2001: 52). In his memoir, *I Stole Freddie Mercury's Birthday Cake*, Hardee wrote:

> I think the comedian Tony Allen is usually credited with coining the phrase, 'Alternative Cabaret'. But in 1978, years before the Comedy Store, the local yacht club at Salcombe in Devon was putting on mainstream acts and the landlord at the nearby Ferry Inn put a notice in the local paper advertising, 'Alternative Cabaret at the Ferry Inn' meaning an 'alternative' to the yacht club's cabaret. *That* was the first time the phrase was used, as far as I know.
>
> Hardee 1996: 89

No direct evidence has been put forward to support this claim, but in any case, even if the phrase was used in Salcombe in 1978, it wouldn't have carried the meaning that it would go on to have. The phrase 'alternative comedy' often provokes the question 'alternative to what?' There are many valid ways to answer that question, but 'the yacht club's cabaret' would not be one of them.

The journalist Andy Beckett provides a useful explanation of the word 'alternative' in his book *Promised You a Miracle*: 'In Britain in the early 1980s "alternative" was a loaded word. It was widely taken to mean left-wing, counter-cultural, rebellious, separate from the mainstream' (2016: 331). This was precisely the meaning that Tony Allen took when he chose the word. Speaking on a podcast in 2017, he recalls: 'I came from a sort of counterculture background. I was squatting at the time and I was an anarchist ... everything was "alternative" ... It was used as a sort of counterculture ... prefix to every sort of cultural thing, really. So it was just obvious that we called it Alternative Cabaret. That's what I called it' (HistComPod 2017a).

Allen remembers being steeped in the alternative culture: 'The area that I lived in, in Ladbroke Grove ... had everything you could imagine that makes up a community – there was an alternative version. So there [were] alternative medics, there were alternative shops, there were alternative anything you can name' (Allen 2016). In July 1979, at almost exactly the time he was forming Alternative Cabaret, he was involved in a protest by the West London Anti-Nuclear group against fuel waste from Bradwell and Sizewell being

## Introduction

transported through the capital. A report in *The Guardian* quoted his reasons for being involved: 'If the economy is run by the multi-nationals, you've got to have nuclear stations, because they are big industries. I certainly don't want that. I'm involved because I want to advocate an alternative life style' (Hebert 1979). In his book *Attitude*, he recollects that 'a bunch of my mates were editing the info-directory *Alternative London*, so that name was in my head when I booked our cabaret package to a promoter' (Allen 2002: 116).

This, then, is the original significance of the word when applied to comedy or cabaret. 'Alternative' meant being part of the counterculture and against the status quo. Being an alternative comedian was like being an alternative medic, running an alternative shop, or living an alternative lifestyle. Regardless of Hardee's and Soan's claims, it was Allen who first used the phrase Alternative Cabaret in this sense, and thus he is the originator of the term – whether he wants to be or not. The counterultural origins of the term also draw attention to the new movement's intention to oppose the values and structures of the comedy that immediately preceded it. This was explicitly stated in an article about the Comic Strip in the music paper *Melody Maker*: '*Alternative* comedy, though? Rik Mayall told me it was simply an attempt by young comedians to break away from racist, sexist and mother-in-law stereotypes. Or, as Sayle puts it: "[I]f you want to be really good, you've *got* to do something nobody'd done before"' (Humphries 1981).

### This book

Having stated my intention to argue for alternative comedy's achievements in reinventing the form of stand-up, I should explain how I intend to do this. In terms of scope, I'll be concentrating almost exclusively on live performance, discussing television only in terms of its impact in popularizing the new comic movement and as an occasional source of performance footage where necessary.

I'll be mainly concerned with the period 1979–90, which saw alternative comedy grow from its haphazard beginnings to a thriving sector of the entertainment industry, a well-established network of performers, venues and agencies. The first part of the book is historical, explaining exactly how this happened. There are chapters on influences and origins, key starting points of the new movement, and the spread of the circuit. The second part of the book focuses on how alternative comedy reinvented the form of stand-up. There are chapters on how the alternative comedians learned their craft, stylistic innovation, stage persona, interaction between performer and audience, and the politics of the scene. Finally, the book will conclude with an examination of altcom's legacy, and how it is reflected in today's comedy scene.

As we have seen, alternative comedy sharply divides opinion, and its history is surrounded by a fog of mythology. In order to try to see past this, I have tried to draw on as rich and detailed a research base as possible. This includes books, articles, journalism, and recordings of performances that have been broadcast or commercially released. I have drawn on my own collection of memorabilia, particularly a stack of 1980s music magazines, the rock press having been quick to catch on to altcom's existence. I have also drawn on a range of interviews, some conducted for earlier research projects, some taken from a podcast I make, and some carried out as events for a public audience. I have also conducted new interviews with nearly forty people involved in alternative comedy, from pivotal performers and well-known comedians to smaller acts now largely forgotten, and from agents to promoters who ran venues.

Crucially, much of the research is drawn from the British Stand-Up Comedy Archive, which (as its website explains) 'was established at the University of Kent in 2013 to celebrate, preserve, and provide access to the archives and records of British stand-up comedy and comedians'. BSUCA includes a varied and eclectic range of material, including publicity material, photographs, script notes, business records and – most usefully – unpublished audio and video performance footage. Alexei Sayle, Tony Allen, Andy de la Tour and Jim Barclay are among its donors. Some of the material even relates to my own experiences on the fringes of the alternative comedy circuit at the end of the 1980s.

This emphasizes the careful path I'm trying to tread in this book. On the one hand, I'm writing about something of which I had direct personal experience, even if only at the margins – hence starting by declaring an interest. On the other hand, I have used documentary evidence to bring in an element of objectivity. My aim is, as much as possible, to support my arguments with personal testimony from people involved in the alternative cabaret scene of the 1980s, and – crucially – the facts as recorded in historical documents from the time.

# UK 1979

In 1979, the UK was on the cusp of massive change – in both politics and comedy. On 3 May, Margaret Thatcher's Conservative Party was elected to Westminster, heralding the final death knell for the postwar consensus that had started with Clement Attlee's radical Labour government of 1945–51. Throughout the 1970s, Prime Ministers from both parties – Edward Heath for the Conservatives, Harold Wilson and James Callaghan for Labour – had been dealing with increasing economic problems and industrial unrest, culminating in the Winter of Discontent (1978–9).

Thatcher's government broke with the orthodoxy that preceded it, based on Keynesian economics, a strong welfare state, a mixed economy with major nationalized industries, toleration of strong trade unions, and relatively high taxation. Instead, it steamrollered forward with a monetarist agenda based on privatization, curbing the power of the unions, cutting taxes, rolling back the welfare state, and above all a chest-beating belief in the power of free market capitalism to solve all problems.

The initial effects were devastating for many. Having inherited an inflation rate of about 10 per cent and unemployment standing at around 1.5 million, inflation shot up to 22 per cent by 1980 (before falling very significantly over the subsequent years) and unemployment rose to 3 million by 1983. With poverty hitting inner city areas and feelings stoked among minority communities by racist policing tactics, April–June 1981 saw rioting in Brixton, Toxteth, Handsworth, Chapeltown and Moss Side, among other places. Nationalized industries were drastically slashed, devastating communities and leading to the miners' strike of 1984–5 – a highly divisive dispute, with violent clashes between pickets and police, ending in humiliating defeat for the National Union of Mineworkers.

One of the Thatcher government's answers to mass unemployment was the Enterprise Allowance Scheme. The concept was to allow people who were moonlighting while claiming benefits to come into the system, declaring their earnings and paying income tax and VAT. In order to qualify, candidates had to be between 18 and 65, have been jobless and claiming benefits for at least thirteen weeks, commit to working at least 36 hours a week on the business, and have access to £1,000 to invest – which could take the form of an overdraft agreement. In return, they would receive £40 per week for a year, to help them get established. The scheme was piloted for 18 months, and although nearly half of the businesses established had failed in that period, it was rolled out nationally in August 1983 (Beckett 2016: 210-14). When it was introduced, nobody could have anticipated that it would become a significant factor in the growth of alternative comedy.

Thatcherism also introduced a more aggressive foreign policy, with a significant ramping up of the Cold War as Britain bought Trident nuclear submarines and allowed American cruise missiles to be stationed at UK air bases. In 1982 Britain's war with Argentina over the Falkland Islands created stark divisions. On the one hand, the right-wing press created a tidal wave of jingoism, transforming Thatcher's political fortunes. *The Sun*'s front page on 4 May 1982 greeted the sinking of the Argentinian warship *General Belgrano* – at the cost of 323 lives – with a one-word headline: 'GOTCHA'. The country's economic woes, with over 3 million people unemployed, had made the Prime Minister an extremely unpopular figure, but the feverish patriotism unleashed by the Falklands War recast her as a national hero. As a *Daily Mail* opinion piece gleefully conjectured, 'The effect of Mrs Thatcher personally could prove profound. The episode looks like vindicating her and discrediting her rivals and critics ... her electoral position could well, within a short time, look almost unassailable. She may emerge not just as the Iron Maiden, but as Iron-clad and unsinkable' (Alexander 1982). This proved correct, as she went on to significantly increase her majority in the 1983 general election.

On the other hand, many on the left opposed the war as a sordid imperialist adventure, and abhorred the triumphalist propaganda spewed out by the popular press. Throughout the time Thatcher was in power the left offered significant resistance, and the early 1980s saw a surge in membership for the Campaign for Nuclear Disarmament reflecting genuine fears that nuclear war might become a reality, and the establishment of the women's Peace Camp at Greenham Common in 1981. Another sign of resistance was the election of a Labour Greater London Council led by Ken Livingstone in May 1981, its radical policies offering a beacon of hope for the left and a thorn in the side for Thatcher, until her government abolished it in 1986.

Meanwhile, pop music had been transformed by the emergence of punk in 1976, but comedy was still largely unreconstructed. In 1979, there were no comedy clubs in the UK, very few comedians performed the kind of autobiographical material which abounds today, and female stand-ups were almost completely unknown. John Fisher's book *Funny Way to Be a Hero*, published in 1973, dedicates just one of its twenty-six chapters to female comics – a chapter entitled 'Are Women Funny?' – and even then, almost half of it is dedicated to the male drag comedians Rex Jamieson and Danny La Rue. Although variety theatre had produced a number of brilliant and successful female comic performers in earlier decades, working men's clubs (WMC) had failed to do the same. Every one of the WMC comedians featured in the 1971 documentary *There Was This Fella . . .* is male. While not a single female comic appears in the show, by contrast there are two black comics (Charlie Williams, Sammy Thomas) and one more-or-less openly gay comedian (Jackie Carlton). This seems to have been an accurate snapshot of the WMC circuit in the 1970s, as the only female comedy star to emerge from it in that decade was Marti Caine – and even she was as much a singer as a stand-up. It was only in the 1980s that female comics like Pauline Daniels, Crissy Rock and Ellie Laine became stars of the WMC circuit. Racist and sexist gags were rife among club comics, and even innovative television comedies like *Monty Python's Flying Circus* and *The Goodies* contained attitudes towards women and ethnic minorities that would be questioned today.

In this context, the birth of alternative comedy in 1979 is as much a watershed as the election of Thatcher, a dividing line that challenged the previous orthodoxies in light entertainment as much as the Conservatives challenged them in politics – albeit taking things in opposite ideological directions. Unlike Thatcherism, altcom had no single figurehead, but a number of individuals played crucial roles. Alexei Sayle quickly marked himself out as the scene's breakout star, becoming well known on television before anybody else, with a style blazing with alternative comedy's special qualities – aggression, surrealism, metacomedy, left-wing politics, and a keen interest in the latest trends in youth culture. Tony Allen was never a household name, but became a kind of spiritual leader of the scene, promoting radical, anarchist ideas about what it should and shouldn't be. In his account, though, it was the outrageous liberties with form taken by his namesake Keith Allen that initially gave altcom its identity. Keith Allen had been an actor, and spent just a short time performing stand-up on the nascent circuit before going back to acting. In this sense, he was typical of the early alternative comedians. Other important figures like Andy de la Tour, Pauline Melville and Jim Barclay also came from and went back to acting, but nonetheless were important pioneers of this new style of comedy.

Alternative comedy's impact was not as immediate as that of the Tory government, but by 1982 it was a national phenomenon. On 2 November,

## Alternative Comedy

the opening night of Channel 4 featured the first episode of *The Comic Strip presents . . .* , a long-running series of comic films for television created by performers from one of altcom's most iconic early venues. Just a week later, the first episode of punk sitcom *The Young Ones* aired on BBC2, written by and starring key alternative comedians. It quickly became known as a classic cult comedy, capturing the imagination of young viewers just as punk had done in music.

This, then, was the UK in 1979 – a country on the brink of radical change in politics and comedy, the effects of which are still seen today.

# PART ONE
HISTORY OF EARLY ALTERNATIVE COMEDY

# CHAPTER 1
# PREHISTORY: INFLUENCES AND ORIGINS

In 1982 or 1983, *The Alexei Sayle Pirate Video* was released into the pre-certification home video market. Even Sayle cannot remember the precise release date or the circumstances of filming, but believes it was a performance at a Manchester music venue called the Gallery. It's a single-camera shoot with minimal edits, but it captures Sayle's act in full flow, boiling with silliness and comic ferocity. At one point, he mentions an American comedian of an earlier era: 'Di- difficult time for comedians though, the '50s, difficult time for comedians, the great, erm – the great *American* comedian, erm, Lenny Bruce, erm –' Suddenly, he snaps into an impersonation of an imaginary Mancunian comedian, screwing his face into a cartoon sneer and yelling in a pugnacious northern accent: 'Lenny Bruce, fuckin' came to Talk of the North, died on his fuckin' *aaarrrse!* [laughter] Fuckin' foul-mouthed fuckin' cunt-ah! [laughter] Don't you say fuck in front o' my wife, you fuckin' *bastaaaard!* [laughter, 4 seconds] He was crap, no jokes about fuckin' Pakis, *nothiiiiiing!* [laughter]' (Sayle ND).

Sayle adopts this cartoonish impersonation to parody the attitudes found in stand-up comedy in working men's clubs. Clearly, Lenny Bruce never actually played the Manchester venue Talk of the North – not strictly a WMC although essentially part of the same circuit – but if he had, he would have been seriously out of step with the comedians who did. Bruce was a comic icon, an improvizational taboo-breaker who shook the showbusiness establishment in the 1950s and 1960s, a drug-taking rebel who ran into trouble with the authorities for his unfettered language and scathing routines on such sensitive topics as racism and religion. In Sayle's flight of fancy, the imaginary northern comic despises him for his obscene language and his refusal to tell racist jokes about Pakistanis.

In giving voice to an imagined enemy, Sayle is shining a light onto the conditions that led to the outbreak of alternative comedy in 1979. His routine acts out a war between different types of comic. On the one hand, Lenny Bruce offered a model for the kind of stand-up that alternative comedy was striving to create. On the other, the comics who plied their trade in working

## Alternative Comedy

men's clubs represented everything the new breed wanted to avoid. This chapter is about the prehistory of alternative comedy, its influences and direct precursors. Among these, the stark contrast between Bruce's generation and the working men's club comedians was particularly important. To Sayle and his contemporaries, one represented the future, the other the past.

### 'Look across the Atlantic'

In 1981, when *The Stage* used the collapse of the Comedy Cabaret at the Boulevard Theatre to prophesy the imminent death of alternative comedy, it complained that 'the majority of its exponents have not studied comedy techniques in their natural habitat, the clubs and some theatres' (*Stage* 1981a). In his letter, Andy de la Tour responds:

> [I]nsofar as we have 'studied comedy techniques in their natural habitat' it has been infinitely more rewarding to look across the Atlantic at a whole generation of comedians (Richard Pryor, Steve Martin, Robin Williams et al) who, having started out with the alternative label pinned on them, would seem to have replaced the stand-up joke-tellers as the mainstream in comedy.
>
> De la Tour 1982

In looking across the Atlantic for inspiration, de la Tour recognized that the evolution of stand-up had happened at a different pace in America, and by the late 1970s its comedians were generations ahead of what was happening in WMCs in terms of both form and content.

In America, the evolutionary leap had happened decades beforehand, beginning in December 1953 when Mort Sahl first stepped onto the stage of the 'Hungry i' in San Francisco. Sahl was radically different from the comedians who preceded him. In his autobiography *Heartland*, he recalls that when he decided to become a stand-up he realized, 'I didn't have the equipment. I didn't have a tuxedo. You needed that in 1953, and a line of girls behind you' (1976: 12). A friend recommended he try the Hungry i, a bohemian venue frequented by hipsters. At first he got mixed responses there, but quickly developed a style that worked. Wearing a red pullover and an open-neck shirt, he often based his act on stories from a newspaper that he took onstage with him.

Material was fluid and improvised. As he put it, 'I've never written a syllable except on the stage ... because I don't know how to write it on a typewriter' (1976: 37). He often performed with jazz musicians, particularly Dave Brubeck, and shared with them the ability to create material in the moment. A *Time* article said that he 'takes off like a jazz musician on a flight of improvisation' and described how this shaped his material: 'He does not tell jokes one by one, but carefully builds deceptively miscellaneous structures of jokes that are like verbal mobiles. He begins with the spine of a subject, then hooks thought onto thought, joke onto dangling joke, many of them totally unrelated to the main theme, till the whole structure spins but somehow balances' (1960: 57). Sahl's material had the rhythms of everyday conversation, and came across as observations of the world rather than contrived jokes. As he put it, 'I acted like a human being and talked about those things that affect human beings, rather than talked like a nightclub comedian' (1976: 34).

Jazz informed the content as well as the form of his act. On his album *At Sunset*, recorded in 1955 at a concert with Brubeck, he talks about the sleeve designs of jazz albums:

> And then on the front they have this one guy who poses for most of the albums. And he's not a musician, but he has a – a peculiar type of talent which is in keeping – er, with jazz as a native American art. Eh, that is he has acne and he's thin. You [laughter into applause, 6 seconds, under which:] know one of those – you know that kinda guy?
>
> *Sahl 1958*

This is insider humour. To get the joke, the audience has to be familiar with jazz culture. By joking about jazz, Sahl is observing the world from the perspective of a young man then in his late twenties, and aligning himself with the youth culture of the time. This is not the mother-in-law comedy of an older generation, aiming instead at the laughter of the young and hip. Sahl was also openly political, joking that the papier maché ears of Mickey Mouse Club members were caused by mutations from nuclear testing (Sahl 1959), and sending up the House Un-American Activities Committee: 'Every time the Russians throw an American in jail, the committee throws an American in jail to get even' (*Time* 1960: 58).

Sahl was not alone in challenging the comic convention of an older generation. He noted that by 1957, 'a lot of comedians were coming out of the shadows, because I was showing them it wasn't as cold in the light as they feared' (1976: 37). In 1960, *Time* magazine argued that, 'The biggest symbol of Mort Sahl's success ... is the fact that he is the patriarch of a new school of comedians that has grown up with him' (60). Members of this new school were sometimes dubbed 'sick comedians' or 'sickniks', and they included Mike Nichols and Elaine May, Shelley Berman, Bob Newhart, Jonathan Winters, and – crucially – Lenny Bruce. An earlier *Time* article described their style: 'What the sickniks dispense is partly social criticism liberally laced with cyanide, partly a Charles Addams kind of jolly ghoulishness, and partly a personal and highly disturbing hostility toward all the world' (1959: 42).

As with alternative comedy, more traditional comedians tried to undermine the sickniks by questioning their competence. Joey Bishop bitterly suggested: 'Those guys tried their hardest to make it our way; when they couldn't, they switched' (*Time* 1959: 44). Such sniping was in vain. The sickniks broke the mould of American stand-up and reshaped it in their own image. The more personal, conversational approach largely replaced the traditional gag-based style, and comics like Richard Pryor, Steve Martin and Robin Williams – cited as influences by de la Tour in his riposte to *The Stage* – were the inheritors of the style of comedy pioneered by Sahl. Moreover, by the 1970s a network of dedicated comedy clubs had grown up across America, when such venues were still unknown in the UK.

The most frequently mentioned influence on alternative comedy was not Sahl, but Bruce – as Sayle's gag imagining him performing at Talk of the North might suggest. An early article about Tony Allen compared him with Bruce (Brazil 1979), and Allen later acknowledged that when he first started doing stand-up, the Bruce influence was all too obvious: 'I'm also having problems with the ghost of Lenny Bruce ... It's his voice. It's in my default mode. I've not actually said anything of his yet, but I know it's there, I can hear the albums' (2002: 81). Like Sayle, Allen also joked about Bruce, in one of his most frequently quoted early jokes. This version is from an unpublished recording of Allen compering at the Comedy Store in around September 1980: 'And then I thought, "Tone," I thought – "Lenny Bruce, he finished his career out of his head on drugs, hassled by the police, and dying in a toilet. And that's how you're starting off" [laughter]' (BSUCA).

Although his double act the Outer Limits was very different from Allen's stand-up, Nigel Planer also acknowledges Bruce's influence: 'I'd never been to a working men's club ... Whereas I did know Lenny Bruce's albums' (Planer 2018). Similarly, Nick Revell recalls: 'I'd stumbled across a Lenny Bruce album called *The Law, Language and Lenny Bruce*, which I found in the Woolworth's in Pontefract . . . in about . . . 1974–75 . . . it was completely different to any stand-up I'd encountered' (2017).

This starts to answer the question of how the more evolved form of stand-up comedy managed to cross the Atlantic to influence alternative comedy. The sickniks owed some of their success to the rise of the comedy album, and many of the records they made were big hits. Shelley Berman won a Grammy in 1959, and the following year Bob Newhart's debut album became the first comedy record to reach number one in the Billboard charts. The fact that Lenny Bruce made LPs allowed his influence to spread far beyond those who managed to see him live, introducing his work to anyone from Tony Allen in Ladbroke Grove to Nick Revell in Pontefract.

Bruce's influence has been widely acknowledged by previous histories of alternative comedy, but many of my interviewees also mentioned Richard Pryor. Pryor was a pivotal figure in the development of African-American comedy, often said to be one of the greatest stand-ups of all time. Like Bruce, Pryor made LPs, but his stand-up concert films seem to have made the biggest impact. Andy de la Tour has written of the impact of seeing his concert film *Live on the Sunset Strip* in a Harlem cinema on a trip to America in 1982 (2013: 66-7), but probably the most important influence on the development of alternative comedy was *Richard Pryor: Live in Concert*, widely recognized as his finest work. Released in the USA in 1979, it arrived in UK cinemas in March 1980, when the alternative comedy scene was less than a year old. Nick Revell recalls that when 'the Richard Pryor first stand-up movie came out [it] just blew me away' (2017). For Mark Steel, *Live in Concert* challenged his expectations of what stand-up was: 'It confused me 'cos I didn't really know what it was . . . At that point we thought comedians were people who just told jokes' (2018). At a performance at the Elgin in Ladbroke Grove on 10 April 1980, Tony Allen even discussed the film onstage, criticizing it politically before confessing: 'And the other thing about that, a third thing I thought about that film, I was sitting there *outrageously jealous*'cos I thought he was very funny as well [laughter]' (BSUCA). Clearly, Pryor's technical mastery offered a standard for the alternative comedians to aim for.

## 'Chubby blokes in their frilly shirts'

While America reinvented stand-up as early as the 1950s, in 1979 Britain was still waiting for a similar evolutionary leap. One of the most important conditions that led to the creation of altcom was the state of British stand-up at the time. In the 1970s, the vast majority of comics developed their acts in working men's clubs or related privately owned venues like Talk of the North. The comedy found in such clubs was an important negative influence, and many involved in the early altcom circuit have talked about the importance of what their type of comedy was determinedly not.

In his entertaining memoir, Arthur Smith wrote, 'I felt no affinity with these chubby blokes in their frilly shirts and glittering jackets, slickly marching their jokes by in single file' (2009: 143–4). Nick Revell recalls: 'Technically, that northern club tradition never really appealed to me generally. Because you knew ... it wasn't their material. And that's the crucial thing as well, I suppose – doing your own material' (Revell 2017). Others point the finger at the prejudice found among club comics. Norman Lovett argues that 'the main thing' about altcom was 'it was anti Bernard Manning. It was anti all the sexist comedians. Jim Davidson, especially' (Lovett 2018). Some of the early pioneers even went out into working men's clubs to see the comedy that went on there for themselves. Tony Allen has recalled that, 'When I actually took the time out in 'seventy-eight and early 'seventy-nine to go round and see traditional comedians working, I realized that what was on the television was a really watered-down version of what they were doing onstage, and what they were doing onstage was horrendous' (Cook 2001: 321–2).

Revell's accusation that WMC comics were unoriginal is absolutely right. The gags they told were packaged gags, based on well-established formulas. Jokes were seen as common property, and there was no expectation that comedians should write their own material. A book based on Granada's series published in 1972, *Laugh with the Comedians*, reveals that, 'On the first three TV tapings of *The Comedians*, Ken [Goodwin] found himself going on last. He sat in the studio and heard all the other comics before him. "I had my list of jokes. So every time I heard one of mine told, I had to cross it off. I was adding and subtracting all the time"' (Irwin 1972: 31).

In 1968, WMC comic John Paul Joans wrote an article for *The Stage* criticizing the unoriginality of other comedians he worked with: 'Many of our performers ... persist in following the patterns of comedians of earlier decades who were content to relate jokes about fat ladies, drunks, mothers-in-law and the like. To quote a cleaning lady in an office: "Most of the time we sit there and finish the jokes with them. We've heard it all before."' A 1971 documentary captures Joans arguing with Bernard Manning, complaining that there's 'not one bit of originality' in WMC comedians and demanding, 'Let them be themselves and not carbon copies of each other.' It also includes footage of Manning performing at his own venue, the Embassy Club: 'Fella walked into the doctor's, he said, "Nobody'll talk to me," the doctor said, "Next!" [laughter] Fella walked into a psychiatrist's. [laughter] Said, "My brother thinks he's an orange," he says, "Where is he?" he says, "In me pocket, 'ere." [laughter]' (*There Was This Fella . . .*).

Gags like these show just how different WMC comedy was from post-Sahl American stand-up. There's no need to have heard them before to sense that these are old jokes, untouched by the spark of individual creativity. The form they take and the situations they describe clearly signal that these are jokes, rather than descriptions of actual lived experiences. The gags are disconnected from the performer – they are about an anonymous 'fella' rather than Manning – and there's no attempt to express a personal opinion or offer a social or political critique.

On the other hand, club comedians did express broadly held beliefs – or more accurately prejudices – in their material. As Ken Irwin puts it in *Laugh with the Comedians*, 'They joke about false teeth and parrots and homosexuals virtually in the same breath. They joke about Catholics and Protestants. They joke about Pakistanis, the Irish and the Jews' (1972: 16). The 1971 documentary gives a flavour of the kind of prejudices on offer in a clip of George Roper playing the Embassy Club: 'And me uncle's got a new job now, he's in the IRA. He's a – rear gunner on a milk float. [laughter] You see what they're doing in Northern Ireland with all the Pakistanis? Melting them down and making rubber bullets out of them. [laughter]' (*There Was This Fella . . .*).

This is by no means the most racist example of 1970s club comedy, but in two short gags it manages to stereotype the Irish – playing on the idea that they are terrorists rather than the more usual ploy of suggesting they are mentally defective – and dehumanizes Pakistanis in a comic image that hints at the violence of some of the more extreme gags found on the WMC circuit. It was this kind of thing that Rik Mayall had in mind when he told *Melody Maker* that alternative comedy was about breaking away from 'racist, sexist and mother-in-law stereotypes'.

To be fair, some club comedians went beyond such prejudice and stylistic rigidity, attempting a more challenging approach. Perhaps the best example is John Paul Joans. Starting life as Reginald John Davidge, his career began in the mid-1950s when he worked as an all-round entertainer under the name Reg Gray. By 1968, he had become a stand-up comic under the name John Paul Joans, and enjoyed a successful career until 1977, when he was hit by a Land Rover during a trip to Northern Ireland to support the peace movement, sustaining serious injuries.

### Alternative Comedy

A 1970 review suggests that Joans was both unconventional and popular with audiences: '"CONTROVERSIAL" is a label that has been attached to several artists – none more so than John Paul Joans. However, from the very start I would like to emphasize that, in this case, I use the word controversial very much of a compliment. This Joans fella completely slayed them at Batley the other week' (Towler 1970). Footage in the 1971 documentary shows just what an unconventional club comic Joans was. In place of the usual suit-and-tie or tuxedo-and-dickie-bow, he has a shoulder-length Brian Jones haircut, and wears an orange shirt, a kipper tie, and a long hippie waistcoat. In spite of being slightly too old for it, it's a look that identifies him with the fashion and pop of the early 1970s, and indeed his single 'The Man from Nazareth' got to number 25 in December 1970.

His material is as unconventional as his look. Instead of reeling off a series of packaged jokes, he presents the audience with a flow of comic ideas, interacting with them, improvizing, addressing individual punters – often singling out the younger ones – and playing with their responses:

> There are far worse words than *titty!* [a few laughs] Most people think the worst four-letter word in the world – is to do with copulation, it's not, sirrrr! Copulation is a beautiful thiiing. Ain't it? Right! The worst four-letter word in the world, ma'm, for me – is the word "bomb". A dirty, filthy, nasty, obscene thing, would you agree? Yes! Now which would you rather hold in your hand, sir, a live bomb or a live tit, eh? [laughter and applause]
>
> 'There Was This Fella ...

The questioning of what constitutes obscenity and the abhorrence of war are more Lenny Bruce than Bernard Manning. Indeed, Manning can be heard offstage commenting 'What a load of rubbish!' However, Joans was an anomaly, a lone voice in the wilderness. Unlike Sahl, no others followed in his wake to really challenge the norms of WMC comedy. As a result, before alternative comedy, British stand-up was largely stuck in a swamp of shared standard gags and lumpen prejudice.

### 'So much more erudite than Bernard Manning'

It would be simplistic to think that the negative influence of WMC comedy and the positive influence of post-Sahl American stand-up were all that

## Prehistory: Influences and Origins

went into the creation of altcom. The alternative comedians also looked closer to home, taking inspiration from the comedy produced by performers who had cut their teeth with the Cambridge Footlights and the Oxford Revue. The impact of *Monty Python's Flying Circus* (1969–74) has been acknowledged by a number of key figures from the alternative cabaret circuit of the 1980s, including Rik Mayall, Nigel Planer, Nick Revell, Paul Merton and Arthur Smith. Alexei Sayle recalls:

> [Monty Python] was massively influential … Particularly … that routine that Eric Idle does about Watney's Red Barrel. … Without taking a breath, that long monologue. And I just thought, 'Fuck! That's really something,' you know. The attack of it. But also the kind of subject matter and also the … delivery and stuff … I remember being very struck by that. And then also obviously … the mixture of using philosophy and, you know, the range of references, which was so much more erudite than Bernard Manning.
>
> *Sayle 2017*

There's a clear similarity between the Eric Idle sketch Sayle references here (*Monty Python's Flying Circus*, 1972) and the furious comic rants he would go on to create – including his northern-comic-laying-into-Lenny-Bruce routine. The feeling that Python had raised the intellectual bar for popular comedy is also important, as is its taste for the surreal.

The Oxbridge revue tradition also produced Peter Cook and Dudley Moore who created the foul-mouthed alter egos Derek and Clive in the 1970s. For Mark Steel, they were 'astonishing' because 'no-one was used to swearing' (2018). Derek and Clive's use of obscene language was more gleefully excessive that Lenny Bruce's. The track 'This Bloke Came Up To Me' on their debut album *Derek and Clive (Live)* is an excellent example. This comprises three minutes thirty-one seconds of expletives, the most frequent being 'fuck' or 'fucking'. The premise of the bit is that 'a bloke' has come up to Derek and called him a 'cunt'. The first one minute forty-eight seconds of the track are devoted to debating this situation, and most of the swearing occurs here. To give an idea of the heroic level of bad language, over the track as a whole the pair say the word 'cunt' thirty-five times, an average of once every six seconds. The flavour of the bit can be conveyed with a single line uttered by Dudley Moore as Derek: 'I said, "You cunt!" I said, "You fucking cunt!" I said, "Who're you fucking calling cunt, cunt?"' (Cook and Moore 1976).

## Alternative Comedy

Monty Python and Derek and Clive were obvious influences, but initially the alternative comedians distanced themselves from the Oxbridge revue tradition. The Comic Strip's Peter Richardson told the *Sunday Times Magazine*, 'We're not a group like the Pythons... What we're doing... is intelligent comedy by people who didn't go to university' (1981). When I ask Nick Revell whether having been a member of the Oxford Revue was a problem for him when he first started on the circuit in 1980, he says, 'It wasn't a problem, because I didn't tell anybody. And why would you?' (2017).

In spite of Richardson's statement, key members of the Comic Strip had, in fact, been to university. Indeed, Rik Mayall and Ade Edmondson's double act 20th Century Coyote grew out of a comedy troupe of the same name formed by drama students at the University of Manchester in 1976. Fellow founder member Lloyd Peters has written a detailed account of the troupe's early performances at the Band on the Wall music venue, arguing that the early 20th Century Coyote shows were 'an antidote to the Cambridge Footlights... relying more on vague parodies or grotesque caricature rather than well-constructed sharp political or social satire' (2013: 10) and describing their style as a 'curious comedy sub-genre – a complex and original mix of extended sketches, improvisatory routines, direct audience address, monologues – a grotesque, slapstick sit-com for the stage' (17). Given the later success of Mayall and Edmondson's double act, the significance of the Manchester University drama department should not be overlooked, particularly given that Ben Elton was also a student there at around the same time.

### 'Neither a stand-up comic nor a stage-Scot'

Neither Python, Derek and Clive, nor 20th Century Coyote were working within the form of stand-up comedy, but there were some stand-ups in the 1970s who were challenging the gag-based conservatism of the working men's club comics. A thriving circuit of folk clubs spawned a small group of singers like Billy Connolly, Jasper Carrott, Mike Harding, Max Boyce, and Mike Elliott, who began to expand the comic patter between the songs until it became the main focus of their acts, effectively turning them into stand-ups. Some of the acts who went on to work the alternative cabaret circuit had themselves performed in folk clubs. Tony Allen had compèred and been a 'token poet' at his local folk club in Hayes (Allen 2002: 74), Earl Okin edited his act down from the two half-hour sets he performed on the folk circuit (Okin 2017), and Jenny Lecoat was only sixteen when she started singing in folk clubs on Jersey, where she grew up (Lecoat 2018).

Carrott and Connolly in particular have been widely acknowledged as influences by early alternative comedians. For Alexei Sayle, Jasper Carrott was the 'most influential', because 'he had a show which was only on London Weekend Television ... in which he did anecdotal comedy. And I remember being quite taken with that ... because it was anecdotal and stuff, to still be aware that he was [going] to open up possibilities' (Sayle 2017). The series in question was LWT's *An Audience with Jasper Carrott*, originally broadcast between January and March 1978. The third episode ends with Carrott lurching into a rant about Monty Python, in which he adopts the attitude of somebody who supposedly hates the programme but can't stop talking about it. As the rant progresses, he wanders off the stage to confront the audience directly, barks some of his comic complaints directly at individual punters and even gets tangled up with the TV cameras. Towards the end, he paraphrases Eric Idle's 'Watney's Red Barrel' rant cited by Sayle as a particular influence. Whether or not Sayle saw this episode at the time, its aggression and confrontation anticipate performance strategies that would be explored by alternative comedians.

Carrott and Connolly also foreshadowed altcom in relying more on anecdotes than packaged gags. Connolly told *The Guardian*: 'I like patter. I don't like jokes' (Mackie 1974). This apparent distaste for straightforward jokes meant some journalists found him hard to pigeonhole. In *The Observer*, John Heilpern said Connolly was, 'Neither a stand-up comic nor a stage-Scot with kilt and sporran', but his act was 'rooted in working-class Glasgow, in gang cultures, raw childhood memories, and near-blasphemy' (1979). Connolly wove vivid anecdotal tapestries from the experiences of working-class Glaswegian life that he shared with his core audience. A routine called 'Oh Dear' from his LP *Live!* (1972) recalls having to use the outside toilets in a tenement building as a young child, and 'A Wee Swearie' on *Get Right Intae Him* (1975) features closely-observed impersonations of drunks hanging around in George Square. Meanwhile 'near blasphemy' can be found on *Solo Concert*'s 'The Crucifixion', which transposes the central story of Christian mythology to Gallowgate, allowing Connolly to portray Christ and his followers as rumbustious Glaswegians (1974a). Although he provoked enormous laughs by masterfully playing with the bawdy and the outrageous, he overtly rejected racism: 'I don't do racist humour, which is my idea of being dirty' (Heilpern 1979).

Given all this, it's tempting to suggest that the folk comics of the 1970s anticipated everything the alternative comedians of the 1980s would go on to do. Indeed, Gavin Schaffer has argued that, 'In the context of earlier "folk" comedians like Jasper Carrott and Billy Connolly, little of the Comedy Store material was that original' (2016: 382–3). However, it's important not to overstate this. Although Tony Allen has grudgingly confessed that he 'learned a lot' from listening to LPs by the folk comedians, he has also argued that 'everything about them had failed to acknowledge the punk revolution and the heightened social and political awareness that was all-pervading in the radical arts' (2002: 81). Similarly, Alexei Sayle argues that the 'whole aesthetic' of alternative comedy 'was rock, not folk ... we sort of all wore suits, you know. We didn't really consciously think about it, but we all knew that we didn't want to wear kind of dungarees or [the] comical shit Billy [Connolly] was wearing' (Sayle 2017).

Mark Hurst, who started playing the circuit a little later than Allen and Sayle, was influenced by Connolly's albums in his teens, and went to see him live at about the age of fifteen. He makes an important point when he observes that Connolly 'would do Irish jokes and pub jokes' (2018). While Connolly and Carrott were rightly celebrated for their anecdotes and observations, less famous folk comedians like Bill Barclay and Tony Capstick were just as reliant on packaged gags as the WMC comics – and some of these gags were just as reliant on prejudice and stereotype. Derek Brimstone, for example, told the one about the twelve Irishmen with 'curly hair and little bowler hats and shillelaghs and pipes and wellies' in an identity parade for rape. When the 'bird walks in with these two coppers', one of the Irishmen steps forward and says, 'Dat's her. Dat's definitely the one' (Barclay/Brimstone/Capstick/Harding 1974).

As for Connolly, many of the routines on his LP *Riotous Assembly* (1979) are actually packaged gags expertly spun out into fuller narratives. One track, 'Marvo & the Lovely Doreen' is actually a version of a lion tamer gag told by variety comic Max Miller in his 1957 recording *Max at the Met* (on Miller 1998). The track 'Funny Thing religion ...' on *Cop yer Whack for This* contains a bona fide Irish joke – about an Irishman who sees a helicopter and starts throwing bread to it – although this is somewhat counterbalanced by a non-comic song elsewhere on the LP that satirizes British military intervention in the Troubles in Northern Ireland ('Sergeant, Where's Mine?') (1974b). Clearly, while there were similarities between folk comedy and altcom, there were also important differences.

## Prehistory: Influences and Origins

### 'He came just a bit too soon'

Beyond the folk comedians, there were also a few isolated individuals who anticipated and influenced alternative comedy. The consummately urbane Irish comic Dave Allen is one – his popular television shows of the 1970s included stand-up segments alongside sketches that often targeted organized religion in general and the Catholic Church in particular. His stand-up – performed sitting down – included observational routines alongside packaged jokes, all delivered with a kind of sedate sophistication.

Victoria Wood's career was already established by the time the Comedy Store opened, but it would be incorrect to say that her stand-up predated alternative comedy. John Dowie toured with Wood around 1977, and when I interviewed him, I asked how much of her act was stand-up at this point: 'None. It was all songs at the piano. But what we did then do was ... little two-handed sketches' (2018a). In fact, Wood only started performing stand-up with her show *Lucky Bag*, which she took to the Edinburgh Fringe in 1983, followed by a run at the King's Head in Islington later that year. Interviewed by *The Guardian* before the Islington run, she said, 'Stand-up comedy is the hardest thing to do. I've been doing it for 10 years and I'm only just coming up to it' (Cunningham 1983). A reviewer noted that, 'Miss Wood's new prowess as a stand-up comic is the great feature of the show' (Cushman 1983). By this point, alternative cabaret was so established that she even included a short routine about working in one alongside an alternative juggler who 'juggled with three copies of *The Guardian* and a wok'. In the interval, she said, they used to play alternative bingo: 'It's like ordinary bingo except when you won, you had to shout out, "Property is theft!" [laughter]' (Wood 1983). This is strikingly similar to an Alexei Sayle gag, recorded for the Comic Strip LP in 1981: 'Then for the community, they have a bit of alternative bingo, you don't shout "house", you shout "squat"! [laughter, some applause]' (Comic Strip 1981).

Probably the most significant stand-up outlier – cited as a precursor to the alternatives by Sayle, Tony Allen, Jeremy Hardy and Mark Steel – was John Dowie. In an interview with Stewart Lee, Sayle confesses, 'I always think "poor John Dowie" because he just came just a bit too soon. [We] went to see him at the Bush in '76, '77. I thought, "This is brilliant"' (BritishComedyGuide 2016). Dowie started performing comedy as early as 1969 when, as he notes in his memoir *The Freewheeling John Dowie*: 'I made my start at the Midlands Arts Centre in Birmingham. Some friends and I put together a show of sketches, poems and songs' (2018b: 10). By 1971 he had turned professional.

## Alternative Comedy

In that year, he got an Arts Council grant and took his one-man show to the Edinburgh Fringe. Later, he toured with Wood, and with his band the Big Girl's Blouse, and his songs were recorded for the postpunk label Factory Records.

When I interview him, Dowie is careful to point out that he didn't see his early work as stand-up comedy per se: 'Well it was one-man show. I mean at the time, you've got to remember there were a lot of theatre groups going around doing comedy shows' (2018a). He names companies like David Edgar's General Will and Mike Bradwell's Hull Truck – who would tour plays and 'do a cabaret show in the bar afterwards' – and comedy-oriented groups like Cliffhanger, The Combination and John Bull Puncture Repair Kit. Dowie explains why he saw theatre companies like this as his peers:

> [T]hese people that were going around were all doing comedy, but they were all just doing it in group fashion. So I was like, 'Well I'll do that on my own, but I'll call it a one-man show.' I mean . . . kind of like long, scripted monologue-y type things. And as I did more gigs, then it would become more sketchy and more chatty. But it was still kind of like, 'Now I'm going to be a man from Birmingham. Now I'm going to be a man in a kangaroo suit.' Things like that. It wasn't so much stand-up as solo sketch performances.
>
> *Dowie 2018a*

He explains that his act only evolved into stand-up comedy 'more or less the same time' as alternative comedy: 'It took a while because . . . there was no definition of it that was applicable. [Stand-up] meant more the working men's clubs and frilly shirts.'

What makes Dowie different from Allen, Wood and the folk comedians is that having foreshadowed and influenced alternative comedy, he then became involved in the scene. He was on at the Comic Strip in its first week, after Peter Richardson had seen him at a show at Chapter Arts Centre in Cardiff, and later did twenty-minute sets on mixed bills in the growing cabaret circuit. Being used to doing an hour by himself, he found adjusting down to twenty minutes 'really difficult', but he enjoyed the social aspect of working with other comics. He became known as one of the big names on the circuit, but always felt slightly apart from it. He's also wary of the idea that he might have influenced the alternative comedians: 'They might say that, I wouldn't know' (2018a).

## 'Playing directly to the audience like a comedian'

Dowie's acknowledgement of comedy-oriented theatre groups points to a crucial building block in the creation of the alternative comedy scene. The alternative theatre of the 1970s was not just an influence on altcom, but a direct precursor. A number of companies were experimenting with the kind of popular performance techniques found in stand-up. Tony Allen recalls that 'there was this great striving for young actors in these theatre groups to get political subject across to the working classes and using forms that were familiar. So a lot of the stuff [was] . . . theatre with a lot of sketches and diving about and talking to the audience' (2019). Such shows appeared in venues like the Albany Empire and the Half Moon Theatre, which would go on to play host to some of the earlier alternative comedy shows.

A good example of how these trends fed into alternative comedy is CAST's 1978 show *Confessions of a Socialist*, a later version of which (*Full Confessions of a Socialist*) won an Obie Award for 'outstanding achievement' when they took it to New York in 1980. It was a one-man show starring Roland Muldoon, who describes the form it took: 'I would come on *à la* stand-up and do an hour play, playing all the different parts, on the microphone, playing directly to the audience like a comedian, but playing a character' (2018). Muldoon would become directly involved in the alternative cabaret scene, as would many who had been part of alternative theatre groups.

Keith Allen was in Crystal Theatre of the Saint, and Jim Barclay had worked with Cockpit TIE, 7:84 and Pirate Jenny. Jenny Lecoat credits her time with Moving Parts with making her 'much more . . . politically aware' (2018). The socialist magician Ian Saville was in Broadside Mobile Workers' Theatre where, he recalls, 'I kept getting criticised . . . partly because the magic tricks weren't political enough . . . I argued that because I was mystifying people, I couldn't also demystify them at the same time. But I don't think they accepted that argument!' (2018). Martin Soan and Malcolm Hardee's Greatest Show on Legs started life as an adult Punch and Judy show, which developed into a touring comedy troupe that played pubs and festivals and went on to become a regular act in the early days of the Comedy Store. Both Soan and Hardee also became stalwart solo acts on the alternative cabaret circuit.

Many of the early pioneers of alternative comedy started developing their acts while still working in theatre groups. In September 1976, Peter Richardson and Nigel Planer presented their comedy rock musical *Rank* at the Roundhouse Downstairs in which, according to a reviewer, 'Actors, musicians, creators and interpreters are all inextricably intertwined, and the audience becomes part of the show within a show' (*Stage* 1976). Various characters in *Rank* went on to become part of Richardson and Planer's double act the Outer Limits, like Ken the photographer and Neil the hippie folksinger – who later mutated into a central character in *The Young Ones*. After the Roundhouse run, they took the show on tour, and Planer remembers:

> [T]he actual comedy scenes all got dropped and they didn't work so well in the venues we were playing. Because we supported AC/DC, we supported Motörhead . . . we had an agency called NEMS who was a rock agency booking the gigs in as if we were just another support act for the band.
>
> Planer 2018

Even so, Planer points out that the tour did make one important contribution to the development of alternative cabaret: 'We took our own PA system around, which was the PA system that ended up in the Comic Strip.'

Andy de la Tour first performed stand-up comedy in 1978 as part of a Belt and Braces show called *Red Rock Revue*:

> It was my idea to do that show and I wrote some sketches, but because I can't sing songs, I said to the other members of the theatre company, 'I've always wanted to do some stand-up – and would you mind if I had a go?' And they could hardly refuse me because I'd organised all the gigs, right? So we had tours all over Britain and into that show I put about eight minutes' worth of stand-up and it was me trying to do what my heroes would do.
>
> De la Tour 2016

That same year, Pauline Melville appeared with the Sadista Sisters at the Oval. She joined them after working with Joint Stock and 7:84, and liked working with them because, 'I could do political stuff but that was more surreal. And also funny. And it wasn't just dialogue that said, "I must go and get the shop steward." Or, equally difficult, pretending to be, like, half a million Chinese peasants.' She recollects her first experiments with character-based stand-up during this show:

There were certain things that were getting on my nerves that I wanted to mock, and take the piss out of. And so I said, 'Can I try something one evening? . . . But please be ready to come on with the next sketch. Because I don't know what's going to happen. I'm just going to start speaking.' . . . And they were all standing by because they could have been on, like, thirty seconds later if it was going nowhere. And the first thing I mocked was hippiedom . . . And I started – and it just took off. I mean there were sounds coming from the audience as if I'd burst some enormous bubble and at one point I thought somebody was sitting on some bagpipes, because . . . they were laughing so much. And I only did . . . a few minutes and then it built from then onwards. I would do a bit more each evening.

*Melville 2018*

In June 1976, Alexei Sayle appeared in Threepenny Theatre debut show *About Poor B.B.*, a Brechtian revue directed by Cliff Cocker. He was still working with them in 1978, when he appeared in 'cabaret style revue' at the Roundhouse Downstairs, which he co-wrote with Cocker and Bill Monks (*Stage* 1978). Even as late as March 1980 when he was an established solo act, he was still performing as part of Threepenny Theatre. The group was significant because of the performer-audience dynamic they set up: 'It was remarkable what a difference it made if people could have a drink while they watched the show; it created a proper cabaret-style atmosphere that undermined the solemn way in which productions were viewed in the conventional theatres' (Sayle 2016: 120). Sayle explains that in the 1978 revue 'there were sketches but also there were bits where I would come out of the show and address the audience directly. So I mean that was stand-up to all intents and purposes' (Sayle 2017).

Tony Allen developed elements of his stand-up with the anarchic Rough Theatre, a group vividly described by Heathcote Williams as 'a street theatre group from the Ladbroke Archipelago which specializes in low comedy, political satire, ham oratory, and spontaneous busking . . . and they perform in the pubs, streets, gutters, and community centres of the Corrugated Iron Belt' (1978: 3). Allen co-wrote and performed in a series of plays for Rough Theatre, often in the guise of Cyril Sleazby, one half of a double act with Ormskirk Arthur, played by his co-writer John Miles. Rough Theatre's plays are bursting with popular performance techniques – direct address, fairground barking, clowning, traditional double-act gags, re-written music hall songs.

There were also lines and comic images that would crop up in Allen's early stand-up act. In 1976's *Free Milk and Orange Juice*, a character called Grace describes a political fundraising event that ended in drunkenness and sexual debauchery with 'all these white bums going up and down in the dark like a production line', commenting wryly, 'It was like trying to politicise a plate of tapioca' (Rough Theatre 1977: 76). Appearing at the Comedy Store in June 1979, Allen uses very similar imagery in a routine about a trip to St Ives in 1965: 'I find the beach. It's full of people. Naked. At it. You know, like a panorama of pale, pulsating bums. Like a vast plate of tapioca pudding, you know what I mean?' (BSUCA)

The fact that Rough Theatre worked in the streets is significant, because the alternative cabaret circuit of the 1980s was swelled by a number of street entertainers. Covent Garden was an important breeding ground for performers, and acts that migrated from there to cabaret venues included John Hegley's Popticians, the Vicious Boys, the Flamin' Hamsters, the Long and the Short of It, and Mac McDonald's Human Jukebox. Some of the most important Covent Garden acts hailed from Brighton, among them Pookiesnackenburger, Lynn Thomas, Tim Bat, and Captain JJ Waller. Directly addressing the audience was a core skill of street performance, and Waller describes how he and his fellow performers discovered comic techniques while working in Covent Garden:

> [W]e were pioneering in a way ... I didn't think of myself as being comical. But because I was a bit rough around the edges, I would often make mistakes ... So I think it was kind of an empirical development of the comedy. You know, seeing where a laugh came and then realised that that's interesting and putting that in in the next show. And then slowly devising gags, interacting with the audience ... We created a sort of language, visual and verbally, which quite a lot of people still use today now as standard.
>
> Waller 2016

### 'Does for humour what the Sex Pistols did for rock and roll'

One of the most oft-cited precursors to alternative comedy is punk, which by 1976 had exploded into a tabloid-inflaming national phenomenon. As early as December 1980, the music paper *Sounds* argued that the Comic Strip 'could give comedy the kind of kick up the bum that punk gave to music' (Silverton 1980). The following March, a review in the *New Standard* said that the Comic Strip 'does for humour what the Sex Pistols did for rock and roll' (Spencer 1981). Tony Lidington wrote the first article on alternative cabaret to appear in an academic journal, in which he argues that, 'One of the major sources of inspiration and motivation in the growth of the new cabaret was the practice and ethos behind the "punk" movement' (1987: 108). This has been a common trope in histories of altcom (Wilmut and Rosengard 1989: 12; Cook 1994: 9; Cook 2001: 60, 98).

There were direct links between punk and alternative comedy. Rod Melvin had been a member of Ian Dury's pre-punk pub rock band Kilburn and the High Roads before playing piano in the Comic Strip's house band (and later, keyboards for Jenny Lecoat). Comic Strip shows regularly featured the crazed postpunk acapella foursome Furious Pig, who appeared in a short film about the club directed by Julien Temple, whose best known work is the Sex Pistols' movie *The Great Rock'n'Roll Swindle*. The Outer Limits' Comic Strip set included a routine called 'Anarchy in Dreamland', featuring snatches of easy-listening covers of punk bands like the Sex Pistols, the Clash, the Jam, the Stranglers – and even Furious Pig. Malcolm McLaren's Bow Wow Wow were due to play their second gig at the Comic Strip before being stopped by the GLC.

All of these connections involve just one venue, but there are many more. Keith Allen drummed for the Tesco Bombers and 'had a hand in the legendary ICA Punk Festival 1976' (Kohn 1981: 45). Tony Allen toured with anarcho-feminist punk band Poison Girls, and later Mark Hurst did the same under his early stage name Mark Miwurdz. Norman Lovett began his career, initially as a comic singer, after being spotted doing a support act for his friend's band: '[I]n the audience was the lead singer of 999, Nick Cash ... He said, "How about doing some gigs with us?" ... And I did a few gigs with them, and their fans liked me, so that was the beginning of the punk thing' (2018).

However, the links went much deeper than this, with punk and alternative comedy sharing roots in the squatting culture of the 1970s. Squatting – occupying empty properties and using them as housing – was an important part of London youth culture. In 1975, the *Daily Mail* estimated that there were 40,000 to 50,000 squatters living in the capital (19). Tony Allen – who was involved with Heathcote Williams's squatting support group, the Ruff Tuff Cream Puff Estate Agency – claims that there were 100,000 people squatting in West London alone (2016). In his vivid memoir about life in the 1970s London squatting scene, Richard Dudanski gives some idea of the idealism involved: 'The ideals of freedom behind the young person culture that grew throughout the 1960's, saw the beginnings of a squatting movement where the motive of Liberty blended with what previously and in less affluent times had been a dire necessity of the poor and the homeless' (2013: 8). The squatters of Freston Road even tried to secede from the United Kingdom, renaming their area the Free and Independent Republic of Frestonia.

This kind of Utopian thinking was not shared by the wider population, and there are plenty of examples of the popular press gnashing its teeth about squatting. In the *Daily Express*, Tory GLC councillor Frank Smith complained that, 'London is becoming a scroungers [sic] paradise' (Craig 1975). The *Daily Mirror* warned, 'Today an Englishman's home can very quickly become a squatter's castle' (Ward 1975). The *Daily Mail* ran a scaremongering double-page spread with one of its subheadings screaming, 'THE MENACE THAT'S NO LONGER A PROTEST – IT'S AN OPEN REVOLUTION'. Its description of the situation reads like a negative inversion of Dudanski's: 'Today, the genuinely needy are vastly outnumbered by layabouts and by politically-motivated revolutionaries – more concerned with smashing the idea of property-owning democracy than with solving the problem of homelessness' (*Daily Mail* 1975: 19).

The London squatting communities were a breeding ground for punk. Joe Strummer's pre-punk pub rock band the 101ers formed in a squat at 101 Walterton Road – with Richard Dudanski on drums. Strummer recalled playing regularly at a venue they set up above the Chippenham pub: 'We called it the Charlie Pig Dog Club, cos there was a dog in the squat that was a cross between a pig and a dog. Then every Wednesday night we'd go up there, and charge 10p to get in, I leafleted all the squats in the area' (Savage 2009: 249). One of the acts that appeared on the bill with them there was Rough Theatre. Tony Allen recalls, 'We would do little sketches ... Little things just to introduce people' (2016). Sometimes they would make a bigger contribution – in 1974, they performed a 35-minute version of their play *Heart of a Patriot* there (Rough Theatre 1977: 33). The 101ers would later have a residency in the Elgin pub on Ladbroke Grove, which went on to host a club run by Alternative Cabaret in 1979–80.

Although Threepenny Theatre once played a candlelit show at the National Theatre of Frestonia, Alexei Sayle was not part of the squatting culture. For Tony Allen, on the other hand, the Notting Hill squatting community reflected his anarchist politics and informed the development of his stand-up act, as he revealed in an early interview: 'This area has always been a bit bohemian, pretty bizarre. I reproduce a lot of their lifestyle on stage, and I think that's political in itself' (Brazil 1979).

## Prehistory: Influences and Origins

Squatting helped to stimulate popular culture in a very practical way, by providing free housing for would-be artists. Allen argues that 'because it was a squatted community, you didn't have any housing problems and therefore you didn't have any money problems', and suggests that punk grew out of the 'anarchist do-it-yourself movement' of squatting culture (2016). This DIY ethos has often been identified as a key element of punk, Dave Laing writing of its '"do it yourself" attitude which refused to rely on the institutions of the established music industry' (2015: 24). Similarly, the notion that anybody could become a performer or start a venue – just as Joe Strummer did – was a crucial factor in the growth of the alternative cabaret scene in the 1980s, as we shall see.

Punk influenced altcom in other ways too. When Joe Strummer first saw the Sex Pistols play, he was struck by their attitude to the audience: '[H]ere was this quartet who were standing there going, we don't give a toss what you think, you pricks, this is what we like to play, and this is the way we're gonna play it. Regardless of whether you like it or not' (Savage 2009: 256). Alexei Sayle didn't feel a particular affinity for punk music, but acknowledges, 'Where they definitely had an influence, I think, was . . . the kind of combative attitude you had to the audience, you know. I think that was . . . a direct follow-on from punk' (Sayle 2017).

Like many others, Sayle also acknowledges the influence of punk poets like John Cooper Clarke. As Ben Elton puts it, 'everybody loved John Cooper Clarke' (2018). Seeing Clarke performing with bands inspired Mark Hurst to start performing his own poetry as Mark Miwurdz: 'That was the spur . . . seeing somebody in the environment that I was used to being in, which is [the] local band scene. And thinking, "Oh, you could do that with bands, because he does it"' (2018). Punk and dub poets were not just an important influence on alternative cabaret, they also became part of the scene. Benjamin Zephaniah, Attila the Stockbroker, Seething Wells and Little Brother all performed in cabaret venues in the 1980s, and even more established figures like John Cooper Clarke and Linton Kwesi Johnson would occasionally appear.

### 'There was this vacuum'

Clearly, there was no shortage of factors that fed into the creation of alternative comedy. The distaste for the working men's club style that dominated the form of stand-up at the time, the influence of sickniks like Bruce and folk comedians like Connolly and Carrott, student comedy, one-offs like John Dowie, alternative theatre, Covent Garden street entertainment, squatting culture, punk, and performance poetry all had an impact.

Trevor Griffiths's 1975 play *Comedians* portrays a night school class for budding stand-ups, and one of them – Gethin Price – has an approach that eschews gags in favour of an uncomfortable confrontation with the audience. The character of Price led William Cook to describe *Comedians* as 'a play that anticipated – with astonishing foresight – the coming of Alternative Comedy' (1994: 10). Certainly, the pioneers of altcom were aware of the play. Tony Allen saw it in 1976 and describes it as 'oddly prophetic' (Allen 2002: 81). Alexei Sayle recalls Allen organizing a screening of the televised version of *Comedians* in a community centre, for members of the Alternative Cabaret group (Sayle 2017).

However, despite a plethora of influences and precursors, the period immediately before alternative comedy sprang into life is often described in terms of *lack*. Keith Allen has argued that, 'Comedy for people of my generation was nowhere to be found on the cultural map' (K. Allen 2007: 229). Paul Merton has recalled being obsessed with comedy from early childhood and facing a fundamental problem: 'I knew that I wanted to be a comedian but I had no way of achieving this ambition. I was sixteen, it was 1973, and there simply were no comedy clubs in London' (2014: 51). For Tony Allen, 'There was an enormous vacuum and it had to be filled' (2002: 81). The image of a vacuum crops up again and again. Alexei Sayle's version is vividly dynamic: 'There was this vacuum. That needed filling … That complete absence of anything … It is like air filling a vacuum, there was a kind of swooshing noise. We filled that space' (Sayle 2017).

By 1979, many of those who would play pivotal roles in creating alternative comedy were already starting to perform their own acts, but in isolation. What needed to happen was something that never happened for John Paul Joans – for them to find each other and realize they were not alone. As Pauline Melville puts it, 'It was really in the air. Because we all were trying it on our own and then we all discovered that other people were doing it. Which was extraordinary, really' (2018). Once this happened, it led to what Arnold Brown describes as 'the big comedy bang. People kind of wandering around in space and then suddenly – collision' (2016).

# CHAPTER 2
# THE BEGINNINGS OF ALTERNATIVE COMEDY

The Comedy Store opened at the Gargoyle, 69 Dean Street, Soho, London on 19 May 1979 – just sixteen days after Margaret Thatcher was elected Prime Minister. The coincidence is seductive. Alternative comedy is often caricatured as a torrent of anti-Thatcher jokes, so it seems as if the two events must be connected – as if the Comedy Store opened as a conscious act of defiance against the incoming figurehead of a radical Conservative government. Clearly, that cannot be the case. The earliest press reports announcing the opening of the Store appeared months earlier, and in any case, the people behind the Comedy Store had no real political motivations. But the fact that this coincidence has been remarked on before (Cook 1994: 1; Double 1997: 214) shows how the early history of alternative comedy has been mythologized. The problem is that it exaggerates the importance of both Margaret Thatcher and the Comedy Store in the creation of alternative comedy.

In July 1979, Thatcher made a speech to the Conservative Political Centre Summer School at Trinity College, Cambridge, in which she said, 'Nations depend for their health . . . upon the achievements of a comparatively small number of talented and determined people' (Beckett 2016: xv). Although she was trying to justify lowering taxes for the rich, the idea that the actions of a small number of talented individuals can make a significant impact is surprisingly apt when it comes to shifts in popular culture. As George Melly observed in his study of the pop arts first published in 1970, 'It is impossible to nail down the exact moment in which a movement is born. All movements of any value are initially invisible like the germs of an epidemic, and are "caught" at approximately the same time by a number of people often unknown to each other' (2008: 11). This chapter is about how the talented individuals who had each caught the germs encountered each other and what they did to precipitate the outbreak of the oncoming epidemic.

# Alternative Comedy

## The Comedy Store

Don Ward is often described as a former comic, having some experience in this area as a young man, acting as a feed for the comic actor David Lodge at Parkins Holiday Camp in Jersey and performing with concert parties like the Fol-de-Rols. However, he only really found his focus when he took charge of the premises at 69 Dean Street, which contained both the Nell Gwynne Theatre and the Gargoyle nightclub. In December 1968, Ward was advertising for 'Waitresses/Personality Girls' to appear at his 'Exclusive West End Club' (*Stage* 1968). The following July, a *Stage* critic praised *Striptease Exposé*, the first show he had seen at the Nell Gwynne since Ward took over, noting that he had 'started his career as a comedian-compère-vocalist in theatre clubs when the strip boom first hit London a decade ago' (Hepple 1969). In 1971, *The Stage* attributed a 'spate of comedy [breaking] out all over the West End' to Ward putting comics like Alan Mills – described as 'one of the best representatives of the new comedy school' – on at the Gargoyle (Hepple 1971). If this seems like the early fluttering of an ambition to start some kind of comedy revolution, it's worth remembering that in the decade or so before the Comedy Store opened, Ward's main business was striptease – making him an unlikely progenitor of a self-proclaimed non-sexist movement.

    The Comedy Store was the initiative of two men – Ward and an insurance salesman called Peter Rosengard. Their partnership ended acrimoniously, so it's difficult to unpick who is most responsible for its creation, although there is evidence to suggest that it was essentially Rosengard's vision. A press report from April 1979 describes the Comedy Store as 'the brainchild of Peter Rose' (Myerson 1979a) – this being a name that Rosengard went by at the time – and Arthur Smith has argued, 'I don't think Don really realised what was going on at the time ... Rosengard was the intellectual inspiration behind it' (Cook 2001: 25).

    What's certain is that the original inspiration was American. A *Daily Mirror* article from May 1979 notes that, 'It is a copy of the Comedy Store on California's Sunset Strip', and quotes Rosengard confessing, 'I saw it while on holiday in Los Angeles last year ... The whole thing was ridiculously funny ... I told myself that Britain urgently needs an injection of laughter like this' (Lewis 1979). By coincidence, Ward had also been to the LA Comedy Store on a holiday in 1978: 'I went onto Sunset Strip ... and [the] Comedy Store ... I saw a series of comics coming on, one after another ... And being a host of my own thing, I then looked at it and I thought, "I could do this"' (2018).

Rosengard's efforts were central to the Comedy Store's success. Ward acknowledges: 'Peter was a very interesting man, he worked for Abbey Life ... I recognised some talent in this guy and this guy was talented at selling' (2018). This talent is very clear from the press coverage Rosengard secured. *The Stage* ran an article about the Comedy Store as early as 12 April, over a month before it opened (Myerson 1979a), and it had reached the mainstream tabloid press – in the form of the *Mirror* article cited above – by 2 May. On 29 March, Rosengard put an advert in *The Stage*: 'COMEDIANS WANTED for new comedy club opening shortly in West End' (*Stage* 1979a). There's no attempt to explain the concept of a comedy club, even though none had existed in Britain before. In America, the first comedy club, Pips, had opened in 1962, and by the 1970s the concept was well established, but Rosengard's advert was taking a chance in assuming that the term would be understood in the UK. Generally though, he was impressively hardnosed. He cheerfully admitted to taking the concept and the name from the LA Comedy Store, but casually brushed aside the threat of legal action from its owners:

> I got a letter from ... Beverly Hills lawyers, saying, 'Sir, it has come to our notice that you are about to open a club or just opened a club, bearing the same name as Mitzi Shore's club, long established at Comedy Store in LA. We tell you to cease and desist.' And I just picked up the paper and chucked it in the bin, and that was it, never heard from them again.
>
> *Rosengard 2017*

The opening night of the Comedy Store received impressive media coverage, and was generally deemed a great success. It was covered in publications as varied as *The Stage*, *The Guardian*, *Punch*, and *Performance Magazine*. There was also a report on the BBC's early evening current affairs programme *Nationwide* the following Monday.

However, Rosengard and Ward struggled to make the Comedy Store's business model work, taking a punt on a number of sometimes contradictory approaches. By December 1979, they were announcing plans to expand to three or four nights a week even as Rosengard acknowledged they'd had to scrap their Sunday nights shows because 'the West End is an empty desert on Sunday' (Myerson 1979b). In May 1980, they announced that they were going to open the Magic Store in the Nell Gwynne, a club for magicians along the same lines at the Comedy Store, and claimed that they had not yet recovered their initial investment in their first venture (Petty 1980a). The

## Alternative Comedy

Magic Store apparently never proceeded beyond the planning stage, and neither Rosengard nor Ward even remember the proposal. However, they continued to tinker with the Comedy Store. In November 1981, Ward announced that comedy would replace strip shows in the Gargoyle for five nights a week (Petty 1981c), and in January 1982 he said he would run gay comedy nights on struggling Wednesday nights (*Stage* 1982a).

It's somewhat ironic that they found it so hard to recover their investment given that they didn't initially pay their acts, and only gave Alexei Sayle £5 per show to compère for them. The idea of expecting comedians to perform for free was part of the original American model – but by coincidence, at the very moment the London Store was about to launch, comedians were picketing outside the LA Store in a strike to establish the right to be paid for their work. *The Stage* carried a report on the strike in LA by Colin Crompton, a well-known working men's club comic: 'On the eve of the opening of a Comedy Store in London ... at the original Comedy Store in Hollywood the comedians are on strike. For the past six weeks a picket line of some 20 comedians has been marching up and down outside the club carrying placards which bear such slogans as "No Bucks, No Yucks"' (1979).

The lack of payment at Rosengard and Ward's club quickly came to the attention of Equity, which discussed it at their AGM in March 1980: 'The issue of the Comedy Store was raised. Archie MacMillan said that Equity has told the management there that their present showcase policy is unacceptable and members of the union have been told to boycott it' (Morley-Priestman 1980). Some of the alternative comedians refused to play there without payment. Pauline Melville remembers: 'I wouldn't go there because I was a Marxist and I wouldn't go without being paid ... And on the first night the Comedy Store paid, I was there' (2018). Although many of her contemporaries did play the Store for free, there was a hard economic logic to paying the acts. Interviewed in December 1979, Rosengard acknowledged: 'We still need more comics and can't in fact offer a completely new show each week. What we do now is have a hard core of regulars plus two or three newcomers each week' (Myerson 1979b). Andy de la Tour recalls that the management 'realised ... quite quickly, that this was going to be a disaster unless some of the [comedians] became regulars ... Unless there was a few of us who could be guaranteed to come each week, there was going to be no show ... So that's when we insisted we got paid' (2016).

By November 1981, Ward's partnership with Rosengard had come to an end (Petty 1981c). According to Ward, he wanted to run shows on other nights except Saturday, and told Rosengard that for this to happen he would have to become a full partner: 'He didn't and I dissolved the partnership. I returned his money, his 500 quid. And for a few years, we didn't really speak' (2018). Rosengard's account is similar, but in his version, he was the one suggesting running five night a week, but he didn't like what a full partnership with Ward would entail:

> Don said, 'Give me £40,000 ... for my fixtures and fittings and your half-share of the lift maintenance and the rates and the rent.' So I looked at the lease ... he was going to be kicked out within a year, the lease was ending ... Anyway, as soon as he realised I wasn't going to give him any money ... I got a letter from a lawyer.
>
> Rosengard 2017

Both agree the split was acrimonious. Rosengard set up a rival comedy club, the Last Laugh, at the Barracuda, and in December 1981 he said he was 'providing tough competition for his former partner, Don Ward' (*Stage* 1981b). In fact, Rosengard's rival club closed after only a few months.

However, he was right about the Gargoyle's lease ending. The original London Comedy Store closed on 23 December 1982, when the rent was increased from £14,000 to £50,000 per year (*Stage* 1983a). Ward announced that it would re-open soon at the Subway Club in Leicester Square. In fact – although he did stage shows in the intervening years – the Comedy Store wouldn't open as a permanent venue in Leicester Square until July 1985.

### 'A showcase for aspiring comic unknowns'

The coverage of the Comedy Store in 1979 shows that it wasn't set up to be an alternative venue and Rosengard's intentions didn't include fomenting any form of comedic revolution. Instead the Store was intended to be, as *The Stage* put it, 'a showcase for aspiring comic unknowns to try their luck before a live audience' – or as Rosengard explained, 'a place where people can get up and be terrible' (Myerson 1979a). Adverts offered 'UNKNOWN COMICS ... A GREAT CHANCE TO BE SPOTTED' (*Stage* 1979b).

In its first months, the Comedy Store was portrayed as simply a showcase for new acts. There was often a tongue-in-cheek suggestion that budding comics currently stuck in conventional careers might be ushered to stardom after appearing at the Store. In the *Daily Mirror*, Jack Lewis wrote, 'You might think your husband is a born comedian – especially with his stories of why he was late home. Soon, he will have a chance to prove it. And that goes for the staid pin-stripe City brigade as well as the shop-floor jokers who are always convinced they can do better than that chap on the telly' (1979). Tom Tickell, a *Guardian* journalist who performed there on the first night (and a number of times afterwards), began his article on the opening weekend, 'Have you heard the story about the dentist, the caretaker and the journalist who turned into comedians on Saturday night?' (1979). The image of the dentist would-be comedian was particularly enduring, probably because of Comedy Store adverts aimed at 'Comedians, aspiring comedians, frustrated dentists etc.' (*Punch* 1979).

The opening night delivered exactly the kind of motley array of showbiz hopefuls and oddball eccentrics that this kind of advertising might have been designed to attract. Infamously, there was a gong by the side of the stage. When the audience decided they'd had enough of whoever was performing, they could shout 'Gong!' and when it was struck, the act had to leave the stage. This put a lot of power in the hands of a drinking audience, and Tom Tickell described how, 'The pace got faster, the audience got drunker, and baying for each act to end almost before it had begun. A beautiful act from Footlights at Cambridge – and many others – just did not stand a chance' (1979). With entertaining chutzpah, Rosengard filleted Tickell's review to make it sound like a positive endorsement when he quoted it in an advert the following week: 'A beautiful act from Footlights of Cambridge ... and many others' (*Stage* 1979c).

The *Nationwide* report captures the showcase for new talent in action. The footage shows a middle-aged Cockney adopting Max Miller's delivery and failing to get laughs with jokes like, 'I've only got five minutes, even the wife gives me six.' A rotund man with an improbable beard gets some laughs by putting a floral-patterned tub onto his head and then makes squeaking noises. A reporter interviews an awkward looking man in a grey suit while over his shoulder we see Rik Mayall drinking beer from a pint mug and Ade Edmondson smoking a cigarette – who were just there to see the show. Cliff Shore,[1] a dapper middle-aged man who would become a regular – despite popular demand – is gonged off after making a joke about a lesbian ('What part are Lesbia d'you come from, dear?'). The audience bays aggressively, and Alexei Sayle bangs the gong. Shore says, 'They're asking for more.' Sayle replies, 'Yeah. They're asking for more, they're the ones who come here for their 200 hours community service [laughter]' (*South Bank Show* 1993).

## The Beginnings of Alternative Comedy

After the opening night, Rosengard declared, 'I think we've unearthed quite a number of really talented new artists – and that's what the whole thing is all about' (*Stage* 1979d). However, it wasn't yet clear exactly what they had unearthed, and although the opening weekend included performers who would go on to be associated with alternative comedy – Alexei Sayle, Arnold Brown, Lee Cornes – the majority were cut from a different cloth.

There were performers who would go on to become successful in careers outside of the alternative circuit, like Sandi Toksvig, Emma Thompson, Theatre de Complicité's Simon McBurney, as well as Clive Anderson – who became a regular at the Comedy Store for a while before becoming a television and radio presenter. There were comic performers who would remain part of the scene for a while before moving on to perform elsewhere, like the character comedian Peter Wear and the musical eccentric Bob Flag. There were others who kept trying in spite of apparently lacking the requisite talent, like Cliff Shore, or Phil Munnoch – an advertising copywriter who billed himself as 'Vernon Vomit – the Punk Comic' (Callan 1979). There were even non-comic acts, like the Glaswegian singer-songwriter Paul Goodman, who regularly went down well in spite of the fact that, as one journalist put it, he 'attempts no jokes' (Burn 1980).

What's significant about the opening of the Comedy Store is that along with the Cliff Shores and Paul Goodmans, this new venue brought together a number of performers who wanted to try something different with stand-up, and had already started exploring ways of doing this. Looking back on its tenth anniversary in 1989, Andy de la Tour argued: 'There's a danger of the whole thing being mythologised. The Store brought together a dozen people who may not otherwise have met – but the connection with the Store soon finished' (Connor 1989: 17). Even Kim Kinnie – who became effectively the Comedy Store's artistic director – acknowledged that, 'Tony Allen and Malcolm Hardee had been doing Alternative Comedy before the Comedy Store opened. What the Store did was form a central focus and give them a platform' (Cook 2001: 270). De la Tour describes how fortuitous the timing of the opening was, coming straight after his initial forays into stand-up with Belt and Braces:

> [W]hen we finished that tour, which then would've been early 1979, I remember thinking, 'This is so frustrating, I've actually done a bit of stand-up. And there's nowhere I can do it. I mean, where else can I do it?' . . . quite soon after, I heard about the Comedy Store and I thought, 'This is weird kind of synchronicity, serendipity of life.' And so when I

43

## Alternative Comedy

> went down the Comedy Store for the first time, [I] met people. There were ... several basically vaguely left-wing actors, performers all kind of somehow gravitating towards the same place. It's weird how the Comedy Store met a need.
>
> De la Tour 2016

For Nigel Planer, the new venue offered the possibility of developing the comedic elements of *Rank*:

> [W]hen those Peter Rosengard posters went up with the smiling mouth ... I was doing Neil as my kind of party piece ... So I dared Peter [Richardson] to go down there to the Comedy Store ... That was it really, the beginning of it. That's where we first saw Rik, first saw Alexei ... [I] said, 'Oh I'll do Neil' ... We then immediately went back and wrote the Outer Limits, that week.
>
> Planer 2018

The fact that the Comedy Store brought together such a range of performers – some focusing on politics, some more on the artistic possibilities of cabaret – is what put it at the centre of the comedy big bang. When Rosengard is asked if he intended to change comedy, he replies: 'I'd never seen a comedian ... I didn't have any vision ... It was just, what's the word, organic' (2017).

However, it was perhaps not quite as organic as he suggests, because these people were brought together by more than just chance and canny advertising. There was also conscious intervention – not by Rosengard or Ward, but by Alexei Sayle and Tony Allen. Sayle quickly became aware that 'the Comedy Store needed more than just me doing innovative material if we were going to survive.' When Allen first performed there, he knew that 'this was who I'd been waiting for: another comic like me but not like me ... he was clearly someone who was trying to do a similar thing with comedy' (Sayle 2016: 173–4). According to Allen:

> Both Alexei and I knew that the one thing the Store needed was a large input of radical acts ... We needed more allies, so I now made it my business to get as many fringe theatre actors, buskers, speakers and musos down to the Comedy Store to at least see the show, if not persuade them to get up and do something.
>
> Allen 2002: 98

## The Beginnings of Alternative Comedy

Keith Allen and Jim Barclay confirm that it was Tony Allen who persuaded them to go along to the Comedy Store (K. Allen 2007: 229; Barclay 2016), and both would go on to be key figures in early alternative comedy.

In spite of this, it was some time before the Comedy Store became a fully-fledged alternative venue, and other types of performer continued to play there for some time. A magazine article entitled 'The Other Comedians' describes the acts at the Store in December 1980: 'There are sexist comedians, feminist comedians, hopelessly drunk comedians, polite, youthful comedians from Oxbridge, sad, failed comedians and, occasionally, talented comedians who give as good as they get from the hecklers' (Hughes-Hallett 1980: 74). Occasionally, television comedians of the old school like Les Dawson and Lennie Bennett came along to perform. Bernard Padden made his Store debut the night Dawson turned up: 'I remember people having great affection for Les Dawson, in that particular audience. They wanted him to perform ... He did, I think, about five minutes of comedy ... and went down really well' (2017). Bennett, on the other hand, got into trouble with hecklers and was gonged off.

Tony Allen talked about the relationship between the alternative comedians and the more traditional ones in terms of conflict: '[I]t was like a civil war in the Comedy Store for about a year, with all these mother-in-law type comedians' (1988). Jim Barclay made a similar point:

> [E]very comic act who'd been touting himself around the clubs, and still wasn't breaking through, like all those people that advertise in the back of *The Stage* for example, they'd turn up, and they'd say this is the way forward, and for six months there was a tussle between what they were doing and what we were doing, and it became clear that what we were doing was what the audience wanted ... and eventually they went ... back to the back page of *The Stage*.
>
> Barclay 1990

In fact, the civil war went on for longer than either Barclay or Allen recall. An article published as late as November 1981 announces a change of booking policy: '[T]he more traditional comedians who rubbed shoulders with the new wave in the early days will be shunned. "They weren't getting the laughs", explained Ward. "The establishment comedians are open-mouthed at the new lot who really have something to say to kids today"' (Petty 1981c). It was not until this point, then, that the Comedy Store became a fully-fledged alternative venue.

## Alternative Comedy

One of alternative comedy's key defining features was its commitment to non-sexist, non-racist comedy. In 1979, when stand-up was still dominated by WMC comics making jokes about melting down Pakistanis to make rubber bullets, this was a radical departure. Rosengard claims that he introduced the idea of non-sexist, non-racist comedy when he opened the Comedy Store: 'I never said, "I'm going to open up a non-sexist non-racist comedy club." There was a press conference or something before the opening, and somebody said ... "Does anything go? Can anybody say anything?" I said, "They can say anything they want to say as long as it's not sexist or racist"' (2017). There's some evidence to support this, particularly the *Daily Mirror* article from May 1979, which quotes Rosengard saying, 'We won't be doing too much censoring. We leave that to the audience, anyway', and notes, 'There is only one rule – racial gags are out' (Lewis 1979).

Whether that rule was really followed is another matter. Certainly, a review of the first night at the Comedy Store notes that, 'Too many of the clean jokes were about foreigners and too many of the dirty ones about sex and foreigners' (Thorne 1979). Sexism and racism continued to rear their ugly heads throughout the period of civil war. This may be because the non-sexist, non-racist ethos actually came from the new breed of comics. In 1989, Lee Cornes claimed: 'Rosengard couldn't care less what went on from the beginning. The ethos came from the alternative cabaret mob – Tony Allen, Jim Barclay and Andy de la Tour. My stuff was outrageously racist and sexist at the time but no-one mentioned it ... It was only later on that such things got mentioned' (Connor 1989: 16). Asked about where the non-sexist, non-racist element of alternative comedy came from, Tony Allen replied, 'Well, I started that, I mean I was really involved with the Women's Movement and all that sort of thing in the late 1970s' (1988). Alexei Sayle can also take some of the credit, using his control of the gong to root out sexist and racist comedy (2016: 175). He also used the gong to promote the kind of comedy he wanted to see, regardless of audience reaction: 'The first night that Andy de la Tour turned up ... he had this routine ... doing Northern Ireland as a kind of Kenneth More movie ... And the audience were going fucking nuts. And I wouldn't pull him off ... I wouldn't gong him off ... because I was sympathetic to what he was saying' (Sayle 2017).

What becomes clear, then, is that the elements of the Comedy Store that would become alternative comedy came not from the management but from the acts themselves. Ward and Rosengard had created a space, but it was the comedians who came along to fill it who changed the nature of stand-up. In particular, performers like Sayle and Allen consciously intervened by encouraging like-minded performers to come along, discouraging sexist and racist comedy, and promoting the kind of comedy that they wanted to see. In doing so, they curated the creation of the new comedy movement.

## Alternative Cabaret

In early 1981, an article in *The Face* suggested that the Comedy Store was only really a starting point because it 'suffered though from an almost wilful diversification . . . For this reason many of the best acts split and evolved into other groups; Alexei Sayle, Rick [sic] Mayall and Tony Allen all began at The Store and have since moved on into better-suited areas' (Norman 1981: 14). Eleven months later, the same magazine described how 'the Comedy Store's first generation of survivors cast their eyes further afield and split into two factions – [what Rik Mayall describes as] "the agit-prop end: you tell jokes about Thatcher, basically" – and the Comic Strip' (Taylor 1982a: 30). The agit-prop end was the group Alternative Cabaret, whose importance has probably been understated as much as the Comedy Store's has been overstated.

It was Tony Allen's idea to start Alternative Cabaret, and he recalls the thinking behind it:

> We didn't have control over the Comedy Store so we started a group of our own . . . We'd come out of a fringe theatre thing where as soon as there were four people, you created . . . a left wing theatre group . . . and then you got some Arts Council money . . . and you played in pub rooms or in the streets or wherever . . . So as soon as we realised that there was half a dozen people that were cabaret artists and we all liked each other's work, we formed a group . . . and we became Alternative Cabaret.
>
> *Allen 2016*

In the summer of 1979, Allen called 'a few ad-hoc meetings' about forming a group (Allen 2002: 107). A number who were present remember Keith Allen turning up specifically to announce he was refusing to join (Wilmut and Rosengard 1989: 38; Sayle 2016: 178). As Andy de la Tour puts it, Keith Allen, 'came along to tell us he didn't want to be part of it – because he's an anarchist. He ended up doing loads of gigs for us, of course, but he didn't want to be kind of part of a group' (2016). Tony Allen, on the other hand, was a different kind of anarchist, and his energy drove the group forward. Sayle describes him as 'Surprisingly competent as an administrator' (2016: 179), and de la Tour makes a similar point: 'for an anarchist he was actually quite well organised' (2016).

Alternative Cabaret's first flyer has Sayle's monochrome gasmasks design on the front, and typewritten information on the back: 'An Alternative Cabaret show consists of up to two hours of radical, raunchy humour and music ranging through folk, blues, and jazz, with three comedians and two musical acts' (BSUCA). It lists the acts involved at this point – on the right musicians (Chisolm & Stevens, the Blue Lovers, Combo Passé, Gasmask & Hopkins[2]) and on the left comedians (Jim Barclay, Andy de la Tour, Maggie Steed, Tony Allen, Alexei Sayle, Peter Wear, Roland Muldoon). This was a very early line-up, as Muldoon recalls that he only performed with Alternative Cabaret 'a couple of times' (2018).

The group staged its first show on 15 August 1979, at the Pindar of Wakefield on Grays Inn Road. Bob Flag, who organized the gig, claims it was performed under the name Krisis Kabaret, which he'd been using for events he'd been running since at least 1976 (2015: 132). However, both Allen and Sayle agree that the show was performed under the Alternative Cabaret label (Allen 2002: 107–8; Sayle 2016: 180). The following day was in many ways far more important. On 16 August, Alternative Cabaret performed their first show at the Elgin pub in Elgin Avenue, Ladbroke Grove, where Joe Strummer's 101ers had established a residency in 1975. Alternative Cabaret played fortnightly shows at the Elgin from August 1979 to 22 May 1980. Unlike the Comedy Store, Alternative Cabaret's Elgin residency was specifically designed to promote the new alternative approach to comedy, leading Tony Allen to argue that the Elgin was 'actually the first alternative comedy venue' (1988).

De la Tour describes the Elgin as 'a big, marvellous old quite tatty Victorian pub [with] a fantastic side room ... Very, very basic, I mean there was a simple raised podium at one end, basically a microphone or two. That was it. There was no lighting or anything' (2016). Allen recalls the kind of crowd they drew in a bohemian area that was a hotbed for squatting: 'At the Elgin, of course, in Ladbroke Grove, the whole audience were anarchists and revolutionary socialists' (2016).

Because the Elgin drew a regular audience, the comedians always had to perform new material there, forcing them to stretch and develop. This was creatively demanding, contributing to the decision to end the residency after nine months. In a show recorded on 10 April 1980, Allen tells the audience,

'We're packing up this gig in a few weeks' time. Mainly because all the comedians have run out of material. Including me' (BSUCA). What this suggests is that the Elgin was not only the first alternative comedy venue, but also the UK's first new-material night.

It was also important in earning the group some money. During a show on 27 March 1980, Allen can be heard telling the audience:

> As you leave, erm, and I know you'll leave as soon as anything's over, could you put a few, a few pound notes or fivers or, you know, that sort of manner of thing in a, in a glass that Jim's holding at the bar there. Thank you very much. 'Cos we're trying to do this *professionally*. I know it doesn't look like it but we are.
>
> BSUCA

Audience contributions were not the only income generated by these shows, as Allen describes: 'We were getting the Elgin free. In fact, we were getting thirty quid to put gigs on at the Elgin. Because it was packed. And then we'd put the hat round as well, so we were getting sixty quid a week in 1979, which isn't bad as a sort of start-up for a group starting out in cabaret' (2016). Adjusting for inflation, £60 would be worth £298.20 in 2018.[3]

If the financial arrangement seems a bit informal, this was in keeping with Alternative Cabaret's general ethos. Allen says that the Elgin was 'a do-it-yourself version of a club, and a more cooperative way of setting it up' (HistComPod 2017a). The group's approach was a continuation of the kind of DIY, cooperative principles found in left-wing theatre and the squatting culture of the 1970s. As Jim Barclay puts it:

> [A]t that time, the whole notion of creating different modes of ... cooperative ventures in the arts was beginning to come through ... eventually we evolved this rule – one person gets a gig, and they invite who they want from the collective. And it was a way forward which didn't put us at the mercy of any kind of booker or agent. We got the deals that we could. They weren't creaming off a percentage and all the rest of it.
>
> Barclay 2016

Key members of Alternative Cabaret shared a suspicion of arts funding. Sayle believed that 'the best barometer of whether your work was any good was not whether some arts bureaucrat thought you were entitled to a grant but if people were prepared to pay to see it' (2016: 130). Allen took a similar line, arguing that:

> The economics should decide your performances – your style then gets based on reality, not on how much money you've got to spend ... If the Arts Council didn't exist, there would have been a flourishing theatre movement in pubs and a raunchy hard-sell entertainment – much like what we call cabaret. The state is intervening through the Arts Council: if it wasn't there ... entertainment would be more intelligent than now.
>
> *Brazil 1979*

This kind of thinking grew much more from a DIY attitude than the market-driven, grant-slashing Conservative agenda that the Thatcher government were starting to drive through in 1979. Jim Barclay explains how the antipathy for funding was related to the freedom that stand-up offered:

> [Tony Allen] had this thing about stand-up comedy, because you could be much more of [a] cultural guerrilla ... you weren't dependent on an Arts Council grant, you weren't locked into a piece of topical theatre that was no longer topical ... With stand-up, you could actually do it, there and then, on that night.
>
> *Barclay 2016*

The anti-funding attitude spread to less-politicized acts like Rik Mayall, who talked about being proud of 'making a living out of performing rather than existing on an Arts Council grant' (Taylor 1982a: 30).

A later publicity leaflet for Alternative Cabaret is more professionally produced than the original Sayle-designed one. It folds out into a poster-sized photo of the group, inset with three smaller photos. On the back are photos and properly typeset biographies of all of the core acts in the group – which were by this point Tony Allen, Jim Barclay, Andy de la Tour and Pauline Melville, plus the two musical acts Combo Passé and Gasmask and Hopkins. Alternative Cabaret are described as 'a variety of radical comedians intent on extending both content and style of the traditional "stand-up" form [who] banded together to present non-racist, non-sexist entertainment which undoubtedly will precipitate the downfall of capitalism and bring an end to injustice and tyranny wherever it rears its ugly head!' (BSUCA). Although the exclamation mark clearly indicates comic hyperbole, as a statement of intent this is strikingly different from the Comedy Store's desire to be nothing more than a 'showcase for aspiring comic unknowns'. It suggests a radical agenda – to expand the form of stand-up, shun sexism and racism, and possibly even topple capitalism.

However tongue-in-cheek this last aim was, the leaflet does point to the group's roots in the anti-establishment squatter culture of the 1970s. The photo on the front shows them in front of a corrugated iron fence, spray-painted with 'ALTERNATIVE CABARET'. Corrugated iron was ubiquitous in the skirmishes between squatters and local authorities – the authorities using it to keep squatters out of unused buildings, the squatters spraying slogans on it. Allen was a prolific sprayer of witty seditious slogans like, 'SQUAT NOW WHILE STOCKS LAST'. The front cover of *Rough Theatre Plays* shows a photo of the book's title sprayed onto corrugated iron, and their street theatre play *Squat Now While Stocks Last* includes a song about corrugated iron, to the tune of Harry Champion's music hall classic 'Any Old Iron' (Rough Theatre 1977: 30).

On the other hand, the increased professionalism of the later leaflet reflects the fact that in addition to the regular shows at the Elgin, Alternative Cabaret quickly began to generate a lot of work for its acts. Pauline Melville remembers 'doing just endless gigs all over London' (2018). Press listings show just how varied these endless gigs were. In May 1980, Alternative Cabaret supported an 11.15pm showing of *The Big Sleep* and *The Maltese Falcon* at the Ritzy Cinema, Brixton (*Guardian* 1980a). In June, they appeared at the Theatre Royal, Stratford East after an 8pm performance of Howard Brenton's *A Short Sharp Shock!* (*Guardian* 1980b). In March 1981, they had a slightly more conventional booking, doing two weeks at the Old Red Lion pub theatre in Islington (*Stage* 1981c). Student shows were an important source of income, as Andy de la Tour explains:

> I think some student unions got wise to the fact that there was this new thing happening, stand-up comedy. And not only was it kind of a happening, interesting thing, but of course it was also cheap … All they needed to do was to provide a microphone – and they could get some stand-up.
>
> *De la Tour 2016*

## Alternative Comedy

Contracts in BSUCA show how much they were making from student gigs. On 2 October 1980, for example, they were paid £100 (£421.24)[4] to perform from 9.20pm–10.45pm at the LSE's Old Theatre. The following day they received the same fee to perform at UCL in the unlikely timeslot of 1pm–2pm.

The variety of bookings suggests a pioneering spirit in Alternative Cabaret's constant gigging. Inevitably, they sometimes came up against circumstances that made performing difficult. Jim Barclay describes appearing at the Ritzy with Alexei Sayle: 'We were going to do fifteen minutes before the movie. And it was extraordinary because you don't go to the cinema to listen to fifteen minutes of live stand-up comedy! And it was about 11 o'clock at night, you know . . . And it was just indifference' (2016).

By travelling around London and sometimes further afield, they were establishing the idea of running cabaret nights in pubs, students' unions and theatres, and thus laying the foundations for the circuit that would grow up in the 1980s. They also helped to establish stand-up comedy at the Edinburgh Fringe. Alexei Sayle and Tony Allen took up a show called *Late Night Alternative* in 1980, playing ten nights at the Heriot-Watt Theatre, promoted by the theatre company Bristol Express. The following year, Alternative Cabaret took up a show under their own name, with Tony Allen, Jim Barclay, Andy de la Tour, Pauline Melville – and a pianist called Phil Nichol. The financial records show that the show was a hit, with a gross take for its Edinburgh run of £5,249.50 (£19,766.59). This allowed all of the show's expenses to be paid, including travel, venue hire, posters, and performers' accommodation, and gave each of the acts a decent slice of profit. Barclay, de la Tour and Nichol each received £390 (£1,468.52), Tony Allen took £10 less (for reasons which are not recorded), and Pauline Melville took £260 (£979.01) having only done two of the three weeks.

By this time, Alternative Cabaret had moved from being a loose collective to, as Allen puts it, 'a group with a management' (HistComPod 2017a). A letter from Martin Bergman, dated 6 June 1981 – aimed at setting up a tour of universities and polytechnics between September and November – announces that, 'They are now being managed by my company Comic Business Ltd' (BSUCA). De la Tour believes that Bergman 'was shrewd, he was a businessman. Though he may not have liked everything we did or certainly everything we said, he could see that there was potential in Alternative Cabaret . . . he could see . . . that there was potentially [a] huge audience out there' (2018). The money Bergman was asking for suggests a business-like approach: 'Our basic fee is £400 [£1,506.17] per performance,

## The Beginnings of Alternative Comedy

but we would prefer to do two shows on one night with some sort of guarantee plus a box office split.' Financially speaking, this was quite a step up from clearing £60 to play the Elgin just two years earlier. Bergman also produced an LP entitled *Alternative Cabaret*, released by Original Records in July 1981.

In spite of this, eventually, as de la Tour puts it, 'the Alternative Cabaret group dispersed, really. We didn't want to carry on being that group' (2018). Allen explains the reason for the split: 'Alternative Cabaret didn't need its brand to be flashed about because we were all just earning' (2016). The members of the group were established as individual acts and apparently had no need for it any more. Thus, in spite of the pivotal role it had played, Alternative Cabaret came to an end.

### The Comic Strip

A yellowing A4 poster from 1980 advertises a show at the tiny Pentameters Theatre, above the Three Horseshoes pub in Hampstead. The show is running for seven nights over two weeks, 18–21 and 25–27 September. There are drawings capturing the likenesses of four faces that would become well known on television, and between wonky Letraset giving the details of the shows, hand-drawn lettering announces two double acts: 'THE OUTER LIMITS PLUS 20TH CENTURY COYOTE'. In much smaller script, a third act is listed: Arnold Brown (BSUCA). Brown recalls: 'I lived in Hampstead and ... to get me more practice, I started this venue in Pentameters ... They used to have Harold Pinter plays and ... poetry and Michael Horowicz, all these kind of avant garde people. And I said I wanted to put on some shows' (2016).

The show at Pentameters was significant for a couple of reasons. First, Mayall invited his university friend Ben Elton to come and see him there, thus giving Elton his first direct encounter with the alternative cabaret scene. Second, it was a dry run for the Comic Strip, which would open just ten days later. The Comic Strip was the second faction to come out of the Comedy Store, and was initially made up of the five men who performed at Pentameters – Peter Richardson and Nigel Planer of the Outer Limits, Rik Mayall and Ade Edmondson of 20th Century Coyote, and Arnold Brown – plus the Store's first compère Alexei Sayle. Sayle explains why he jumped ship from Alternative Cabaret to join the Comic Strip: 'Very cynical really, because ... when you had four or five blokes all talking about Thatcher,

## Alternative Comedy

I didn't stand out, you know when I was with [the Comic Strip] there was nobody else doing what I was doing' (Sayle 2017).

The Comic Strip venue was initiated by Peter Richardson, who gathered together a core set of acts to perform there. Like the Comedy Store, it was an important enough venture for its imminent opening to be mentioned in *The Stage*, reporting that: 'Richardson came up with the idea when he was doing a stint at London's talent-spotting platform, the Comedy Store. He decided to bring together the best kind of alternative entertainment he had witnessed there' (Petty 1980b).

Something else the Comic Strip shared with the Comedy Store is that it was housed in a strip club – the 200-seat Boulevard Theatre in the Raymond Revuebar. The *Stage* article notes that Richardson had to fight to be allowed to use the name Comic Strip, because, 'It was felt that the word "Strip" would confuse visitors to the theatre'. Indeed, the comic possibilities of the audiences for the strip show and the alternative cabaret show getting mixed up were explored by Sayle in his compering – imitating a befuddled punter saying, 'Sven, Sven, when's the strip going to start, Sven?' (Comic Strip 1981) – and by journalists. In the *London Review of Books*, Ian Hamilton wrote: 'On the night I went there, the tuxedoed bouncer was having a hard time explaining to the punters that Raymond's Revuebar was now in fact *two* theatres. "Turn right for the Festival of Erotica," he'd instruct the plumply cufflinked; "Upstairs for *The Comic Strip*," he'd tell anyone in jeans' (1981).

A large black bomb dominates the iconic Comic Strip poster, chalked with the motto 'HAVE A NICE DAY' as it plummets giddily towards the Houses of Parliament below. Describing the Comic Strip as 'London's newest anarchic cabaret', the poster advertises 10pm shows from Tuesday to Sunday with extra 8pm performances on Fridays and Saturdays (BSUCA). Looking at the poster, Nigel Planer points out the midweek shows: 'You notice it hasn't got our names on it because Alexei refused to do those. So me and Peter had to take over the compèring for three of the nights a week, because Alexei refused to do anything other than Fridays and Saturdays' (Planer 2018).

In contrast with the bearpit hostility of the Comedy Store and the looser vibe of the Elgin, the Comic Strip was a distinct step up in terms of presentation. The venue itself was more formal, and one journalist noted: 'Drinking is allowed but it is more of a theatre than a nightclub' (Hughes-Hallett 1980: 74). Bruce Dessau – who visited the Comic Strip more than once and is now the *Evening Standard*'s comedy critic – makes a similar point: 'Although it was in one of the rooms in Paul Raymond's Revuebar, which was a strip club … it was still theatrical. It was still proper rows of seats and you were, like, sitting in the stalls of a very small theatre' (HistComPod 2017b).

Planer remembers Richardson's eye for detail and the care he took in creating the ambience he wanted in the performance space, with 'torn-off posters', a 'silver curtain' and a band 'looking seedy': 'You know, he made a production. He's a producer, he did a really good job of giving it an image, of giving it a feel for the audience' (Planer 2018). Sayle preferred the carefully-curated loucheness of the Comic Strip to the gigs he had done with Alternative Cabaret: 'It wasn't just a load of hippies going around playing students' unions. . . . It was a load of counterculture people . . . in this bastion of erotica' (Sayle 2017).

The show itself was just as tightly controlled, as Planer explains: '[B]y the time we get to the Comic Strip . . . it became more like a show . . . The running order had to be the same . . . It became quickly apparent that [with] audiences sitting in rows, it had to be slick and it had to come off and you couldn't really be trying new material out there' (Planer 2018). Alexei Sayle argues that 'people would still fuck about and stuff' but like Planer acknowledges that, 'Everybody rigidly settled on their favourite bits' (Sayle 2017).

With a fixed line-up of acts presenting more or less the same material, an element of variety was provided by the fact that the bill would also include guest acts. A listing stuck to the front of Arnold Brown's scrapbook records that on Friday 19 December 1980 the guest acts were Tony Allen and musical duo Trimmer and Jenkins, and the show on Saturday 20 December featured Hermine and French and Saunders (BSUCA). Ben Elton recalls making his stand-up debut at the Comic Strip: 'I auditioned and Pete [Richardson] gave me a couple of . . . evenings early on in the Comic Strip' (2018). Some acts guested regularly, like Trimmer and Jenkins, who recorded a live album at the Comic Strip (1981). Another regular guest, Hermine, was a symptom of Richardson's taste for kookier acts – attracted to the Comic Strip by adverts offering auditions for 'UNUSUAL COMIC PERFORMERS' (*Stage* 1980b). Planer explains why Richardson included such oddballs on the bill: '[I]t's quite a tightly organised show. And for that purpose, he'd make sure that we had a bizarre act in. Like Hermine – amazing! A woman comes on in ten feet of newspaper wrappings in a cone and sings something in French' (Planer 2018). More than one critic noted that having guest acts made for an erratic show. Michael Church (1981) argued, 'the Comic Strip's varying menu inevitably means that dud acts sometimes creep in', and Antony Thorncroft declared, 'There is no consistency in the programme: a few regular performers are mixed with one-offs, so a good night could be followed by a dire' (1980).

However, having guests helped to counteract the fact that the regulars were all men. Other female guests included the American actor Beth Porter and, on the opening night, Pamela Stephenson – then a big television star from BBC2's *Not the Nine O'Clock News*. French and Saunders went from regular guests to become part of the group, and both have argued that one of the reasons they got onto the bill in the first place was to redress the gender imbalance. According to Dawn French, 'Only later did we realise that *any* women who had walked in the door on that day would have got the job. They were desperate for women in the line-up of an all-male comedy group' (2008: 255). Jennifer Saunders's account is similar: 'There just weren't many female acts around; most comedy clubs were bear pits. I think we got the gig by virtue of the fact that we were the first living, breathing people with bosoms to walk through the door' (2014: 51).

The Comic Strip quickly became more successful than either the Comedy Store or Alternative Cabaret, and an important factor in this was that, as Moira Petty noted in *The Stage*, 'Impresario Michael White has pumped money into the venture, following an approach by Richardson' (1980b). White was an important producer, with West End hits like *Joseph and the Amazing Technicolour Dreamcoat* and *The Rocky Horror Show* and films like *Monty Python and the Holy Grail* under his belt. As Arnold Brown recalls, White's involvement attracted celebrities to the Comic Strip: 'Michael White knew people like Jack Nicholson, and they came to see us. Bianca Jagger and all sorts of funny people. Barry Humphries came ... and he knew Dustin Hoffman, and I met Dustin Hoffman for about 30 seconds' (2016). He argues that it was 'that kind of razzmatazz' that made the Comic Strip a well-known venue.

Once they became known as a group, the Comic Strip were treated like a hip new band. They were covered by music papers like *Melody Maker*, which called them 'rock 'n' roll comedians' (Humphries 1981). Even *The Guardian* suggested that 'the regulars from The Comic Strip are now being launched more like pop stars than comics' (Denselow 1981). When their LP was released in 1981, it was greeted with some of the furore that had been stirred up by the Sex Pistols in the previous decade. Boots, WH Smith and Woolworths – responsible for 20 per cent of the record market – all refused to stock it, and London Transport banned advertising for the LP (Petty 1981d).

On 8 August 1981, the Comic Strip performed their final show at the Boulevard Theatre, having played to a total estimated audience of 25,000 during their ten-month run (*Stage* 1981d). On 14 September, they performed at major London live music club The Venue before embarking on a fifteen-date national tour of 'the country's seediest fleapit venues', booked by the rock promoter Asgard (*Stage* 1981d). Again, the decision to play scuzzier performance spaces was a deliberate ploy, as Planer explains:

> Peter [Richardson] insisted that we play unusual places, like porn cinemas ... He wanted it to continue the image of the thing ... He didn't want to play [the] university circuit, he didn't want to play arts centres. He wanted it to look like the dangerous thing you couldn't get hold of ... We got the reaction like a punk band might of sort of, 'We don't like you in our town,' from older people. But in the actual audiences I think people were bemused and shocked and delighted and excited.
>
> *Planer 2018*

Sayle recalls audiences on tour being harder than the ones they had faced at the Boulevard Theatre: '[J]ust because you've been in London ... doesn't mean shit in fucking Ipswich. You know, we met with a very mixed response outside London really ... You're full of yourself because you've been on the cover of *Time Out* twice. And no cunt knows who you are at the Kirklevington Country Club' (Sayle 2017). *Melody Maker* covered the tour, and describes a Monday night gig in Leeds: 'There's a good crowd, but they're as cold as a plate of Wimpy chips, uncertain how to take the Strip. The criticisms that their humour is too London-orientated seems to be true, but their sheer comic talent eventually wins over the crowd' (Humphries 1981). This suggests that they had the performance chops to overcome any cynicism they encountered.

In the spring of 1982, they went further afield with an Australian tour – albeit without Arnold Brown – that took in the Adelaide Festival. *Guardian* theatre critic Michael Billington vividly captured the excitement of the Adelaide shows: 'Twice nightly Sayle, bullet-headed and manic with a face that belongs in a police gazette wanted ad, has been busy biting off the hand that has fed him. He has been lashing out at Adelaide ... at the perils of street entertainment ... and at German expressionist dance-drama, which he characterises with the frenzied cavorting of a hopped-up pachyderm' (1982).

With a hit London show, a controversial LP, coverage in the music press, and tours of the UK and Australia, it was probably inevitable that the Comic Strip would find their way onto television. In fact, alternative comedy's small screen debut wasn't exclusively dedicated to them, but to the scene more generally. Producer Paul Jackson had become aware of the new comedy, and managed to get it onto TV quite quickly. A one-off programme called *Boom Boom Out Go the Lights* was broadcast at 10.20pm on Tuesday 14 October 1980. Jackson had got Alexei Sayle, Rik Mayall, Nigel Planer, Tony Allen and Keith Allen into a TV studio and filmed their acts – along with Paul Jones and the Blues Band, an inappropriately unhip choice for musical guest. The show had little impact on the viewing public – perhaps unsurprisingly, given the late night midweek slot – but the *Financial Times*'s Chris Dunkley wrote enthusiastically about 'startling young nightclub performers who stand in relation to *The Comedians* as Hot Gossip to The Tiller Girls' and concluded, 'The quicker the whole crowd is brought back the better' (1980).

What's significant about *Boom Boom* is that it represented television's recognition of a live scene that had existed for less than 18 months. A second edition followed on 5 May 1981, this time featuring Alexei Sayle, Tony Allen, 20th Century Coyote, the Outer Limits, Pauline Melville and Andy de la Tour – and a rather more appropriate musical guest act, Dexy's Midnight Runners. Taken together, the two editions of *Boom Boom* favoured Comic Strip performers. Alternative Cabaret was represented by Melville, de la Tour and Tony Allen, whereas the Comic Strip had Sayle, Mayall, Edmondson, Planer and Richardson.

By November 1982 it was clear that the Comic Strip was the dominant force in televised alternative comedy, with the *The Comic Strip presents...* debuting on Channel 4 just a week before BBC2 aired the first episode of cult sitcom *The Young Ones*. This wasn't a Comic Strip production, but four of the five main characters were played by members of the group and based on elements of their live acts. Mayall's feminist poet became the would-be radical student Rick, Edmondson's Sir Adrian Dangerous became the crazed punk Vyvyan, Planer's dreadful folksinger became Neil the hippie, and Sayle played a different member of the Balowski family in each episode, incorporating material adapted from his stand-up. The only central cast member not from the Comic Strip was Christopher Ryan, but the character he played – Mike – had originally been based on a creepy persona Peter Richardson had developed in the Outer Limits.

Television divided the alternative comedians. Some felt that when TV producers started turning up at the Comedy Store and the Comic Strip it created an unpleasant atmosphere, like the first flash of lightning on a perfect summer day. Pauline Melville recalls, 'There began to be the feeling that you were being checked out for TV or some other career prospects. I almost immediately began to lose interest ... I just did it for the hell of it. And also because there were certain things I wanted to attack, politically' (2018). Similarly, Maggie Steed – an actor who briefly did stand-up with Alternative Cabaret – remembers how it felt at the Comedy Store:

> There was a sudden change. Not in the material, but in the atmosphere of the place, when it suddenly became known as a place where there was something interesting going on. And people from the television were turning up . . . You'd see people sitting on the stairs going, 'This is a really big night for us' . . . So it started to change. So it wasn't as anarchic.
>
> *Steed 2018*

On the other hand, some willingly accepted TV's embrace. In 1984, Dawn French told *The Face*: 'We didn't start to always stay on the alternative cabaret circuit. People think we've sold out 'cos we're on TV but that's ridiculous. People perform because they're ambitious. The alternative cabaret circuit is a stepping-off point, a place where people start out' (Rouse 1984: 38). By this point French and Saunders had only done a smattering of television – an episode of *The Young Ones*, a single episode of the relatively obscure Channel 4 series *The Entertainers*, and the first two series of *The Comic Strip Presents . . .* However, they would go on to write and star in the sitcom *Girls on Top* (1985–6), and subsequently their own hugely successful sketch show, *French and Saunders*, which would run for six series between 1987 and 2004. In the course of this they enjoyed more television success than any of their Comic Strip contemporaries, becoming the Morecambe & Wise of their generation.

### 'Revolutions by their very nature are not gradual'

The possibility of something like alternative comedy hitting the UK had been there since America reinvented stand-up in the 1950s, but when it finally happened, it happened with remarkable speed. In less than three and a half years, the alternative cabaret scene went from a single London venue to a national phenomenon, broadcast on rival TV channels. On one level, this could be attributed to the efforts of 'a small number of talented and determined people', as Thatcher put it. Individuals like Peter Rosengard, Don Ward, Alexei Sayle, Tony Allen and Peter Richardson all made vital contributions to the comic revolution, and even the impresario Michael White and the TV producer Paul Jackson were important in popularizing it.

That said, it would be simplistic and misleading to put it all down to individual endeavour. After all, John Paul Joans had challenged the conservatism of working men's club comedy, but without a community of like-minded people around him, he made little lasting impact. It was the way these individuals met, interacted, and coalesced into groups, networks and communities that brought alternative comedy into being. Altcom was built on three pillars – the Comedy Store, the Comic Strip, and Alternative Cabaret – each contributing something different.

Despite its reputation as the birthplace of altcom, the Comedy Store was not set up to be an alternative venue and took some time to fully embrace the new comedy it had spawned. Nonetheless, two things made it vitally important. First, it was the UK's first dedicated comedy club, and thus established a new kind of venue in which stand-up could be performed. Second, and probably more important, it brought together the germs of the epidemic (as George Melly put it), or the people who had been wandering around in space to allow the big comedy bang to happen (as Arnold Brown put it). The fact that the Store brought together individuals like Alexei Sayle, Tony Allen and Peter Richardson was what made it really significant, because it was their efforts both there and beyond that really made alternative comedy happen.

The Comic Strip was crucial in popularizing alternative comedy. Its success, as a live show and particularly on television, took altcom beyond London and drew it to the nation's attention. Alexei Sayle argues that:

> Revolutions by their very nature are not gradual, but pressure builds up on the dam and then boom ... Paul Jackson was coming down the Comedy Store and could get stuff on the telly ... I mean television in the end made the difference, really. I don't know what would have happened if we'd had to build it through live work. I don't know whether it would have happened in the same way.
>
> *Sayle 2017*

On a personal level, I wouldn't have encountered alternative comedy as a teenager in a provincial town like Lincoln if it wasn't for TV programmes like *The Comic Strip Presents ...* and *The Young Ones*. However, what's interesting about the Comic Strip becoming the public face of alternative comedy is that in many ways the acts involved were so atypical, as Nigel Planer points out:

I mean what's odd is that us lot, our group, our gang – Alexei is a stand-up, but the rest of us aren't ... You know, myself, Peter, and Rik and Ade I think are exceptions to the fashion that happened rather than the rule ... It's quite a dull form, I think, stand-up, personally ... But if you think about Rik and Ade and myself and Peter ... not one of us is really a stand-up.

*Planer 2018*

Planer argues that they were also unusual in that they played the emerging live circuit for such a short period before being whisked off to the world of television: '[W]e did a year in the Comedy Store. Then we did eight months in the Comic Strip, ten months? We did a tour of Australia and came back and became telly stars.'

Alternative Cabaret was the opposite of the Comic Strip – comparatively unknown among the general public, yet far more typical of how altcom would develop. The residency at the Elgin was the first of the pub-based cabaret venues that formed the circuit that would grow up in the decades that followed. This circuit was further seeded by the gigs Alternative Cabaret performed around London, which helped to establish the idea of running small-scale, DIY cabaret nights. Their successful run at the Edinburgh Fringe also helped to establish stand-up comedy there, now such an important part of the festival but then practically unknown. Despite being the least-remembered of the three, in many ways Alternative Cabaret was the most important in establishing a live comedy scene that continues to this day. Beyond this, the group also embodied the radicalism of alternative comedy, with an explicit mission statement to extend the content and style of stand-up, to challenge sexism and racism, and to 'bring an end to injustice and tyranny'. With all of this in mind, it's perhaps unsurprising that during the 1980s, the phrase alternative cabaret went from being the name of a specific group to a generic label for the entire scene.

# CHAPTER 3
# THE SPREAD OF THE CIRCUIT

In early 1983, Andy de la Tour sent out a letter to fellow performers that paints a vivid picture of the state of the alternative cabaret circuit at this point:

> As you will probably know – especially if you were there – there was recently a meeting of many of the performers currently working the London cabaret scene. The meeting was held courtesy of Colin down at the Sol y Sombra and we have much to thank him for, not forgetting the bloke running the disco there at the same time. The meeting was the first attempt to organise – in the communist sense – the cabaret scene.
>
> BSUCA

As it continues, the tone skips playfully from seriousness of intent to jokiness – after all, many present were comedians. There are references to Marx, but these are clearly tongue-in-cheek: 'This attempt to organise the field will only work if everyone sticks to it. (quote: Marx: Theories of Surplus Value, Vol.9 but I don't need to tell you that).' Nestled among the jokey bits are some serious resolutions:

> a) No jokes at the meetings (immediately broken by Jim Barclay)
> b) As from May we agreed to ask for a minimum of £25 for solo performers for a 20-minute set. Having established this as a minimum, solo performers, double acts, compères etc can then negotiate their own fees above the minimum should they so wish.
> c) This minimum was to apply to all venues except:
>   i. Soly Sombra [*sic*], Crown and Castle, Earth Exchange where we agreed to the present situation of a box-office split.
>   ii. The Comedy Store and New Variety where we have asked for a minimum of £30 for solo performers for a 20 minute set. (also at C.S. – a min of £40 for compering; £45 for double-act).

The letter reports that, 'Promoters/Manafements [*sic*] talked to so far have agreed to these new fee levels. Don [Ward] at the Comedy Store would also like to see some kind of written confirmation that performrs [*sic*] are on Schedule D (i.e. self-employed) tax so that he won't get his collar felt by the Inland Revenue, (previous tax receipt would do; accountant's letter etc)'.

Ultimately, this attempt to unionize the circuit came to nothing, perhaps because the acting union Equity seemed reluctant to get involved. In April 1982, de la Tour complained about Equity refusing membership to alternative comedians (*Stage* 1982b). Undeterred, on 19 April 1983 he wrote to Archie MacMillan – Equity's Variety organizer – inviting him to a meeting between cabaret performers and promoters. There's no record of MacMillan's response.

In any case, the individualistic nature of stand-up made unionizing the circuit inherently difficult. Paul Merton confesses: 'The idea was that everybody should get paid the same. I remember looking around the room, and I said, "Well I don't want to get paid the same as *him*" ... It's just not going to work, because in the end, somebody who's not very good, why should I be paid the same as him?' (2018).

Nonetheless, the paperwork reveals a number of things. First, Ward's response to the demands suggests that the circuit was becoming more professionalized, and starting to move on from the cash-in-hand DIY approach to a situation in which acts declared earnings for income tax. Second, the fact that Ward was entertaining the idea of the minimum rates of pay suggests that relations between performers and club owners were reasonably cooperative – as does the fact that performers accepted smaller venues paying a share of the money taken on the door. Third, and most important, the fact that performers were starting to ask for decent rates of pay suggests that the alternative cabaret circuit was in a healthy state. Indeed, de la Tour's letter to Archie MacMillan estimates, 'There are probably over 20 venues of this kind now.'

Something else that suggests the circuit was thriving is the sheer number of people in the contacts list. There are forty-one acts here, and whilst most are solo, there are also double acts, a triple act, and even a quadruple act – taking the total number of performers to fifty. This is not to say that all of them were making a living from the circuit. Some had other sources of income, like acting or street performance. Talking about this period, Arthur Smith wrote: 'The cabaret scene was flourishing, but was still so small and poorly paid that no performer yet considered playing it to be much of a career move' (2009: 150). However, the list doesn't include everyone working in alternative

## Alternative Comedy

cabaret at the time. The fact that over fifty people were playing the circuit at this point suggests that if it wasn't exactly rude with health, it was at least impolite.

The contacts list is a fascinating document, giving a good idea of the nature of alternative cabaret in 1983. It shows well-known names of the future (Clive Anderson, Ben Elton, Paul Merton[1]) rubbing shoulders with acts who are now largely forgotten. Indeed, one of them, Ian Kelly, remains totally obscure. Unlike the other forty acts I have entirely failed to find any information on him. Of the rest, it's worth noting that all four comedians that appeared on the Alternative Cabaret LP and in their 1981 Edinburgh run are listed (Tony Allen, Jim Barclay, Andy de la Tour, Pauline Melville). By contrast, the only members of the Comic Strip here are Arnold Brown and French and Saunders – Sayle, Mayall, Edmondson, Planer and Richardson having moved on. The also-rans of the Comedy Store's early days are also largely absent. Presumably people like Peter Wear, Cliff Shore, and Paul Goodman had given up or found other places to play, although Bob Flag is still listed.

The most common type of act is solo stand-up. Even taking a fairly strict definition, there are eighteen of these, making up 44 per cent of the total.[2] The next most common category is street performers, of which there are seven (17 per cent).[3] Then there are double acts (four, 10 per cent),[4] and poets (three, 7 per cent).[5] The remaining nine acts include a couple of musical comics, an impressionist, a bizarre clown, a sketch group, a male feminist comedy troupe, and three who are hard to categorize.[6] The range of acts represented suggests that the cabaret circuit was not just healthy but also artistically diverse.

In this chapter, I'll explore how it developed from here throughout the rest of the decade, looking at the spread of pub-based venues, the role played by the publicly subsidized CAST New Variety, the emergence of agencies like Off the Kerb, the growth of comedy at the Edinburgh Fringe, and the phenomenon of touring shows.

### Rooms above pubs

Newspaper reports from the mid-1980s suggest that once the circuit had become established, it spread quickly. A *Sunday Times* article noted that, 'The new cabaret – or "new variety" or "alternative comedy" – has been one of the few boom areas in live entertainment in the past two or three years. Last week in London, for instance, you could have taken your pick from some 40 shows – half as many again as last year and twice as many as two years ago' (Williams 1984).

One factor that helped the circuit to mushroom was that it was relatively easy to set up a regular cabaret night. It's been argued that for all its left-wing pretensions, alternative comedy encapsulated the Thatcherite ethos of small businesses driven by thrusting entrepreneurs (Cook 1994: 10; Smith 2009: 158; Thomas 2015a), but in fact this description doesn't fit most of the people who ran the venues. As Steve Gribbin explains, 'A lot of them were rooms above pubs ... And they were done on a shoestring' (2018). Jenny Lecoat suggests that the DIY ethos encouraged people to set up cabaret venues: '[I]t came out of all those people who were music fans ... and there was that sort of punk mentality of anyone can do this ... And of course stand-up shows are much cheaper to put on than bands or theatre. So it made sense that the whole thing was going to spread' (2018).

The first of the DIY-type venues started to appear not long after the Comedy Store first opened at the Gargoyle. Kim Wells set up a weekly night at a vegetarian restaurant called the Earth Exchange in Highgate as early as February 1980. Julian Clary did his first alternative cabaret performance there, appearing as Gillian Pie-Face, and many acts fondly remember its gentle, hippie-ish audience. Mark Steel recalls: 'It was on a Monday night and ... the brilliant thing about doing the Earth Exchange was you got ... a free vegetarian dinner ... Economically that was like quite important ... And then there'd be a collection, and you'd get eight quid or something' (2018). In 1981, Jean Nicholson started the Crown and Castle cabaret. The Finborough Arms started as a venue in 1982, claiming to be 'The first pub in London to present cabaret' (Conway and McGillivray 1988: 153), and the Hemingford Arms started running cabaret in December the same year.

Some of these London clubs developed strong reputations. Malcolm Hardee's Tunnel Palladium – at the Mitre, near the Blackwall Tunnel – held its first show on 8 January 1984, with the Greatest Show on Legs, Skint Video, and Fiasco Job Job on the bill. It quickly became known for its hostile, anarchic atmosphere, with well-organized hecklers regularly doing battle with the acts. Jongleurs – which started at the Cornet in Battersea on 4 February 1983 – was another matter. Initially it was known for its booking policy, presenting 'a mixed bill of singers, groups, comedy acts, jugglers, fire eaters, classical and jazz musicians'. Maria Kempinska explained that she wanted to 'make it into a real variety show' rather than concentrating on 'comedy-oriented performers' (*Stage* 1983b). It didn't take long before

## Alternative Comedy

Jongleurs became known for something else – the 'Battersea hoorays and Sloanes' who dominated its audiences (Williams 1984).

Although alternative cabaret remained a mainly metropolitan phenomenon throughout the 1980s, it didn't take long to start spreading beyond London. Alan McGowan set up a monthly cabaret called Wit's End[7] at the 250-capacity Pavilion in Brighton in 1981, claiming it was 'the first club outside of London presenting ... alternative comedy' (Sweeting 1982: 21). More clubs sprang up within striking distance of the capital – the Square in Harlow, the Old Town Hall Arts Centre in Hemel Hempstead, the Friday Alternative at the South Hill Park Arts Centre in Bracknell, the Zap Club in Brighton. Gradually, outposts of the cabaret circuit began to appear further afield – Spotz in Nottingham, the Tic Toc Club in Coventry, Cabaret a Go Go in Newcastle. A club called Brickies opened in the Bricklayer's Arms in Bournemouth, a local listings magazine describing its promoters as 'pioneers of New Variety and New Wave comedy on the Costa Geriatrica' (Ward 1984).

The listings magazines *City Limits* and *Time Out* recognized the size and importance of the circuit when they began to list cabaret separately from theatre, and *The Alternative Theatre Directory* followed suit in 1988. Its 'Cabaret Venues' section gives some idea of just how big the scene had grown by this point (Conway and McGillivray 1988: 151–9). London now had thirty-three weekly cabaret venues, most of them running throughout the year. Between them they put on forty-seven shows per week, the most popular nights being Fridays (fourteen shows) and Saturdays (fifteen shows). Some clubs had specialist remits, only programming poetry (Apples and Snakes), or playing to specialist audiences – gay and lesbian (Fallen Women) or women-only (Cave of Harmony).

The total weekly audience capacity of these clubs, based on maximum capacity of venue multiplied by number of shows per week, is 6,735. This is capacity rather than actual attendance, and one venue, the Rub-a-dub Club at the Greyhound in Sydenham, notes that although its capacity is 150, its average attendance is only sixty. However, the figure doesn't include fortnightly or monthly clubs like the Rosemary Branch or the Bearcat, or bigger venues that programme comedy like the Albany Empire and the Hackney Empire. Meanwhile, the 'Cabaret Artists' section (99–109) lists as many as 128 acts. Although a few of these did not play the alternative cabaret circuit as such, the vast majority of them did. What this suggests is that in the half-decade after Andy de la Tour's attempt to set up a trade union for cabaret performers, the circuit tripled in size.

Something that might have encouraged so many performers to start out as cabaret acts was the simple economics of the situation. Putting together a stand-up or ranting poetry act required almost no capital outlay. The benefits system was still generous enough to provide a financial cushion while the act was becoming established. Then there was the fact that, as William Cook noted, 'Many comedians even started out courtesy of Maggie's own Enterprise Allowance Scheme' (1994: 10). This was never designed to be a source of arts funding, but in 1987 Anne Carlisle noted that 'after a period some artists began to realise that the rather broad requirements for eligibility to the scheme meant that it could also encompass being self-employed as an artist' (23). Steve Gribbin and Brian Mulligan of the musical comedy double act Skint Video were both on the scheme, and Gribbin recalls: 'So was everybody we knew. It's ironic that it enabled us to do [what we did]. It was the ultimate Thatcherite scheme' (2018). What Gribbin sees as irony could also be seen as inventive subversiveness – using a scheme aimed at promoting capitalist self-reliance to grow a left-wing performance scene.

## CAST New Variety

Another important factor in the expansion of the circuit was the intervention of Roland and Claire Muldoon of the pioneering left-wing theatre company CAST. Jenny Eclair argues:

> [T]hey are the most under-thanked, underestimated couple in the whole history of alternative comedy ... They created a whole network of CAST New Variety ... and they were really right-on about having women on the bill and all that sort of thing. I mean they were so ahead of their time. The Comedy Store always sponges up all the praise and all the glory for creating however many comedy names, but it wasn't, it was Roland and Claire Muldoon.
>
> *Eclair 2018*

Like the comedians on the Enterprise Allowance Scheme, CAST took a cannily subversive approach to funding, at odds with the anti-funding attitudes of Tony Allen and Alexei Sayle. Roland Muldoon recalls, 'One of the great arguments of this time, people ... used to believe it was market forces and all the rest of it that somehow made it happen. And it didn't. It was subsidy ... that's the answer really to why it took off' (2010).

CAST – an acronym standing for Cartoon Archetypical Slogan Theatre – formed in 1965, but didn't get their first Arts Council Grant until 1976. They felt ambivalent about funding. On the one hand it allowed them to pursue theatre full-time, but on the other they worried about funding leading to government interference with their plays (Itzin 1980: 18). Ultimately though, Roland Muldoon acknowledged, '[I]t remains essential that labour-intensive theatre be underwritten by increased funding' (Itzin 1980: 19).

CAST had always been interested in a performance style directed straight at the audience, and by the early 1980s, their work was becoming increasingly cabaret-like – particularly a show called *Sedition 81*. Shortly after this, one of the leading actors had to drop out of their Arts Council funded play, *Hotel Sunshine*. They cancelled the rest of the tour and used the money to start running the first of their New Variety venues at the Old White Horse pub in Brixton. *The Stage* gushed, 'Hot on the heels of London's alternative comedy cult, the variety world has spawned its own "new wave" performers', as it announced that the opening night, 22 January 1982, would feature Akimbo, Mr Clean, Brid Keenan, the Chip Shop Show and others (1982c). Tickets were cheap – £1.50 (£5.20) full price, 90p (£3.12) for students or social security claimants. Roland Muldoon compèred many of the shows, and Claire's role was 'spotting and encouraging the new talents' (Muldoon 2013: 33).

The Arts Council was unhappy that CAST had used their *Hotel Sunshine* grant to subsidize New Variety, leading to what *The Stage* described as 'a showdown' (1982d) and what Roland Muldoon remembers as the funding body going 'apeshit about it' (2018). As a result, there was no more Arts Council money. Instead, in the summer of 1982 CAST secured a grant of £25,000 (£86,672.91) from Tony Banks at the radical Labour-run Greater London Council. The following September, the GLC gave them another £82,000 (£271,816.17).

In 1984, when the GLC faced abolition, one of its responses was to give CAST money to run a campaigning New Variety tour around Greater London. In the *NME*, Dave Quantick wrote, 'You go along, sign a petition if you want, buy a ticket and see a lot of New Variety acts. Have fun and support the GLC ... a noble cause, a good idea, and you should go' (1984). The *Live 32 Borough Touring Show* involved twenty-eight shows between 8 and 31 March, and another thirty-three in April. The venues were diverse – anywhere from the Half Moon Theatre to Lambeth Town Hall, from South Mitcham Community Centre to the Dolphin in Romford. The acts were equally varied, with bills including comedians like Pauline Melville, poets like Benjamin Zephaniah, musicians like Billy Bragg, street performers like Captain JJ Waller, and one-offs like the socialist magician Ian Saville.

In 1985, CAST were still receiving a GLC revenue grant of £65,000 (£193,467.31) for New Variety, plus another £15,000 (£44,646.30) to run an Arts in Danger week at Hounslow's Montague Hall. Even after the GLC was finally abolished in March 1986, CAST were still able to secure other sources of subsidy, particularly the London Borough Grant Scheme. Roland Muldoon explains how crucial all this funding was to the running of the New Variety circuit:

> A. We paid, with a grant now. B. We backed it up with paid technicians. And then we set up a collective, in each place we performed, of people we also paid, who every week would set up ... So we used the money to build up a base, to pay for the staging and the lighting and the equipment. So our shows were always really well technically [produced] and also we paid people ... And being a leftie organisation, we were quite principled in all of that.
>
> *Muldoon 2018*

A CAST circular dated 26 July 1982, handwritten by their administrator Warren Lakin, announces: 'GOOD NEWS – NEW VARIETY HAS GOT A GRANT FROM THE G.L.C. . . . . . THIS MEANS MORE VENUES; SHOWS; AND WORK FOR PERFORMERS IN LONDON' (BSUCA). The new season was due to start on 17 September, with venues in Brixton (Fridays), White City (Saturdays) and Wood Green (Sundays). Lakin pointed out, 'ALL THIS MEANS WE CAN NOW OFFER CONSECUTIVE GIGS'. As the letter suggests, CAST's public subsidy sped up the growth of the circuit by significantly increasing the number of venues and thus the amount of work available.

It also meant that New Variety gigs paid more generously than other venues, hence being singled out for a higher guaranteed fee in the proposed comedy trade union's demands. The fact CAST paid good money undoubtedly helped to make being a cabaret performer more financially viable, as did the sheer volume of work they could provide. In 1985, Claire Muldoon told *The Stage*, 'The GLC years will be remembered as the years where numerous acts were able to break out of the bland ghetto of popular entertainment and reach popular audiences without compromising their material' (*Stage* 1985).

By late 1986, CAST was able to add an enormous jewel to the crown of its New Variety circuit. The Hackney Empire is one of the few of London's majestic music halls to survive the death of variety in the 1950s. Built in 1901, it presented variety for more than half a century before closing down in 1956 and being converted into first a TV studio, then a bingo hall. When Mecca Bingo closed the Hackney Empire, it was offered to CAST, and through a process of careful negotiation and wily wrangling, they managed to bring it back to life as a theatre, staging the first New Variety show there on 9 December 1986. Roland Muldoon recalls the challenge it posed: 'All of a sudden we had a twelve hundred seat venue, not a two hundred seat one, in Hackney ... I couldn't sleep, you know. We had no money' (2010). At one point CAST had as many as eight new Variety venues, and in 1985 they started calling themselves 'The London Circuit' (*Stage* 1985) – a phrase that came to refer to the alternative cabaret scene as a whole, and was still very much in use when I started performing.

As well as helping the cabaret circuit to grow, CAST also helped to make it more diverse. They promoted female performers and ethnically diverse acts, and – as the name New Variety suggests – they also prized artistic diversity. Olly Crick, who was half of juggling duo the Long and the Short Of It, argues, '[T]he Comedy Store was alternative comics, but CAST was New Variety. So there would be a band or a musical act. There would be a variety act, magician or juggler. One or two stand-ups maybe ... or there'd be a stand-up and a compère who also did a bit of stand-up' (2018). Mark Hurst, then a ranting poet known as Mark Miwurdz, first encountered the London cabaret scene when CAST started booking him:

> There was hardly any stand-ups on the New Variety when I got there. I was still doing poetry but half poetry, half stand-up. And it was always great because you would be the only male single stand-up on the bill, usually. There'd be a musical act, a mime act, a juggler, some sort of speciality act playing the spoons or slack-wire walking or something.
>
> *Hurst 2018*

A flyer advertising four New Variety shows at the Cricklewood Hotel in October 1982 (BSUCA) supports Hurst's memories. Each bill features four acts, sixteen in total, and none is a fully-fledged stand-up comedian. There are eight musical acts (Proper Little Madams, Pookiesnackenburger, Pearls & Swine, Holloway All-Stars, Mr Sprat's 21st Century Pop Motets, Jumping Jazz Rats, Akimbo, Jazira), three street acts (Captain JJ Waller, Controlled Attack, Tim Bat), three poets (Mark Miwurdz, Little Brother, Attila the Stockbroker), a comedy sketch group (Mountbatten's Plimsoll), and a musical poetry act (African Dawn).

As the decade wore on, stand-up began to dominate the alternative cabaret circuit, and thus became more common on New Variety bills. In 1993,

Muldoon complained, 'I wanted jugglers, magicians, balancing acts, on the bills, and in the early days we got them. But somehow comedy got the upper hand and has now become a kind of industry standard' (Hepple 1993: 11). A flyer advertising seven shows at the Cricklewood Hotel in November and December 1987 (BSUCA) shows that stand-up had already got the upper hand by this point. There are still double acts, jugglers, street performers, poets and musical acts, but now eleven of the twenty-three acts listed are solo stand-ups.

## Agencies

Something else that helped the circuit to grow was the emergence of agencies and promoters, touting for work for the acts they represented. As befits alternative cabaret, the people who ran them took a punk DIY approach, learning how to operate as they went along. One of the earliest was Pranksters, run by Jonathan Richards and Ivor Dembina – who still runs comedy events today, as well as being a veteran stand-up comedian. Pranksters began as a company that offered bespoke pranking – as the name might suggest – with Dembina recruiting performers from the alternative cabaret circuit to carry out the practical jokes. They soon changed tack, instead going for a more straightforward plan.

By May 1984, they were advertising themselves as 'Alternative Comedy Promoters' in the trade press (*Stage* 1984), and around this time, they produced their first brochure. By today's standards it's a slightly amateurish attempt at marketing, a distinctly homemade-looking document. The pages are cheaply reproduced and bound between two sheets of thin card. Each page features between one and three acts, with a copier-degraded photo and a typewritten blurb for each of them. There's also an introduction, explaining the idea of Pranksters to the uninitiated:

> PRANKSTERS is the leading promoter in the field of alternative cabaret. It puts together complete packages of first class live acts for any venue in the country ... PRANKSTERS is more than simply a theatrical agency. It provides a creative input, advising artists about their material, planning the running order and overall presentation of the show and making all the necessary arrangements to ensure the success of every gig.
>
> *BSUCA*

## Alternative Comedy

Dembina recalls the thinking behind Pranksters:

> I was mindful of the complaint from the acts that they only had one gig a week ... And out of that, we decided to have a brochure of acts put together. We'd do two things. One, we'd run our own little gig. And two, we'd try and sell little packages of entertainment ... to whomever wanted it. And you know, we were just floundering around ... We didn't do marketing or market research.
>
> *Dembina 2018*

A flyer from 1984 advertises a Pranksters package show called *HA! – THE PACKAGE*, with a bill made up of David Cohen,[8] Cecilia Scanlon, Ivor Dembina and Steve Edgar, appearing at the Finborough Arms (10 November), the Richmond Cabaret Club (12 November), the Pindar of Wakefield (14 November), the Zap Club in Brighton (16 November), and the Crown & Castle (24 November) (BSUCA). In this case, the show was marketed to existing cabaret venues, but as Dembina explains, Pranksters also put shows into venues that were new to this type of entertainment:

> We were among ... the first people to commodify it ... It was not like we were setting up a business to get rich ... We didn't really know what we were doing, but we thought, 'This is great. We reckon there's a demand for this' ... We didn't have an office, I think we did it out of my front room. You know, with a phone and ... a typewriter. Yeah, we typed the invoices, we didn't even have computers. And of course the acts liked it because we were quite well organised, comparatively. The gigs themselves had [an] enjoyably loose feel ... What we brought to it was, we were going to take this what was essentially London-centric thing and offer it out elsewhere to whoever wanted it, like colleges, arts centres, anyone ... We were selling it like meat, but underneath it, we really did believe in the product as well.
>
> *Dembina 2018*

The contradictions in what Dembina says highlight the spirit of the 1980s cabaret circuit. This left-wing former playwright talks of commodification and selling comedy like meat – but on the other hand, not wanting to get rich, not knowing what he was doing, and running the whole enterprise out of his front room. Where he describes the Pranksters gigs as 'enjoyably loose',

## The Spread of the Circuit

Mark Thomas once described them as 'really ropey college gigs . . . put out . . . as the cheapest comedy around' (Cook 1994: 205).

In spite of this, Pranksters' ramshackle approach to promotion undoubtedly increased the opportunities for acts to get paid work, and encouraged newcomers to the circuit. Jeremy Hardy remembered an early performance at a Pranksters venue: 'In February 1984, my second ever open spot was, I think, ten minutes for Ivor Dembina . . . he did an open mike night somewhere in Archway . . . I did ten minutes. I think that's the first time I ever got paid. I think I got eleven quid for that, so bit excited by it' (2018).

Pranksters produced three editions of their brochure, which chart the growth of the business. The second two were produced by the Lasso Co-operative, so the text is properly typeset and the photos properly reproduced – suggesting that Richards and Dembina were developing a more professional approach. Moreover, each edition contains more acts than the last. The first features twenty-three acts, the second forty-eight and the third fifty-nine – an increase of around 256 per cent, which both reflects the growth of the circuit more generally and suggests that Pranksters were helping to stimulate this.

They were not the only ones making homespun attempts to promote alternative cabaret. As well as establishing a circuit of gigs, CAST also set up the New Variety Cabaret Agency. Like Pranksters, they produced a brochure of acts, a shiny card folder containing loose A4 sheets with poorly reproduced photos and typewritten text (BSUCA). However, the most significant of the pioneer agencies was Off the Kerb. Since the early 1980s, Off the Kerb has grown into one of the biggest and most powerful comedy agencies, representing acts like Michael McIntyre, Phill Jupitus and Josh Widdicombe. Agencies like Off the Kerb, and their rival Avalon, have come to represent the circuit's metamorphosis from an anarchic DIY scene to a professional and highly commercialized business. Off the Kerb's founder, the late Addison Cresswell, started his career as the entertainments officer for Brighton Polytechnic, and the attitudes he expressed might suggest a chest-beating capitalist, keen to exploit the alternative cabaret scene:

> I can't work with comics who say, 'I don't want to be famous.' . . . Why get on the stage in the first place if you don't want to be famous? I've go [sic] no time for these idiots. You can be famous for five minutes at the Comedy Store, or you can get yourself on the fucking telly, and do the business. You can do big tours round the country, or you can be a very big fish in a tiny little pond.'

*cited in Cook 1994: 267*

## Alternative Comedy

In spite of the rhetoric, Off the Kerb started with the same kind of amateurish enthusiasm as Pranksters or the New Variety Cabaret Agency. Jeremy Hardy points out that while some saw Off the Kerb as 'this huge, awful corporate comedy machine', in fact it was 'being run out of an office next to Addison's bedroom, with a layout table on it because Addison was basically a graphic designer and made really good posters' (2018).

Joe Norris, who runs Off the Kerb today, got involved in the mid-1980s when Cresswell was promoting the Red Wedge Comedy Tour, designed to encourage young people to vote Labour. He recalls the kind of spirit that drove Off the Kerb in its early days:

> There was that kind of do-it-yourself punk rock [mentality] ... You only wanted to do a good job for the people you represented and if you did a good job, we'll see what happens afterwards. I don't think there was that kind of, 'Yeah, we can make a business out of this' ... Addison was never going to wear a suit ... Addison was always like, 'No, if I want to go and have a meeting with someone, I'll turn up in my jeans.' ... It did come out of left-wing politics as well, I mean those kind of radical ideas that people were talking about ... as a reaction to what was going on from 1979 onwards.
>
> *Norris 2018*

Similarly, Mark Hurst marvels at the contrast between how Off the Kerb started out and what it grew into:

> I remember [Cresswell] staying in his little flat in Peckham before he expanded, and he was just working out of his kitchen. And putting all these handbills together with all these sort of fringey acts ... But how weird for him to see a direct route to making an absolute fortune out of it ... He didn't just come along and see a load of comics who'd got really polished and brilliant, and think, 'I'm going to push these to go on Channel 4.' ... He was down at the Deptford Engineers Trade Union Club watching a load of acts, and up at the Fringe when everybody was still doing their humble little sets. But had a big vision for it, which he followed through.
>
> *Hurst 2018*

Ambitious agencies like Off the Kerb allowed alternative cabaret to move beyond an established circuit of regular clubs, taking the acts further afield to other kinds of venues, often in universities and colleges.

### Festivals and tours

Another stimulus for the growing circuit was that festivals started to host alternative cabaret acts. Glastonbury's 1983 line-up, for example, included a cabaret tent playing host to acts like the Greatest Show on Legs, Tim Bat, Captain JJ Waller, and Attila the Stockbroker. The following year, Tony Allen, Sharon Landau and the Popticians were among the acts appearing at the Elephant Fayre in Cornwall.

However, by far the most important festival was the Edinburgh Fringe. Arthur Smith has recalled how alternative cabaret 'begun to colonise the Edinburgh Fringe programme and the festival would never be quite the same again' (2009: 160). After *Late Night Alternative* in 1980 and Alternative Cabaret in 1981, the colonization really started gaining momentum in 1983. In 1990 John Connor wrote, 'Of all the years of the decade, 1983 is the dream one' (27), and argued that the 'grouping of [Ben] Elton, [Rik] Mayall and [Andy] de la Tour at the Assembly Rooms was the comedy toast of Edinburgh that year' (42). De la Tour recalls how the show in question – entitled simply *Standup Comedy* – came about:

> David Jones was mainly a kind of fringe theatre person ... He approached me, because I think he'd done stuff at Edinburgh before – fringe theatre, you know. And he approached me about doing a show at Edinburgh ... So my immediate thing was, 'Let's do it with Ben' ... So I spoke to Ben about this and we decided we should be three of us, because none of us had enough material for any longer.
>
> De la Tour 2018

They initially wanted the third comic to be a woman and approached Jenny Lecoat. However, plans changed when Mayall expressed an interest, as de la Tour explains: 'When I next saw Ben, he says to me ... "Rik really wants to come with us to Edinburgh." ... We were completely opportunistic as well, we both thought Rik was brilliant of course, but we knew that Rik was, by this time, already famous' (2018). A document dated 10 May 1983 (BSUCA) suggests that the plan had actually been for the third act to be 20th Century Coyote, but presumably Ade Edmondson pulled out at some point. Nonetheless, the trio of Mayall, Elton and de la Tour went to Edinburgh, played for three weeks – rather than two as originally planned – and proved to be a commercial hit. An undated financial summary (BSUCA) shows that each performer was paid £2,387.82 (£7,915.22) for three weeks' work.

At this point it was normal for Edinburgh stand-up shows to involve a package of acts, and in 1984 there was a handful of such shows. However, there were also appearances from some of alternative comedy's biggest stars. Nigel Planer and the Big Karma Tour appeared at St Mary's Hall for a three-week run, and Alexei Sayle did two nights at the Edinburgh Playhouse.

Package shows continued to dominate through the rest of the decade. For example, in 1987 Ivor Dembina took the first of three shows under the title *Comic Abuse* to the Pleasance, in which he appeared alongside Dave Cohen, Felix Dexter,[9] and impressionist Phil Cornwell. The same year, Arnold Brown became the first alternative stand-up to win the Perrier Award (now the Edinburgh Comedy Award), in a show called *Brown Blues*, which also featured singing duo Jungr and Parker. Even as alternative cabaret gained this kind of official recognition, its joyfully amateurish spirit was still very much alive – as indicated by a flyer for *Brown Blues*, photocopied on simple white paper, with a grainy photo of the performers and all of the information handwritten in black felt-tip (BSUCA).

Doing a solo show was beyond most of the stand-ups working in alternative cabaret, but package shows allowed them to move beyond the familiar circuit venues. Jenny Eclair remembers touring with Rory Bremner and Mark Steel: 'We did a few gigs together, because we'd done an Edinburgh together. And that was organised by Colin Watkeys, who had ... taken over the Finborough Arms. And we went out under the name *Dubious Entertainment* ... Mostly to universities. Colleges and universities ... freshers' balls, all that kind of stuff. Some of them were hideous, some of them were so rough' (2018). Jenny Lecoat, who toured with Simon Fanshawe and Oscar McLennan as *Three of a Different Kind*, makes a similar point: '[W]e used to do a lot of colleges [and] universities ... I mean it was the Wild West, absolutely. You would turn up at a gig and you'd say, "Well we asked for a PA system," and they went, "Oh, we didn't know what that was. We've got you an amp but didn't know you needed a microphone"' (2018).

However, package shows could also bring advantages for the performers. In 1984, Nick Revell, Arnold Brown, Norman Lovett and Paul Merton toured in *Brave New Comedy*, starting even before the show went to the Fringe.

Revell recalls: 'We toured on and off for about 15 months. And we're getting some nice venues, varying sizes of audiences ... they've come to see *us*, it's not that they've come to the venue because there's something on here every month that CAST put on, they've come to see *us* ... that was quite liberating' (2017). Paul Merton, who was the last to be added to the line-up, recalls:

> I think the suggestion was for the *Brave New Comedy* thing that I should open every time, and I was very happy to do that because I saw that again as an opportunity to get more gig time, and opening isn't always the easiest of things, but I was very happy to do that as the others had come up with the idea of the show anyway ... So I opened for the whole year.
>
> *Merton 2018*

This, then, is what comedians had to gain from touring with a package show – an audience that had specifically come to see them, a regular income, and an abundance of stage time to hone and develop the act – particularly for Merton, having to consistently face the tough opening spot.

While packages became important because few comics had enough material to sustain a whole evening, a few pioneers did put together full-length shows. Towards the end of 1981, Keith Allen was nearing the end of his short but influential time on the alternative circuit when he put together *Whatever Happened to the AA Man's Salute*, described by *The Guardian* as 'a new kind of one-man show ... deal[ing] with some of his more surprising obsessions' (Harron 1981a). It opened at the Hampstead New End Theatre in late November and subsequently went on tour.

In 1984, Jim Barclay became one of the first of his generation to take a full-length solo show to the Fringe. He explains that *Four Minutes to Midnight* was a chance to stretch the form of stand-up and have a greater political impact:

> I thought, 'What I need to do is a longer one-man thing, about one theme,' which turned out to be nukes. Which I did a few times. Took it around, took it to the Edinburgh Festival ... It's easier because the audience have paid their money, they know what they're going to get ... I wrote that show specifically to take the audience on a journey. So in an ideal world they were slightly different when they came out than when they went in, which is what theatre should do.
>
> *Barclay 2016*

## Alternative Comedy

By building the entire show around a single theme, Barclay was anticipating the themed stand-up shows that have come to dominate the Edinburgh Fringe in the last ten years.

However, alternative comedy's most dramatic leap beyond the boundaries of a circuit of small pub-based clubs was when the performers who had become TV stars went out on tours put together by rock promoters like Phil McIntyre. McIntyre worked with heavy metal bands like Gillan and Iron Maiden before branching out into comedy. In 1983, he put together a 23-date tour of *The Young Ones*, featuring Rik Mayall, Ade Edmondson and Nigel Planer, but he also worked with smaller names – it was McIntyre who promoted *Brave New Comedy*.

Perhaps most significantly, he worked with Alexei Sayle, who was the first alternative comedian to do a solo tour in big venues. Sayle was following a precedent set by Billy Connolly (Sayle 2016: 273), but touring was still quite a novel move for a stand-up comedian. Sayle's first tour began on 27 May 1982 at the Theatre Royal, Bury St Edmunds and continued throughout the month in venues like the Liverpool Everyman, the Towngate Theatre, Basildon, and the Plough Arts Centre, Torrington. These were mid-sized venues, with capacities generally ranging from 200 to 500, but when the tour resumed in September, he was playing bigger venues like Southampton Guildhall, Birmingham Town Hall and Nottingham Theatre Royal. Most of these venues had capacities of over a thousand. Sayle worked with various promoters, but eventually settled on Phil McIntyre because, as he explains:

> It was very hit and miss. Because you're pioneering . . . you never knew with the local promoters . . . who was a fantasist and who knew what they were doing . . . Phil McIntyre pretty much made it clear that he would really like to be the sole promoter . . . he understood the game enough to not have you performing on beer crates. So it was difficult and . . . I hated it when a gig didn't work properly, you know, when the promoter didn't know what he was doing, you know, or the crowd were out of control, or I didn't have authority or I had to fight for authority.
>
> *Sayle 2017*

In bringing the new comedy to a wider audience, playing thousand-seater theatres instead of comparatively pokey venues like the Comedy Store or the Comic Strip, Sayle was indeed a pioneer. An *NME* review from December 1982 almost suggests that there was an element of missionary work here, with Sayle continuing to develop as a comedian whilst winning over a larger, broader audience: '[H]is show contains a good 50 per cent new material and features sometimes radical rearrangements of the rest. He's managed to take a wide cross section along with him' (Watson 1982).

## 'Briefly, I was the most successful stand-up comedian'

The reason Sayle was able to tour like a rock star was that he was the first of his generation to become well-known on television, thanks to a regular spot on a late-night show called *OTT*. This adult adaptation of anarchic cult children's programme *Tiswas* was a notorious flop, but at a time when there were still only three TV channels, being on *OTT* was still enough to make him famous. *The Young Ones* further boosted his reputation, but the first series hadn't even finished airing when he finished the last few dates of his 1982 tour on 12 December.

Although he and most of his fellow performers from the Comic Strip became successful enough to move beyond the emerging circuit within a couple of years, this pattern was not repeated by others. By May 1985, a *Guardian* article was noting the frustration comedians felt at not being able to move beyond the circuit:

> [A]ctually breaking through to the big time at the moment remains virtually impossible since there is no established career pattern for this kind of comedy and very few big venues interested in promoting it. Many up-and-coming artists would like to follow Alexei Sayle's example in using the power of television appearances to pack big live venues but that kind of shortcut contains many pit-falls.
>
> *Shearman 1985*

These pitfalls were, as Sayle put it in the same article, that, 'Faking cabaret just doesn't work on TV'. He may have been thinking back to his experience of *Boom Boom Out Go the Lights*, and since that had aired, further attempts at cabaret-format TV shows had failed to attract big audiences. In this sense, the problem was that television had failed to create a programme that successfully captured the appeal of alternative stand-up comedy.

When the first series of *Saturday Live* started airing in January 1986 – after a pilot the previous January – it didn't seem to be any more roadworthy than any previous attempt to create a television vehicle for live cabaret.

## Alternative Comedy

*Saturday Live* was a ninety-minute variety show with an uneasy mix of existing stars (Rik Mayall, Ade Edmondson, French and Saunders), American stand-ups, vaguely satirical sketches, and musical guests, all filmed in front of a large audience milling about in a vast, hangar-like studio decorated with garish neon-lit 1980s frippery. To add a touch of jeopardy, it was – as the title suggests – broadcast live. All things considered, this was by no means the most flattering format to present alternative comedy to a wider audience. Even Ben Elton – resident comic for the first series and subsequently the regular host – criticized it for 'having no teeth and no politics', feeling that it was too constrained by the TV company's caution in the light of an obscenity bill going through parliament: 'We were under a microscope. It was children's censorship. Every Saturday morning I'd have to do my act in front of a lawyer. You couldn't say "dick" for example' (Myers 1986: 12).

In spite of this it was a hit, running for three series between 1986 and 1988, the third renamed *Friday Night Live* to reflect its new position in the schedules. Crucially, the show offered guest spots to a representative range of acts from the cabaret circuit, including stand-ups (like Paul Merton, Jenny Lecoat, Nick Revell), speciality acts (like Steve Rawlings, Randolph the Remarkable), impressionists (like Chris Barrie), and even genius eccentrics like Andrew Bailey. Some, like Jo Brand and Julian Clary, became stars directly as a result of appearing on the show. Clary recalls in his autobiography, 'Those seven minutes on live television suddenly seemed to be having enormous consequences. For the first time I felt a little bit famous' (2005: 199).

It also drew attention to the cabaret circuit as a whole. Nick Revell recalls: '[H]onestly, you could feel the difference in the audience at the Comedy Store . . . Once [*Saturday Live*] started, there was a period where people were like, "These guys have been on telly. Or they might be." And you could feel this kind of respect. It was extraordinary . . . There was a sense of excitement and anticipation' (2017). For Ben Elton, *Saturday Live* was the decisive step in the expansion of the circuit:

> The real sea change in culture was *Saturday Live*. That's when it exploded. It didn't explode in '81 and '82, it continued to limp along . . . Somebody would put on an evening in a pub and one would go to it . . . [but] I think if people thought of alternative comedy, they thought of television, they thought of *The Young Ones* and *The Comic Strip*. But the stand-up thing was still staggering along, really. My memory is that it exploded with *Saturday Live* . . . Between *Saturday Live* in '86

and *Friday Night Live* in '88, suddenly every graduate wanted to be a stand-up comedian as far as I could see.

Elton 2018

For the regulars, the effects of being on the show were transformative. Fry and Laurie got their own series in 1989, Harry Enfield in 1990. Ben Elton became the face of *Saturday Live*, and this allowed him to follow Sayle into big-venue national tours. He had already supported Rik Mayall on tours of Britain and Australia between 1984 and 1986, but the success of *Saturday Live* made him a headline act. Between 14 November and 11 December 1986, his first solo tour sold out twenty-seven dates in university venues and large theatres, many of which seated well over a thousand people. Elton puts it simply: 'Clearly I had something because I ended up, you know, being very successful as a stand-up comedian. Briefly, I was the most successful stand-up comedian' (2018).

Being the most successful comedian to emerge from the circuit made Elton the target of criticism from his peers, some of it savage (Double 1997: 214–19). However, his success was another factor in the spread of the circuit. As the host of *Saturday Live* and as a touring comic capable of playing to over 25,000 people in less than a month, he undoubtedly helped to popularize the comedy scene from which he sprang.

## 'Rik and I did a season in Ibiza'

Like the beginnings of alternative comedy, the spread of the circuit in the 1980s could be attributed to the actions of a small number of talented individuals like the Muldoons, Ivor Dembina, Addison Cresswell, Phil McIntyre, Alexei Sayle and Ben Elton. However, as with the beginnings of alternative comedy, it would be simplistic to put it all down to individual endeavour, as the circuit's expansion was driven by broader trends, some of them in contradiction with one another.

Perhaps the most important of these was the economics of alternative cabaret. It was cheap to start a club or put an act together, particularly with the cushion provided by the Enterprise Allowance Scheme. The DIY ethos, rooted in the 1970s squatting movement and subsequently punk, created the feeling that anybody could do this, and having to make it up as you went along was no barrier to getting involved. The burgeoning circuit of cabaret gigs in pubs populated by an ever-expanding number of acts was further boosted by the contradictory forces of public subsidy on one hand, in the form of CAST New Variety, and the emergence of a kind of homemade private entrepreneurship on the other, epitomized by agencies like Off the Kerb. What united the public subsidy wing and the fledgling entrepreneurs was a kind of subversive DIY spirit, whether this involved repurposing an Arts Council grant without bothering to get permission, or running a promotion company from a front room despite having no knowledge or experience. Finally, although some of the new breed of alternative entertainers were suspicious of television, the exposure it offered undoubtedly helped the live scene to flourish.

What's remarkable is just how much it flourished. The London circuit massively expanded in terms of both acts and venues; packages of acts toured beyond London, alternative comedians appeared at rock festivals and colonised the Edinburgh Fringe, and appearances on TV allowed the biggest stars to fill major venues when they toured. Some have dismissed alternative comedy as a small metropolitan scene, dominated by an elitist middle-class audience (Schaffer 2016: 394), but what this ignores is the extent to which it outgrew the boundaries of the London circuit in the 1980s.

The audiences who came along to watch, say, Alexei Sayle at the Sunderland Empire on 22 May 1983, or Rik Mayall and Ben Elton at Blackburn King's Hall on 30 April 1985, would not have seen themselves as part of a tiny metropolitan elite. Certainly, that thought didn't cross my mind as I watched Elton headline at the University of Exeter's Great Hall on 24 November 1986, any more than it did when I saw The Damned play there. In the mid-1980s, alternative comedians even started playing working-class holiday resorts in Spain, as Elton recalls: 'Phil [McIntyre] said to us, "Variety's basically dead. The working class no longer go to British seasides. They go to Spain. Why don't we go and play Spain?" . . . And Rik and I did a season in Ibiza, only a two week season, and then Andy de la Tour and I did it the following year' (2018).

The fact is that the mid to late 1980s saw alternative comedians play to large and varied audiences, in a scene that was utterly transformed from what it was like just a few years earlier when de la Tour attempted to unionize it.

# PART TWO
## ALTERNATIVE COMEDY PERFORMANCE

# CHAPTER 4
## 'BITS OF ME HAVEN'T BEEN FINISHED YET': REINVENTING STAND-UP FROM SCRATCH

During a demented routine about childhood at the Comic Strip, Alexei Sayle's sentences start to buckle under the pressure of his breakneck delivery. Stumbling over his words becomes an opportunity for further laughs, as he comments on his verbal mishap with the same manic energy:

> I'm getting mixed up now, me fuckin' brain's gone! Berp berp berp berp! Sorry a minute, I'm an experimental comic an' bits of me haven't been finished yet! WHOO WHOO WHOO!! [laughter] Biddibiddibiddi! Bip-bib-bib-bib-bib-bib! What's the point of me writing material if you laugh at me going, 'Bib-bib-bib-bib-bib-bib-bib-bib-bib!'? [laughter]
>
> *Sayle 1998*

Apart from gleaning extra laughs on the spur of the moment, what Sayle says is also a revealing comment about how alternative comedy was seen and how it saw itself.

Some have argued that the new comedy scene was stylistically conservative, simply continuing with the form and content established in variety theatre and working men's clubs (Peters 2013: 6–7; Schaffer 2016: 383). However, this is not how either the comedians or the critics who commented on their scene saw it at the time. A magazine article about the Comic Strip from December 1980 declares, 'Alexei Sayle, the one indisputable star the club has so far turned up, owes nothing to anyone' (Hughes-Hallett 1980: 75). Similarly, a *Times* interview with Sayle the following October argues that the Comic Strip's success 'owes more to the tradition of rock music than to those of comedy and Sayle is quite clear that he personally owes nothing to any known comic tradition. "I can't think of any comics I like", he muses for a moment, "none at all"' (Appleyard 1981a). Generally, alternative comedy was seen not as a continuation but as a new start, a 'Year Zero' (*Vox* 1993: 69).

Sayle still argues that he wasn't much influenced by earlier comedians today: 'I didn't own any comedy records. I didn't particularly pay attention to comedians, except in the sense that ... I could see what they were doing ...

### Alternative Comedy

What was being attempted. Where they were going wrong' (Sayle 2017). Although, as we have seen, others in the scene were paying attention – and collecting comedy albums by the likes of Lenny Bruce – there was a general contempt for the working men's club comedy which predominated before the new scene sprang into existence. Some were more sympathetic to the earlier variety tradition, but not Sayle, who tore into it in his stage act: 'Actually, people are always going on about, erm – about the British music hall, you know, and erm – how and why it died out. *I'll* tell you why it died out, 'cos it was *shite!* [laughter, 6 seconds]' (Sayle 1983).

Given the lack of respect for earlier traditions, it's unsurprising that alternative comedy saw itself as appearing from nowhere. Sayle, who was at the epicentre of the alternative comedy explosion, puts it this way: 'To, you know, lapse into megalomania here ... I was inventing an art form from scratch, you know, in Britain for the first time. I was inventing this thing ... I just kind of made it up as I went along, really. And there was no template' (2015).

Inventing from scratch brings with it both the excitement and the fear of the blank canvas. On the one hand there is the excitement of being an 'experimental comic' – on the other, the fear that 'bits of me haven't been finished yet'. This was what the alternative comedy pioneers faced. They had the artistic freedom that comes when there are no expectations. Yet they also had the daunting task of trying to acquire the craft skills that stand-up demands, without an older generation of performers to learn from.

There were distinct echoes of punk here. TV Smith – lead singer of the Adverts – wrote of the early punk scene that 'the question of how well or badly we could play didn't matter anymore ... The doors had opened for people with ideas; the renegades and mavericks who took an alternative view of the way bands should look and sound' (cited in Laing 2015: v). As with punk, the alternative comedians often prioritized discovery and imagination over skill for its own sake. They learnt in public as they reinvented the existing art form of stand-up. Understandably – perhaps thrillingly – the results were mixed, bare competence rubbing shoulders with moments of comic genius. In fact, the lack of craft skills and the reinvention of form can be seen as two sides of the same coin.

### 'Nobody really knew what they were doing'

Learning to perform stand-up comedy is never easy. Getting a laugh is not an exact science, and acquiring the skills to be able to do it consistently means learning in public. In this sense, what the alternative comedians were doing was not unusual, and their accounts of how they learned are similar to those of any other stand-up. In particular, they learned from experience, as Tony Allen explains that 'the *best* thing to do to be a stand-up comedian is to get a lot of stage time' (HistComPod 2017a), and recalls that he would compère the Comedy Store when Sayle couldn't do it to quickly build up his experience.

The importance of stage time is widely recognized by comedians, and the importance of getting in front of an audience as often as possible is that it allows, as Jenny Eclair puts it, 'real trial and error . . . It's a real suck it and see. Unfortunately, you never know what's funny until it's in front of an audience' (2018). Maggie Steed remembers a similar process: 'I sat down and wrote stuff. And then tried it out. And then cut it and wrote some more' (2018). Maria McErlane, who performed under the glorious stage name Maria Callous, argues that the process of failing can be particularly valuable: '[T]hose "stiffing it" gigs . . . actually, you learn more from them than the ones that go well' (2018).

All of these accounts could apply to any new comic, but what made the learning process particularly difficult in the early days of alternative comedy was that, as Nick Revell explains, 'You had no tradition of older performers' (2017). Whether in the variety theatres of the mid-twentieth century or on today's live comedy circuit, it is not unusual for more established performers to pass on the wisdom of their experience by giving tips and advice to newer acts (Double 2012: 159–61; Double 2014: 2–6). By contrast, when alternative comedy began there were no older, wiser comedians around to pass on their knowledge. As a result, when Sayle started performing with Threepenny Theatre, he had 'no conception of exactly how I should write down the thoughts that were in my head' because 'there was nobody who could tell me how to get humour onto paper' (2016: 127).

This meant that there was a whiff of amateurism throughout the early years of the alternative cabaret scene. Jenny Lecoat candidly admits, 'I really am not very impressed with my work at that period, quite frankly. Not that anybody else's work was necessarily that great at that time, either. It was a very mixed bag' (2018). Alexei Sayle returned to stand-up in 2012, and prepared for this by going out and watching shows on today's live comedy circuit, commenting: 'Everybody that I've seen seems much slicker than in my day . . . They all know what they're doing in a way that we didn't, both for good and ill. When we were good we were fantastic. But when we were bad we were fucking catastrophic' (Williams 2012). Recordings of early shows at venues like the Comedy Store, the Elgin and Pentameters in the British Stand-Up Comedy Archive bear this out. Some capture comedians getting laughs which any gig-sharp performer would be happy with today. In other cases, a whole set might come and go without being much troubled by laughter.

One of the things comedians found especially challenging was being able to perform longer sets. John Dowie is modest about his influence on alternative comedy, but he acknowledges it 'To the degree that, "Well there's a bloke out there doing an hour. Let's go and see what he's doing"' (2018a). Having performed full-length solo shows since the early 1970s meant he was a role model for those who wanted to stretch their act beyond the twenty-minute set that would become standard. For John Hegley, starting to perform hour-long sets was a significant moment in his development as a performer:

> [Maria Callous] and Phil Herbert said, 'You've done twenty minutes. What else can you do?'... One night... Andy Arnold said, 'Would you like to try and do a solo show at the Bloomsbury?' And I thought, "On my own? What, an *hour?*" ... I suppose you had to think, 'Well it's a broader canvas. You're going to have to address it differently.'
>
> *Hegley 2016*

The general amateurism among alternative comedians went deeper than simply not being able to hold the stage for longer than 20 minutes. It might have been somewhat unfair for *The Stage* to attack them for being 'neither as good nor as professional as the mainstream variety', but there was a grain of truth in it, particularly in terms of the simpler aspects of stagecraft. A review of French and Saunders at the Edinburgh Fringe in 1983 provides a good example: 'French and Saunders disappointed me a little. Though blessed with exceptionally good material and attractive presences, their presentation struck me as uneven and disjointed. Performers who have to announce when they have come to the end of a sketch still have a fair amount to learn' (Hepple 1983).

When American comics like Charles Fleisher, Will Durst and even Robin Williams came over to perform at venues like the Comedy Store, the professionalism they brought with them from their far more established circuit drew attention to just how primitive the skills of their British counterparts were. Paul Merton recalls how difficult he found it to even negotiate the mike stand:

> Americans ... they'd take the microphone off the stand. A lot of the people didn't know how to take the microphone off the stand, so you

didn't want to fiddle around with it. I never really got the hang of it, because you didn't want to be doing that in front of an audience ... and a couple of times I had to crouch because the compère had forgotten to do it.

*Merton 2018*

While visiting Americans helped to introduce skills to the British scene, one alternative comedian learned by going out to see the more established American scene for himself. In Andy de la Tour's letter to *The Stage* in 1981, he had talked about looking across the Atlantic for inspiration. In 1982 he was able to actually do this: 'I applied to the Arts Council for something called the performers' bursary, which they used to hand out to professionals to develop their skills ... So almost as a kind of laugh, I put in a submission' (2016). A letter from the Arts Council dated 19 July 1982 formally offers de la Tour a bursary of £500 (£1,733.46): 'The bursary is offered to enable you to undertake a study of stand-up comedy in the United States of America from July to September 1982' (BSUCA).

This allowed him to visit comedy clubs in San Francisco, Los Angeles and New York. Along the way, he jotted down notes on assorted scraps of paper or the backs of flyers and two-drink minimum signs, now held in BSUCA. Some of his comments criticize comedians for presenting 'Vaguely topical rubbish' or being 'V. racist', but he is pleased when he comes across more political comedians. Seeing Richard Belzer at the Comedy Store in LA on 21 August, he writes: 'One of the best of all so far. A New York comic, well known from "Catch a Rising Star". Much <u>harder</u> & more political, a lot of free-wheeling – like Tony Allen at his best.' Looking back, he also recalls being 'delighted ... there were many more women comics than there were at the time in Britain' (2016). He is particularly impressed by Elayne Boosler, seeing her at Catch a Rising Star in New York on 29 August: '[P]erhaps the best so far of all. Well known now; so very funny – open[ed] set with brilliant "self-deprecating" stuff, lots about food, living alone, etc. Earned the right to be political, & turned allsorts of things on their head (men & cars, current affairs, sex).'

His comments about Paula Poundstone at Comedy Nitely in San Francisco epitomizes his overall impression of the American circuit: 'Very good improv., etc. Shame no consciousness.' He recalls being disappointed by the general lack of 'consciousness': 'The material wasn't particularly radical. I think in some respects, those few of us in Britain were doing stuff which was more overtly political than the stuff we were seeing there.' On the other hand, he acknowledges that 'the technical standard of a lot of the comedians was very, very high. And I have to be honest, it was higher than what I was witnessing and what I was doing in Britain. We were still, to some extent, novices' (2016).

## 'You're learning together'

American comedians weren't the only ones whose acts could be watched to glean bits of performance know-how. Although alternative comedians tended to despise comics who had cut their teeth in working men's clubs, there's some evidence that they learned from watching the more traditional acts who appeared at the Comedy Store in its first few months (Cook 2001: 51). Even Alexei Sayle, who supposedly owed 'nothing' to older comedians, acknowledges:

> I mean some of it I understood right away was the same as being one of them old-style hacks ... stand-up comedy even if you're talking about, you know, lifestyle or Maoism or whatever, it's the same as being one of them old geezers, you know, it's the same art form. So I knew ... that you could take some of what they did.
>
> *Sayle 2015*

Another source of traditional showbusiness know-how was Kim Kinnie, who became the Comedy Store's booker when it moved to Leicester Square in 1985. Kinnie's background was in strip shows, but many comics who played the Store under his reign have spoken of the importance of the support and guidance he gave them. Kevin Day acknowledges that Kinnie 'made me what I am' advising him on 'material, pacing, delivery and stuff like that' (2018). Mark Thomas argues that Kinnie 'was really amazing at actually encouraging people and getting new comics to come along ... he'd always have advice for them' (2018).

However, while American comedians and traditional comics might have been good for picking up skills like microphone technique and other aspects of basic stagecraft, perhaps the most important element of the learning process was the sense of shared discovery. Alternative comedians not only found out things for themselves, but also from *each other*. They learned from their fellow performers by watching them develop and evolve, as Jim Barclay explains: '[T]he great thing about it was a lot of the performers were discovering stuff for themselves, everybody watched everybody else's act, and it was just exciting to see how people developed and what they did' (1990).

There was something instinctive about this collective learning process. As John Hegley puts it, 'You learnt a lot from everybody else. But again, it was without thinking about it very much ... It's a bit like learning the language from listening to the radio. You're not sort of having any lessons' (2016). Similarly, Andy de la Tour argues, 'I suppose instinctively, obviously everyone's learning. And you're learning together, and you're picking up stuff and ... you're watching other people perform' (2016). In some cases though, there was more to it than learning through osmosis. Tony Allen has recalled how he, de la Tour and Barclay learned from each other in a slightly more organized way, by offering each other feedback and support: 'All three of us were struggling to understand what we were doing and we gave each other valuable feedback and helped nurse each other's wounds' (2002: 100).

Newer acts could learn from more established ones, even if being more established meant having only a few months of experience. Jennifer Saunders has written of the advantage of going on first at the Comic Strip and thus being able to stand at the back and watch the other acts: 'This is how we learned how to do it. They had been at it longer than we had, and were incredibly confident and funny' (2014: 53). Certain key performers were particularly important in the collective learning process, because they quickly became particularly adept and inventive. Barclay recognizes that:

> The big inspirations for all of us were Alexei [Sayle] and Keith [Allen] ... because they had a real kind of bravado which drove them through. And they were on top of their material so well and so clearly setting something up new ... in totally different ways ... You'd sit there every night thinking, 'Oh, I see what they're doing now.'
>
> Barclay 2016

For Tony Allen, the influence of his namesake Keith was particularly important: 'Keith Allen was a delinquent iconoclast and without his inspiring risk-taking example, the whole Alternative Comedy thing may well have collapsed due to ineptitude in the first twelve months' (2002: 103). What was important about Sayle and Keith Allen was that, in Barclay's words, they were 'so clearly setting something up new'. Whereas American comedians or even the more traditional hacks who appeared at the Comedy Store could demonstrate basic stagecraft skills, Sayle and Allen were exploring the creative possibilities of the form of stand-up comedy and leading the way for others to do the same.

In a sense, stagecraft skills and exploring the possibilities of form were opposite paths. Stagecraft skills can be seen as norms that become set within an established tradition. By starting from scratch, alternative comedy was free from the norms – and the constraints – that tradition brings with it. It was this lack of norms that allowed Sayle and Keith Allen the liberty to explore artistically and politically – as Allen has acknowledged: 'An incredible freedom comes from operating outside the normal field of expectations. I loved being on stage without the constraints of either a recognizable act or the disciplines of a script. I could do anything – and, believe me, I did' (K. Allen 2007: 230).

Of course, operating outside the normal field of expectations always involves the risk of failure, and in this sense, the amateurism and inventiveness of early alternative comedy are two sides of the same coin. A 1981 article about the Comic Strip hints at this idea: 'The Strip make comedy dangerous again, and even their failures are compensated for by their very attempts at *trying* something different' (Humphries 1981). Andy de la Tour makes a similar point, relating alternative comedy's specialness with its disrespect for earlier traditions, and its desire to not simply replicate them: '[T]here's no doubt the comedy of those early years had something special even if many if not most acts were far from hilarious. It was its differentness, its unselfconscious disrespect for all that had gone before, good and bad' (2013: 18).

### 'Well that's it!!'

Unpublished recordings of performances at the Elgin are shot through with this sense of freedom, newness and collective discovery – and with the vulnerability that comes with this. A recording of Alexei Sayle on 17 January 1980 (in the BSUCA archive) captures one of the stars of the early scene at a stage in his development where his inexperience is still audible alongside the qualities that had already made him influential. Having got big laughs by putting on a pair of glasses to demonstrate his uncanny likeness to the iconic German playwright Bertolt Brecht, he ends the act with a surreal anecdote about his youth:

> I remember one time, you know, I was in, I was in this, in this club, you know, in Liverpool, like this in the mid-Sixties when I was a teenager, you know, and I was – I was doing all the latest dances of the time, you

know, I was doing the Waaa-tusi, you know, and the er, Monkey Climb, you know, and the Stalin tank, you know. [laughter] And er – it was 1968, you know. And er – and er – those – this, this girl come up to me right, and she said, er, I was dancing away like, you know, she said er – doing the Twist like, you know, and she said er, she said er, "Ere! Ere! Are you, er, are you, er, Bertolt Brecht?' [laughter, 19 seconds] And er – I said, er, 'Yeah!' Er. [laughter, 5 seconds] She said, er – 'Aren't you dead?' [laughter] I said, 'No, I've just had a fortnight off, you know.' [laughter] She said, er – said, 'Did you write all them plays, you know like, er, you know *The Mother* and er *Threepenny Opera* and all that?' I says, 'Yeah!' She said, er – she said, 'Did you er, did you er.' She said er – [quiet laughter] (It's only a prop, anyway, you know.) She said, er – (Thirteen pence, quite cheap that, innit?) She said, er, you know, 'Did you er – invent all that stuff about alienation in the theatre and all that, you know, when you was in Augsburg in Germany?' I says, 'Yeah!' She went SMACK!! [laughter, 10 seconds] I was down there on the floor, like, and I said – I said, 'What's that for??' I said, 'Is that, is that 'cos of me, er, principled stand, you know er, er during the war, you know, or er – or er, you know, particular stands in me plays that you didn't like?' She says, 'No, that was for the fucking Blitz.' [a few laughs] Well that's it!! [brief laughter into applause]

*BSUCA*

Unsurprisingly for new material, there are gags that don't quite hit home, and a vague sense of grasping about for a laugh. The obvious example is the clearly improvized reference to a prop and its cheapness, transcribed here in parentheses. This is an audio recording, so the comic point of this is not entirely clear because we can't see what he is referring to, but in any case it doesn't get a laugh.

A much more glaring symptom of inexperience is that when the last gag of the routine gets a mere smattering of laughter, he has nothing in the bag to manufacture a more respectable laugh to finish on, and simply resorts to yelping, 'Well that's it!!' in a voice that suggests he is both surprised and amused to have to end the act like this. Such an ending brings to mind French and Saunders having to announce when they had finished a sketch.

What forces Sayle to acknowledge the relative failure of the final gag is that the laughter it gets is so puny by the standards of what he has achieved moments before. In particular, the response to the girl in the club asking him if he is Bertolt Brecht is truly remarkable. To get a full nineteen seconds of laughter in a pub-based comedy club with a comparatively small audience is unusual, but it's not just the length but also the quality of the laugh that makes it stand out. There's an unruliness to it, the audience sounding slightly astonished as well as delighted by the surreal image of teenage girl mistaking the young Sayle for a communist playwright rather than, say, a pop star. Shortly afterwards, the laughter that greets the sudden comic violence of the girl punching him – 'SMACK!!' – lasts for ten seconds, and is just as unruly. To get more than one such response in such a short routine is impressive given the size of the gig, particularly for a performer who had started as compère of the Comedy Store just eight months earlier.

Yet the ability to get such big laughs is not the only remarkable thing here. What's also conspicuous is how many of the building blocks of Sayle's distinctive comic voice are already in place. Even as early as January 1980, he is the working-class Scouser obsessed by communism, who can wield highfalutin references as easily as naming obsolete dance crazes. His act creates a fantastical comic world where intellectualism lives next door to slapstick violence, putting Brecht cheek-by-jowl with the Watusi. The quality of imagination, the breadth of reference, and the surrealism had been largely absent from the stand-up that had predominated before alternative comedy, but they would become key features in Sayle's act.

Indeed, this specific routine became a regular part of his repertoire, and he would later perform it in one of his spots for series two of *The Young Ones*. By this point, the anecdote has evolved and mutated, becoming shorter and tighter, and swapping Brecht for Mussolini as the person he's mistaken for. This later, more developed version boasts a subtly revised punchline, allowing him to finish on a proper laugh. When he asks the girl why she has just butted him in the face, she replies, '"That's for the invasion o' Crete!" [laughter]' (*Young Ones* 1984).

Even though the act at the Elgin ends with an anti-climax, the audience's enthusiasm is audible in the quality of their applause as Sayle leaves the stage, and the isolated cheers that keep erupting from within it. The sound the audience make suggests that for all its rough edges, they have thoroughly enjoyed the act they have just seen. Whether they realized it or not, what they were recognizing is that even if bits of Sayle hadn't been finished yet, he was an experimental comic, making them laugh in new ways. Indeed, it seems likely that it was precisely because he was so raw and unpolished – unencumbered by the inherited techniques of tradition – that he was able to be so startlingly fresh and inventive. He was not alone in this – experimentation with form would become one of alternative comedy's defining features.

# CHAPTER 5
## 'ANTI-MATTER COMEDY': STYLISTIC INNOVATION

In the middle of a high-octane rant at the Comic Strip, Alexei Sayle appears to be on the brink of shedding light on the new live comedy scene over which he holds sway: 'Now people often say to me, "What is alternative comedy?"' Quick as a flash, without leaving a moment for reflection, he violently changes tack: 'And I say, *"Fuck off, you nosey cunt!!"* [laughter]' (Comic Strip 1981). It's the suddenness and cussedness that makes the joke work. The surprise necessary to get the laugh comes from the rapidity and needless aggression with which Sayle squishes an idea he has barely yet established. However, there's something else going on here. What the joke hints at is that alternative comedy might resist being pinned down with anything as conventional as a definition, avoiding established structures and violently refusing to go where the audience expects.

In his influential book *On Humour*, Simon Critchley argues, 'Joking is a game that players only play successfully when they both understand and follow the rules' (2002: 4). To illustrate the point, he gives examples of what happens when someone breaks 'the tacit social contract of humour', like interrupting the joke-teller or walking away before hearing the punchline. What seems to be happening in Sayle's joke is that he – the joke-teller himself – breaks the social contract of joking, by presenting material that doesn't fit any established pattern.

Indeed, while alternative comedy might be difficult to pin down, one of its key defining features was that it shunned most of the structures that dominated stand-up in the 1970s, preferring to find newer, fresher ways of getting a laugh. As Jenny Lecoat puts it, 'Standards were different. Everything was new ... It was very experimental. It was an exciting time to be around' (2018). A review of the second night of the Comedy Store declares, 'The standard on my visit the Sunday before last was encouragingly high, even the amateurs doing their best to break away from the one-liner and Irish jokes syndrome' (Hepple 1979). This suggests that there was an attempt to challenge existing structures even at the very beginning, long before the alternative comics had won what Tony Allen called the 'civil war' against more traditional performers.

## Alternative Comedy

By the time the Comic Strip was up and running, alternative comedy had really broken away. An article about that venue from the beginning of 1981 describes what went on there: 'Comedy striptease is precisely what occurs; humour in performance is anatomically revealed in a harsh, often downright aggressive style ... It is a kind of anti-matter comedy – the sort that makes you laugh while actually rearranging large chunks of your brain. And unlike most of the stuff touted as comedy today, you need your wits about you' (Norman 1981: 12). It's an impressively astute description, identifying some of the most important aspects of what alternative comedy was doing differently from what preceded it.

Part of what made it unpredictable was the variety of different types of act that came under the banner of alternative cabaret. Jeremy Hardy points out that 'the alternative cabaret scene as it was called then, rather than alternative comedy, was very mixed ... it was a lot of people not doing straightforward stand-up' (2018). For Tony Allen, '[W]hat was good about that period is that people were trying all sorts of things. We hadn't yet decided that it was stand-up comedy that was the central thing of this new wave of cabaret' (HistComPod 2017a). Lecoat makes a similar point: 'If you go to a comedy club now, it's one stand-up after another, largely. But in those days, stand-up was just one of the things that you'd see' (2018). Many involved in the scene in the 1980s look back fondly at its greater diversity. Mark Thomas relishes the fact that: '[Y]ou went along and you didn't know what you were going to see. And I loved that, I really loved the excitement of it all' (2015b).

What united the diverse acts in alternative cabaret was the idea of doing things differently and breaking away from the showbusiness norms that had been built up over decades. This chapter will examine the various ways that alternative comedy experimented with the form of stand-up and other genres of act. Perhaps the easiest place to start is with the street entertainers who quickly became part of the alternative cabaret scene.

### 'I'm fully aware my act is stupid'

Charlie Holland, of juggling duo the Long and the Short of It, believes that there were essentially two types of street act on the circuit:

> Part of the thing was that skill-wise, there were people who were very skilled, and there were quite a lot of people who didn't have a level of

skill but what they did was they built entertainment around the level of skill that they had... it goes back to that thing of wanting performers with character and attitude, rather than people who were technically superb but totally dull.

*Holland 2018*

Performers with more character and attitude than skill seem to have predominated, examples including Tim Bat, described by a reviewer as 'a very funny bowler-hatted juggler' who 'joins in a hymn to eggs while juggling several of them and finding good use for both a flaming torch and a frying pan'. The same review describes JJ Waller as 'a gleaming demon in a Tarzan outfit' who 'swallows fire, lies on a bed of nails and finally escapes from a strait jacket suspended from the ceiling while leading the company in "My Way"' (Coveney 1983).

Waller describes the basic approach of his act: 'It's kind of like how you do it really, not what you do ... It wasn't really alternative in any other sense than ... I wouldn't be able to do it.' Not being able to do it might mean making sure that when he was hauled upside down in the straitjacket, coins would shower down from his trouser pockets. It might also mean continually postponing the promised feat: 'It was all stop-start. So I was about to do it, then I thought of something else' (2016). Similarly, Holland recalls that the Long and the Short of It enjoyed 'working in places that were stupidly small for what we were doing' because it allowed them to play with the difficulties which such a venue presented:

Downstairs at the King's Head in Crouch End would be a classic example, with a ceiling height of, I don't know, seven or eight foot. And we'd have the five foot giraffe unicycle which I was going to juggle the knives on the top of. And ... you could spend the best part of an evening really, looking at the top of the unicycle, looking at the ceiling, looking at Olly [Crick], looking at the top of the unicycle, looking at the ceiling, looking at Olly, looking at the audience.

*Holland 2018*

This kind of thing is what was known in variety theatre as a 'cod act', in which the entertainment stems from a performer's failure to carry out the kind of feats they are supposed to be presenting (Double 2012: 186–87). What made the alternative cabaret cod acts different was both their prevalence over straightforwardly skilful speciality acts, and the sheer brass-necked audacity with which they stretched the concept.

A common technique – not just among acts who had started on the street – was to present something that lacked any conventional sense of skill as if it were a marvel worthy of the audience's adulation. An excellent example is Philip Herbert's street and cabaret act, Randolph the Remarkable. Notionally a fire-eater, Randolph the Remarkable mostly presented bizarrely mundane feats, like the ones he performs on *Saturday Live* on 14 March 1987. An unashamedly rotund figure, a shower cap on his head and his tummy safely contained within a blue sweatshirt emblazoned with the name of his act, he announces: 'My first feat this evening, attempting a right-footed tippy-tippy-toe entrance into the bowl – [laughter] of lukewarm water.' Having warned them that he risks 'a nasty fall into the bowl' and breathed in as if preparing himself for danger, when he eventually puts his foot into the lukewarm water, the audience cheer and applaud. He then announces, 'I must – now remove my protective clothing.' Peeling up his sweatshirt, the audience laugh as he begins to reveal his tummy, and – subtly encouraged by him – some of them shout for him not to get any more naked, while others emit ironic wolf-whistles. Now topless, he instructs them: 'Please do try and control your obvious sexual desires. [laughter].'

After a few comparatively simple stunts with his fire eating sticks – laced with more gags – he announces his final trick: 'I shall attempt for your pleasure and delight, a full stomach entry into the bowl of lukewarm water. [laughter].' The build-up that follows is meticulous. He explains the stunt, asks a member of the audience to check his stomach for asbestos, polythene, wiring, trapdoors, padding or double-sided Sellotape – getting a number of laughs in the process – then announces, 'my stomach has been confirmed'. The audience groan as he fondles the weight of his belly, and he admonishes them as if genuine danger is involved: 'Please! I do require absolute silence.' He then dangles his stomach into the blue plastic washing up bowl, wiggling from side to side to squeeze it right in before raising his arms for applause, declaring, 'My stomach has entered the bowl!' After the cheering and applause have died down, he confesses, 'Can I quickly say at this point, I'm fully aware my act is stupid. [a few laughs] A lot of people come up to me after the show, they say, "I did enjoy your act, it was truly remarkable, but do you know you're stupid?" [laughter].' Finally, he completes the trick. The bowl is stuck to his stomach by suction alone, and he stands up in stages to flaunt this, each stage bringing more cheering, applause, and eventually whistling (*Saturday Live: The Best of Series Two*).

## Stylistic Innovation

By framing his underwhelming skill in this way, Herbert manages to elicit the kind of adulation which in other contexts might only have been earned by a much more spectacular feat. He cues the audience's responses using the established grammar of the speciality act: emphasizing the danger of the coming feat; getting a punter to confirm that no trickery is involved; demanding 'absolute silence'; raising an arm to directly cue applause. Even with a conventional spesh act, it is the way a stunt is framed rather than the level of skill involved that dictates the response (Double 2012: 167–9). Here though, framing is everything. Being able to use suction to stick a plastic bowl to the belly may be oddly fascinating, but lacks a conventional sense of skill, and thus its entertainment value would be negligible without the framing.

However, there's more to it than that. Part of what makes acts like Randolph the Remarkable entertaining is the sheer audacity they involve. He freely admits that his act is stupid, but the audience play along with the idea that his feats are, indeed, marvels. Their cheering and applause are as playfully ironic as their wolf-whistles when he disrobes. He holds sway over them despite emphasizing his lack of conventional sex appeal and acknowledging the stupidity of his act. By doing so, he subverts established showbusiness conventions, sending up more conventional speciality acts and perhaps even the very idea of framing skill in this way.

### 'These two Popes go into a bike shop'

What street acts like Randolph the Remarkable did for the conventional spesh acts's stunts, alternative stand-ups did for the kind of material used by more conventional comedians. As we have seen, working men's club comics like Bernard Manning told straightforward jokes, starting with lines like 'Fella walked into the doctor's' or 'Fella walked into a psychiatrist's'. The anthropologist Mary Douglas labelled and defined this kind of gag: 'The standard joke, starting for instance with "Have you heard the one?" or "There were three men, an Irishman, etc.", contains the whole joke pattern within its verbal form ... The joke pattern can be easily identified within the verbal form of standard jokes' (1999: 151).

This is an important point. Standard jokes announce themselves as such, their form – and to an extent their content – clearly labelling them as jokes. There's no mistaking them for normal discourse, and they often give the listener simple clues as to how their comic narrative will develop. Once we

## Alternative Comedy

have heard that a fella walked into the doctor's, we know roughly what kind of thing might happen next, just as we know a joke about an Irishman will tend to hinge on his supposed lack of intelligence. This is the kind of thing Critchley meant when he described joking as a game in which players have to understand and follow the rules. In standard jokes, the rules are usually simple to grasp.

Alternative comedians didn't entirely shun the standard joke. Performing with Alternative Cabaret at the ADC Theatre, Cambridge, on 29 May 1981, Jim Barclay tells the audience:

> Know what I'm gonna be? I'm gonna be wacky and zany! 'Cos I'm *fucking* wacky and zany. [a few laughs] A wacky and zany comedian, 'ere we go! Wacky and zany jokes, right? What is the difference between a cactus – and the Houses of Parliament? A cactus has all the pricks on the outside, eh? Ha ha ha ha! [laughter, 6 seconds] Wacky and zany, innit, eh? [laughter] Here's another! What has a pelican – the Inland Revenue and the South East Gas Board all got in common? They can all stick their bills up their arses, eh? Ah ha ha ha! [laughter, 11 seconds]
>
> *BSUCA*

The gags here are straightforward standard jokes, using a simple riddle format and hinging on double meanings of words or phrases. However, even here, the gags are framed in a way that makes them a bit less straightforward. Onstage, Barclay was a distinctive figure, in yellow tights and a garish jacket, on his head a joke bowler hat sporting both a fake nail-through-the-head and deely-boppers.[1] His delivery was all cheery Cockney blokeyness, with a hint of mania. There's a slight belligerence in the way he tells them he is '*fucking* wacky and zany', which suggests his wackiness and zaniness might be in some way ironic. The fact that the jokes are being barked out as proof of his wacky and zany qualities frames them in much the same way as Randolph the Remarkable frames his stunts. Like Randolph's raised-arm gesture cuing applause, Barclay's cheerily aggressive 'eh?' and his own laughter cue the audience's laughter – and that in itself is part of the joke. The proof of this is the fact that he gets a laugh after the first joke by saying, 'Wacky and zany, innit, eh?' This un-punchline-like statement only works as part of the distancing frame he has placed around the jokes.

Many went further in undermining the structures and conventions of earlier traditions of stand-up, and alternative comedy was shot through with metacomedy of various types. First, there were the gags that playfully

## Stylistic Innovation

subverted showbusiness conventions, repurposing its more administrative elements. Keith Allen's approach to compèring a show at the same venue on 16 January 1981 is a good example:

> Ladies and gents, will you please put your stumps together, for – [laughter] 'Sa little joke for all the sympathisers of certain members of the police force, namely down in Catford. [uneasy laughter] A certain area where the long arm of the law has got progressively shorter. [laughter, some clapping and shouts of 'Aww!', 6 seconds in total] Don't get too sorry, because they, er – will undoubtedly be welding the gun on his stump. [laughter] Be a lot easier for him to shoot innocents, don't worry about that. [one or two laughs] Ladies and gents, will you please take all your clothes off. [laughter]
>
> BSUCA

Here, there are not one but two twists on the time-honoured tradition of asking the audience to put their hands together, the first rather horrific (stumps instead of hands), the second inappropriately sexual (take your clothes off). However, these are rather gentle subversions compared with the sick joke thrown in between them, a reference to PC Stephen Hickling, a nineteen-year-old policeman who had lost part of his right arm when Catford police station was bombed in May 1980 (*Guardian* 1980c). Understandably, the joke somewhat divides the audience, bringing laughter and applause from some, groans from others. Whatever the morality of telling such a joke this is a bold ploy, given that the compère is expected to unite the audience before bringing the next act on. Certainly, it's not the sort of joke a compère would use on, say, *Sunday Night at the London Palladium*.

Second, alternative comedians sent up the conventions and structures of stand-up itself. Alexei Sayle excelled at this. In the middle of a freewheeling, expletive-rich routine performed in the character of a distinctly ungenial Cockney mod poet, he sends up that staple of stand-up in variety theatres and working men's clubs, the catchphrase: "'Ere! Good catchphrase that, innit, eh? – "Shit piss bollocks wank cunt fuck it." [laughter] Beats me last one, which was, "Don't tell Mr Mugabe." [laughter].' In another routine, this time in his usual stage persona, he sends up a different piece of stand-up furniture – the segue:

> This is about the nature of comedy. Now – I think it's very hypocritical the way comedians make tenuous links between bits of material, you

## Alternative Comedy

know, like, erm, 'Talking about bicycles, here's a story about the Pope', you know. [scattered laughter] [mock-innocent tone:] Actually, talking about the Pope, erm. [laughter] These two Popes go into a bike shop, right, and one says – [laughter]

*Comic Strip 1981*

The last line is ostensibly the beginning of the next joke, but in fact it is a fake first line of an imaginary joke. As well as sending up the segue, Sayle is also ridiculing the very form of the standard joke.

### 'A gooseberry in a lift'

The most popular form of metacomedy was gags and routines that worked by subverting standard joke structures. Rik Mayall and Ade Edmondson's frenzied double act 20th Century Coyote excelled at this, often by applying real-world logic to the fantastical cartoon world of the standard joke. A classic example is their take on the knock-knock joke, in which Mayall says 'Who's there?' and Edmondson responds with, 'Open the door!' (Comic Strip 1981). Although Critchley argues that joke-tellers must 'both understand and follow the rules', clearly this gag works precisely by *not* following the well-worn rules of a knock-knock joke. In another case, they wreak similar destruction on the riddle:

Mayall: Mr Cooper's new joke!
Edmondson: Huh. Don't tell it. Huh.
Mayall: It's a good one, it's a good one. What lies at the bottom – what's *yellow*, and lies at the bottom of the Atlantic Ocean?
Edmondson: I don't know, what?
Mayall: Sand! [laughter, 5 seconds, under which the next line is spoken]
Edmondson: I told you they wouldn't like it.
Mayall: I didn't write it, it was written by hippies, wasn't it? [laughter]

*Fundamental Frolics 1981*

Here, the riddle format sets up the idea that the answer to the question will be something jokily incongruous, perhaps involving a pun. When it turns

## Stylistic Innovation

out instead to be something straightforward and factual – lent an extra plainness by being a single blunt syllable – this is surprising enough to get a good, strong laugh. There's also an extra layer of metacomedy here. As with Jim Barclay's wacky and zany gags, the way they frame the joke distances them from it. They are telling 'Mr Cooper's new joke' – even though it is never made clear who Mr Cooper is or why they are having to tell his joke – and after it has been told, they blame its poor quality on the hippies who wrote it. Thus the joke itself becomes just one part of the absurd onstage world they are creating.

Their most celebrated metajoke saw them take several minutes to frantically dismember a single short riddle. The first surprise is that they throw the supposed punchline away right at the start:

Mayall: I'll tell the gooseberry joke.
Edmondson: What's the gooseberry joke?
Mayall: What's green and hairy and goes up and down?
Edmondson: What?
Mayall: A gooseberry in a lift, it kills 'em, I'll tell it. [laughter] Good evening ladies and gentlemen, I'd like to tell the gooseberry joke.

*Comic Strip 1981*

Before Mayall can get any further, Edmondson derails him by applying real-world logic to the fantastical punchline: 'But how does a gooseberry get into a lift? [laughter]'. Unsatisfied by Mayall's exasperated reply – 'How the fuck do I know? It's a joke, it's implicit!' – Edmondson proceeds to come up with logical objections to all of Mayall's increasingly ludicrous explanations. Supposing somebody had taken the gooseberry into to the lift, says Edmondson, '[H]ow's he going to press the fucking *buttons*, he's a fucking gooseberry!! [laughter]'. Not that Edmondson's own statements are entirely free of ludicrousness. When Mayall suggests the gooseberry might have 'little gooseberry arms', Edmondson replies, 'Gooseberries don't have any fucking arms!' – leading Mayall to demand, 'How many gooseberries do you know? Eh?' After a pause, Edmondson says he knows three gooseberries, and when challenged to name them, the only name he can come up with is 'Derek Gooseberry'. This infuriates Mayall:

Mayall: That's a fucking lie! [laughter] You made it up! All right, go and get the fucker, I'm dying to meet him!! [laughter]

## Alternative Comedy

| | |
|---|---|
| | Come on Derek, your mother wants you!! Let's see Derek Gooseberry, your mate! |
| Edmondson: | *DEREK!!!* [laughter] [pause] Oh, he's got a headache. |
| Mayall: | Oh he's got a headache!! [laughter] That's very fucking convenient, isn't it? |

*Comic Strip 1981*

Having accepted that gooseberries don't have arms, Mayall comes up with another explanation: 'All right – maybe it jumped up and nutted a button?' Edmondson objects that gooseberries have 'fuck-all legs', and is only convinced of the validity of the joke after Mayall has come out with a convoluted explanation involving 'a contraceptive gooseberry bush'.[2] This allows Mayall to finally tell the joke, which by now has become irretrievably mangled:

> I'll tell it. [extremely fast:] Good evening ladies and gentlemen, what is it when there's a man and a lady who don't wanna have a baby but they wanna do the bits – so they've got a rubber gooseberry bush and they're trembling with fright in case they get seen – shakes a gooseberry off, hits one of the buttons, lift goes up and down. What's that? [pause] [laughter, which rises and then extends more quietly for six seconds] *A GOOSEBERRY!* [with Edmondson joining in:] *A BLOODY GOOSEBERRY!! A BLOODY GOOSEBERRY!! A BLOODY GOOSE-A-BERRY!! GOOSE-A-BERRY!!* [to Ade:] Get out! [laughter into applause]

*Comic Strip 1981*

There's a lot going on here. The basic comic premise is not the joke itself but the pair's failure to tell it properly. As a result, many of the laughs come from the brilliance of their characterization as maniacs in purple suits, yelling at each other with increasing desperation, sometimes spilling over into brutal slapstick violence. As with alternative spesh acts, there's also the feeling that they are ridiculing a more traditional style of entertainer, in this case one who would use such formulaic joke structures. The device of giving away the actual joke right at the beginning is almost Brechtian, and in amongst all the shouting and craziness that follows, the idea that established joke structures are being revealed and critiqued is made explicit by the line, 'How the fuck do I know? It's a joke, it's implicit!' It must have been routines like this that

Neil Norman had in mind when he wrote about 'comedy striptease' in which 'humour in performance is anatomically revealed in a harsh, often downright aggressive style'.

20th Century Coyote were by no means the only act to subvert traditional joke structures. Long before he adopted the stage name Paul Merton, Paul Martin had a short routine in which his dad tells him he wants to be a memory man, in spite of not being able to remember his name and calling him Terry instead. This is largely a pretext for a metajoke that plays on a very specific type of riddle: ''E said, "Terry – whoss the difference – between a memory man, and an undertaker?" I said, "I dunno, dad," 'e said, "Well – a memory man remembers convoluting facts from rear of his cranium. And an undertaker buries people." [laughter]' (*Let the Children Play* 1984).

Merton explains how the joke works:

> The first bit sounds like it's very wordy, so it's going to be a play on those words . . . It's like the old joke . . . 'What's the difference between a barrow boy and a dachshund? Well a barrow boy bawls his wares on the pavement. And a dachshund wears his balls on the pavement.' So it's that. So the first bit, it sounds like this is going to be clever! A clever twist on those words.
>
> *Merton 2018*

In this specific form of riddle, then, the first half of the answer is the set up for the second half, which reincorporates many of the words but with certain letters rearranged. Merton subverts this by replacing the expected wordplay with a bluntly logical statement containing no rearranged reincorporation – which makes the whole joke come across as a kind of non-sequitur. What's interesting about this is that for the joke to really work, the audience must be familiar with this specialized form of riddle, or the whole thing might come across as simply perplexing. Metajokes like this are relatively demanding on the audience, requiring them to recognize both the original set of rules involved in such gags, and to see how the rules have been broken in this twisted version. As Neil Norman pointed out, the audience needed their wits about them.

This might make metacomedy sound rather cerebral, the kind of thing that might get more of a wry chuckle than a belly laugh. In fact, the recordings show just how potent it was in terms of getting laughs. When Mayall finally tries to tell the gooseberry joke in a garbled rush, the silence that follows his urgent, 'What's that?' gets six seconds of laughter, and the final, desperate,

'Get out!' gets laughter and applause. In a sense, 20th Century Coyote didn't simply make fun of established joke structures, they also started to reconfigure the standard joke so that it worked in an entirely different way. Another routine from the Comic Strip provides a good example:

Mayall: I saw an old man, outside. Well not so much of an old man, more of a – a middle-aged man, actually. *He* had a cabbage. The bastard!! [a few laughs] Walking along the road, as bold as a parrot. With a cabbage on a lead. [a few laughs] Hm? Fucking looney! [a few laughs] I confronted him. 'Middle-aged man!' I cried. 'Why do you walk along the road with a cabbage on a lead?' Hmm?? [a few laughs] *Bastard!* [a few laughs] He looked up at me with little piggy eyes. And he said, 'It's *not* a cabbage!' Eugh! [the sound of some physical business] [laughter]
Edmondson: He said it was a cauli, didn't he?
Mayall: It's a – *YOU FUCKHEAD!!!* [laughter with a smattering of applause, 23 seconds]

Mayall and Edmondson 1998

Essentially, this is another joke that works by failing to tell the joke properly. Mayall takes over forty seconds to deliver the set-up, with a pause-laden delivery more suited to a Beckett play than a silly gag. This only gets small bursts of laughter, mainly from his puzzlingly angry interjections. After all this effort, Edmondson ruins the joke for him by giving away the punchline, and Mayall's furiously sweary response gets an enormous laugh from the audience. What's interesting is that the sabotaged gag is essentially so weak – a simple pun based on the homophone collie/cauli(flower). It's unlikely that such feeble wordplay could get such a huge laugh in a more straightforward gag, but reconfiguring it into a ruined joke hugely increases its potency.

In some cases, there was a political dimension to subverting jokes. Performing at the Watney's Brewery Sports and Social Club in 1983 for Channel 4's *Interference*, Jim Barclay tells the following metajoke: 'I've been talking to a very eminent – stand-up comedian in America – Mr Caspar Weinberger. [laughter] I'd like to do one of his jokes now, it's a cracker, I'm sure you'll love it. Here we go – "I say. I say. I say. Even an inaccurate cruise missile – is an effective deterrent." Haha! [laughter]' (PawsOfTheSphinx 2015).

## Stylistic Innovation

The key to understanding this is that far from being a comedian, Weinberger was Ronald Reagan's hawkish Secretary of Defense. The 'joke' that Barclay lightly misquotes is not a joke at all, but something that Weinberger actually said: 'Even an inaccurate missile is quite a deterrent' (*Observer* 1982). By reframing it as a joke, Barclay lampoons the mindset of the pro-nuclear lobby, which can spin even the most legitimate concerns about nuclear weapons – their ability to actually function – into support for the theory of deterrence.

Tony Allen took a different approach, critiquing not right-wing politicians but the implicitly right-wing values contained in comedy itself. At Pentameters on 24 September 1979, he performs a tight parody of bigoted working men's club stand-up: 'This Pakistani squatter takes my mother-in-law to an Irish restaurant. [laughter, 4 seconds] He says to the West Indian waiter, he said, "Waiter, waiter, there's a homosexual in my soup," and the waiter said, "Whaddya expect for thirty pence, a Jewish – businessman?" [laughter, 8 seconds].' By cramming so many stereotypes into such a small space, he creates a highly effective *reductio ad absurdum*. Not only does he suggest that this species of standard joke is formulaic and lazily prejudiced, he also gets two big laughs along the way. This would become an early signature gag for Allen, appearing in different versions in a number of recordings, and quoted on the original Sayle-designed Alternative Cabaret flyer.

### 'Hardened criminals jumping out the fridge'

Beyond parodying and reconfiguring established conventions and joke structures, alternative comedians moved beyond them by entering the realm of comic surrealism. This was not entirely new, as variety comedy had occasionally touched on the surreal. However, in altcom, comic surrealism was more widespread – and sometimes wilder – than anything seen in earlier British stand-up. Paul Merton's comedy was often described as surreal, and a routine performed at Jongleurs in 1987 gives a good idea of his style:

> I live opposite Brixton Prison and someone, I don't know who – has dug a tunnel from E-wing to the back o' my fridge. [laughter, 4 seconds] I can't sleep at night. Hardened criminals jumping out the fridge all hours o' the morning. [laughter] Half o' them want minicabs. [laughter]

The only way I can get any sleep is go through the tunnel and sleep in E-wing, it's bloody empty! [laughter] I got this book at home. A book about the paranormal. I didn't buy it, it just *appeared* in my room one night. [laughter, 4 seconds] I dunno what it is about where I'm living, but I often get visitors from outer space, it's one o' those things, you know I – I had a blob come round the other week. [laughter] Horrible it was, green, purple, thousands of eyes, you know. And the thing about these superior beings is they never let you forget it. Stand in the middle o' the living room, 'I come from a civilisation millions of years ahead of yours. I could show you a thousand things in the blink of an eye that you'd never – *Fuck me, you got prisoners coming out your fridge!*' [laughter, 9 seconds]

Live at Jongleurs 1987

To identify what's surreal about this, it's worth thinking about the connections between comedy and surrealism more generally. In his masterful version of the incongruity theory of comedy, Arthur Koestler calls the conceptual process at the heart of making jokes 'bisociation', defining this as '*the perceiving of a situation or idea, L, in two self-consistent but habitually incompatible frames of reference, M1 and M2*' (1970: 35). In other words, a joke occurs when something (L) allows two 'frames of reference' which are not normally connected (M1 and M2) to collide. Applying this idea to Jim Barclay's joke about a cactus and the Houses of Parliament, the first frame of reference (M1) is the physical properties of plants, and the second (M2) is the moral character of politicians. The thing that allows them to collide (L) is the double meaning of the word 'pricks', which can refer to the physical properties of cactus spines, or suggest that the Houses of Parliament are full of idiots.

Incongruity and juxtaposition are also important in Surrealist art. As Robert Short wrote, '[B]y juxtaposing elements which reason would deem to be irreconcilable, [Surrealism] disrupted conventional expectations and sabotaged the passive enjoyment of the world. The Surrealists frequently found that the power of an image was in direct proportion to the incongruity of the entities which it brought together' (1980: 87). He also explained what was new about the way Surrealists used juxtaposition: 'Omitting the mediating and distancing "like" and "as" of the customary poetic simile, the Surrealist image attained a startling new directness' (Short 1980: 87). In other words, unlike a poet comparing two different things to form a simile, Surrealists juxtaposed irreconcilable elements without offering any rationalization. To relate this to Koestler, they brought together two frames of reference without needing to have an L to justify the collision.

All of this can help us to understand what qualities comedy might have that would lead us to find it surreal. These would seem to be that the frames of reference in the bisociation should be as wildly divergent as possible, and the justification for bringing them together as slight as possible. In Merton's routine, the bizarre image of 'Hardened criminals jumping out the fridge' bisociates the frames of reference of jailbreak narratives (M1) and domestic appliances (M2), with little more justification (L) than the fact that he lives opposite Brixton Prison. This is made all the more startling and direct because it is presented as actual experience, rather than safely contained within the identifiable structure of a standard joke. Merton portrays himself as actually living in a world where books mysteriously appear from nowhere and aliens pop in for a visit. He explains how he came up with this gag, and why he had a preference for surreal comedy:

> I was living in a bedsit. I didn't have a lot of life experience, so . . . I'd make things up. So yeah, I did live near Brixton Prison. So the logical thing is, 'OK, somebody breaks out of the prison and they come to where you are. Where would they be? Will they build a tunnel to the front door? No. So it's through a wall. So if it's through a wall, it must be out of the fridge or out of an oven or something.' And a fridge felt funnier . . . I'd left school and worked in the Civil Service for a while and then sort of lived in a bedsit, didn't know many people. So, you know, I tended to sort of write imaginatively.
>
> *Merton 2018*

Whereas Merton developed a surreal style as a response to lack of life experience, in other cases comic surrealism grew out of the fact that alternative comedians drew on a broader range of references than working men's club comics, with their standard jokes about a limited set of subjects – 'false teeth and parrots and homosexuals', to recall Ken Irwin's description. According to Pauline Melville, this was because 'a lot of people were much better educated than most comedians. You know, the northern comedians hadn't been to university. Whereas nearly everybody had . . . So you would get names like Magritte the Mind Reading Rat,[3] which you wouldn't get in a northern club' (2018).

Alexei Sayle's art school education helps to explain his genius for coming up with surreal juxtapositions of high and low culture, imagining residents

## Alternative Comedy

of tower blocks discussing Chekhov or Cockney geezers describing Jean-Paul Sartre as the 'best centre forward West Ham ever had' (ND). With his skinhead haircut and a tight suit highlighting his corpulent frame, Sayle would go into bizarre rants that juxtaposed his knowledge of art and philosophy with extreme comic violence. For example, he had a routine about getting into an argument with a barman over an exhibition of Futurist art at the Hayward Gallery:

> Anyway, right, you know, as he was topping up the spirit bottles with water, he says, er – 'You're not going to the Futurist exhibition are yer?' I says, 'Yeah!' I says, 'Why not?' I says, *'Excusez moi*, lad! [laughter] But in my humble opinion, this Italian art movement was the first, and it was arguably *the* most radical of the revolutionary art movements of the Twentieth Century – *bollock-brain!*' [laughter] So he's standing there, right, an' he's crunching up the crisp packets in his hands, you know the way they do, like? [laughter] He says – 'Yeah, but don't you think it was intrinsically fascistic – in its outlook – Futurism? I mean don't you think that it degraded the human spirit, in its abject homage to the machine age?' Well have you ever heard anything so stupid in all your *life?*? [laughter] I said to him – I said to him, I said, 'Listen, lad,' I said, 'Listen – can't you see – that the Futurist love of machinery was only a form o' romanticism?' Then before he could say anything else stupid, I pulled him over the bar and nutted him one!! [laughter, 8 seconds] Things like that are always happening to me, though, you know. [laughter]
>
> *Sayle 1998*

Here, the two frames of reference that collide are styles of speech – intellectual discussions and violent pub arguments – and there's no apparent justification for bisociating them, beyond the wildness of Sayle's persona and his established habit of juxtaposing high and low culture.

It might seem that there's a touch of elitism in gags that include intellectual or high culture references, that mentions of Futurism might alienate a less educated working-class audience. Indeed, Sam Friedman has suggested that 'the main legacy of the Alternative Comedy Movement has been to … introduc[e] more "highbrow" niches, styles and artists', thus creating a new tier of high cultural capital comedy (2014: 25). However, this was not the first time that university and art school influences had seeped into popular culture, infusing it with references to twentieth-century art movements and political

## Stylistic Innovation

theory. Many of the early punks had also been to art school, leading the poet John Cooper Clarke to argue that punk was 'the nearest thing that there's ever been to the working classes going into areas like surrealism and Dada' (cited in Savage 1997: 46). What Clarke is suggesting is that far from alienating working-class rock fans, punk made Dada and Surrealist influences accessible to them. Similarly, Sayle – who considers himself working-class – has argued that his routines only really require superficial knowledge: '[O]ne of the comedian's tricks is to pretend to be much more erudite than you are ... I know very little about any philosophy, Sartre, you know, my knowledge is minimal. It doesn't matter. It is a fake, it's a trick, but you know, it's about finding the telling phrase, the right name' (2003).

That said, Sayle also sent up the kind of working-class punters who preferred the bigotry of WMC comedy to his own surreal approach. Performing in Manchester in around 1983, he notes that the audience have gone a bit quiet, and imagines the northern bouncers commenting on his comedy: '"Tell you, if I want fuckin' surrealism, I'll go to a fuckin' art gallery, that's what. [laughter] Tell you what I want from a stand-up comic, I want fuckin' racial hatred, that's what I want. [laughter] Racial hatred and a chicken dinner for two quid, that's what I want" [laughter]' (ND). Coming from a comedian whose working-class identity was expressed in the thickness of his Scouse accent, this comes across not so much as an attack on working-class people, but on the inadequacy of the entertainment aimed at them.

### 'I could do anything I wanted'

In a 1985 *Times* article, Lisa O'Kelly argued that, 'When it exploded six years ago alternative cabaret was unhampered by any precedent and its irreverent verve had free rein.' This free rein gave performers the liberty of exploring, sending them on voyages of discovery into new ways of getting a laugh. Sometimes the experimental nature of what they were doing onstage became quite overt.

In his Pentameters show on 16 January 1981, Keith Allen tells a long, surreal story – lasting almost twelve minutes in total – which starts with him going out into the countryside to look for revolution. He cuts to a passenger plane, about to crash as the stewardess fellates the pilot, then cuts again to a public school headmaster's study with a schoolboy being reprimanded for smoking, with a suggestion that the headmaster might be a predatory paedophile. Having created the feeling that there is some point to all of

## Alternative Comedy

this – that it might be leading somewhere – he suddenly breaks out of it to confess: 'I haven't got an ending to this act. [laughter] That's true, I haven't. Sorry about that, right now listen – [laughter into 11 seconds of applause].' This is like a particularly brutal shaggy dog story, lacking the normal deliberately anticlimactic punchline in favour of a straight confession – he hasn't got an ending yet, but he tells the story anyway, making it clear that he's still exploring and experimenting. Abandoning the routine in this way is an extreme example of a comedian refusing to follow the rules of joke-telling, and as such – according to Critchley – it should fail. Instead, the audience reward him with laughter and applause.

At the other end of the spectrum from Sayle's berserk energy, there were acts who explored the possibilities of extreme deadpan. Norman Lovett, who pioneered this style, explains: 'I watched Ben Elton rabbiting away at about a hundred miles an hour, and I thought, "That's the speed I'm never going to go at." And of course, I go much slower . . . You don't have to travel fast and get onto the next thing, you can get something out of nothing' (2018). Lovett's first TV appearance, on 6 January 1984, shows the audacity with which he could get something from nothing. While the audience applaud, he saunters on unhurried, puts his glass of water down by the mike stand, and straightens up as the last claps end. He says nothing, looking at the audience and adjusting his clothing for three seconds, before bending down again to pick up his water. That's his first laugh. He sips his water and prods at his left shoulder. He puts his glass down and adjusts its position with his foot. He rolls his tongue around in his mouth. He looks around. He blows air out through his lips. That's his second proper laugh, although there have been little ripples of laughter in between. Finally, around forty seconds after the applause ended, he breaks his silence: 'My name's Norman Lovett. [a few laughs] 'S my real name. [a few laughs] I'd like a pound for every time someone said, "Lovett, I bet you do." [laughter, 5 seconds] 'S I'd have about six or seven pounds by now. [laughter, a few claps]' Lovett 2016).

His delivery has all the hallmarks of conventional deadpan – slow and inexpressive delivery, bored voice, pauses between each sentence. Where he pushes things to extremes is in the length of his pauses. Saying nothing for forty seconds at the beginning of the act is a bold ploy. By doing almost nothing in the silence, he focuses the audience's attention on the very little he is actually doing, turning simple, mundane actions into occasions for laughter. In these moments, he's like the John Cage of comedy. Essentially, it's his deliberate lack of obvious funniness that is the basic joke of the act. He's funny precisely because he is so boring and unfunny. At one point, he even breaks a pause by saying, 'Cor, I'm bored now. [laughter].'

Another who explored the creative possibilities of extreme deadpan was the Irish comedian Kevin McAleer, who presented a bizarre slideshow. Appearing on *Saturday Live* in 1987,[4] he takes over a minute and a half to deliver his first line after arriving onstage. During this enormous pause, he stands in front of a home projector screen showing his first slide – a photo of four baby owls of different heights sitting in a row on a branch, with slightly mad expressions on their faces. He gets laughs, some scattered and confused, some unified and full-blooded, with a series of small, unshowy gestures – using his pointer to tickle an owl's tummy or tracing the shape of another owl's mouth. All of this is performed with the same neutral expression.

When he does eventually start to speak, his delivery is slow and full of pauses, his voice coloured by his County Tyrone accent but untroubled by emotion. He talks about the slide in ways that are straightforwardly weird – like referring to the owls as 'four normal people' or suggesting that they are tied down to an armchair – or odd by virtue of the unnecessary straightforwardness of his description. Pointing at the tallest owl, he deadpans, 'He's the big one. [laughter].' He points to its feet: 'Starts down there. [laughter].' He points to the top of its head: 'And goes right up to there. [laughter].' He points to the shortest owl: 'She's small but she's got a big head.' The audience laugh as they realize this owl has indeed got a large head. He points at another owl: 'This poor bastard. [laughter] No arms.' The audience laugh as they notice that its wings are not showing at all (smorodina 2009). His long, drawn-out delivery forces the audience to pay close attention to the slide, and what he says about it constantly shifts their perception of it, either by pointing out something they hadn't noticed ('big head') or imposing fictional interpretations of it ('no arms'). These perceptual shifts are the gags. All of this is a considerable distance on from the standard joke.

One of the most inventive explorers of new methods of laughter-making was Andrew Bailey. Before becoming a stalwart of the alternative cabaret scene, Bailey had experienced an eclectic career, having been a theatrical dresser and worked for Don Ward on his pre-Comedy Store strip shows. He had also acted, and what appealed to him about cabaret was that it gave him creative autonomy: 'I'd been in all these theatre companies, Theatre of Lies and things. And it was all these directors ... People giving you direction [and] telling you how to do things ... But suddenly the Comedy Store arrived and I could do anything I wanted' (2018).

## Alternative Comedy

Bailey created not just one act but many. An early incarnation was Brian Bailey, who presented finger puppet plays – which according to the Pranksters brochures were 'influenced by Harold Pinter'. One of his most habitual stage characters was Podomovski,[5] a toy-wielding clown who spoke in noises. A typical Podomovski stunt involves taking seven plastic crocodiles, and joining them together by placing one's tail in the next one's mouth, accompanying the process with vocal noises suggesting a great feat is in process. There are 'Hup!'s and 'Ha!'s and simulated drumrolls – 'Drrrrrrrrr!' Eventually he forms them into a full circle of crocodiles, and after a couple of arm gestures which suggest no trickery is afoot, he plunges his hand right through it. There's no obvious point to this feat, but he bows and the audience applaud obediently (Eugenecheese 2014).

A number of Bailey's fellow performers recall how impressed they were with the wildness of his comic imagination. Jenny Lecoat encountered him when she did her first Comedy Store open spot:

> I arrived at the Comedy Store and was there early doing soundchecks, and I walked on and there was Andrew Bailey onstage with Dave Rappaport … One of them was in a birdcage … And someone pretending to push Trill through the cage. And I just thought, 'I don't know what the fuck is going on here!'
>
> *Lecoat 2018*

Paul Merton, who describes Bailey as 'extraordinary', remembers seeing him at the Rosemary Branch, where he took a punter's jacket – which he had previously planted – put it in the fireplace, covered it with lighter fuel and set light to it: 'But what he hadn't checked out was that the chimney was no longer a functional chimney, so the room started filling full of smoke. He jumped out of the first floor window, it looked like to us, but there was a ledge beneath the window which he knew about and we didn't. But nonetheless, the gig … had to be stopped' (2018).

Given how unconventional Bailey was, it's not surprising that he could divide audiences. He recalls overhearing two punters at the Leicester Square Comedy Store: 'I heard these people having an argument about me … One was saying he thought I was funny, and the other was saying I wasn't' (2018). However, despite the strangeness of his comic imagination, Bailey could go down as well as far more conventional comics. On 28 March 1987, he appeared on *Saturday Live* in the guise of Frederick Benson. This character, originally named Harry Benson, is described in the first Pranksters catalogue as 'a Transylvanian personality who has lived in New York's South Bronx and worked there as a playleader' (BSUCA). He wears an implausibly voluminous purple glitter jacket, its gigantic shoulders flanking his whitened face, with lips and eye sockets painted black. The make-up highlights his unhinged facial expressions, mouth gaping as he speaks, eyes wide as he stares at the audience.

He starts the act with some business with a rubber mask and an ironic showbiz dance to Laurie Johnson's 'Gala Premiere', then he slowly approaches the mike, staring at it intently. There's a ripple of laughter. He takes the mike into his mouth, eyes now staring down to one side, and the audience laugh. He takes it out of the stand and makes humming noises through it, backing up and staring from side to side with wild, panicky eyes, provoking another ripple of laughter. After a bit more business, he points at somebody in the audience and with the mike still in his mouth, he speaks to them in a deep voice: 'Luke! [laughter] It's me, your father. [laughter] I've come to say – I'm sorry. [laughter] I'm – so – very – very –'. Now the mike falls out of his mouth but the voice continues – 'sorry' – revealing that it must have been a recording all along. Another laugh. Now Benson speaks, his voice recalling Bobby 'Boris' Pickett's vocal style on the novelty song 'Monster Mash': 'Mind the gap. [laughter into applause, 8 seconds]'.

Later, he addresses the punter he picked out before and says, 'D'you remember, son – that night I came to your bedroom? I was – smoking Roger, your favourite dinosaur.' He pulls a plastic tyrannosaurus from his massive props box, with a cigarette coming out of its mouth. The audience laugh at this sight gag, and the laughter continues as he actually smokes it, by blowing through its tail.

Towards the end of the act, he announces, 'I'm going for a job tomorrow.' He gets out a paper forage hat. 'Little catering job.' He unfolds the hat and puts it on. 'See what you think, son. [laughter] Have a nice day. [laughter] Would you like any – burger with your relish? [laughter] Why do they get the stars? I'm going to say "yummy" every time I sell a burger.' Now he gets a contraption out. 'But I'm also going to use one of these.' He starts to place the contraption on his head, attaching painful-looking clamps to the sides of his mouth, which gets a few laughs. 'It's a smile machine. [laughter] [gets out controls for smile machine] [laughter] Have a nice day. [operates smile machine so that his mouth is stretched surprisingly wide] No! [laughter into applause]' (Thatnuttysound 2016).

In this act, Bailey is going far beyond the norms of stand-up performance, and there are a number of things that make it remarkable. First of all, it's an intensely playful act, with its plastic toys, creepy contraptions, and general pointlessness. Bailey reveals, 'I just do like the mechanics of playing' (2018). Second, although blending horror and comedy is not unknown in popular culture, it's an unusual feature in stand-up. Some of the more grotesque elements, particularly the smile machine, verge on the disturbing even while they get laughs. Third, the mad, staring eyes and the drawling horror-movie voice reconfigure the conventional rapport found in stand-up, by preventing him from establishing the normal pretence that this is just a conversation between performer and audience. Finally, by taking phrases from everyday interactions – like the 'Mind the gap' safety announcement from the London Underground – and placing them in the context of his outlandish act, he reveals the strangeness of things we take for granted. The line 'Have a nice day' is funny because of the distance between what he's saying and how he's saying it. Delivering one of the ritualized sayings of the fast food industry in a mock-horror voice, deadpanning it to remove the familiar intonation, alienates it (in Brechtian terms), and turns it from something 'ordinary, familiar, immediately accessible, into something peculiar, striking and unexpected' (Brecht 1964: 143).

## 'I'll laugh at that when I get home'

Acts like Alexei Sayle, 20th Century Coyote, Norman Lovett, Kevin McAleer and Andrew Bailey were worlds apart from the standard jokes of the working men's club comedian, but they also went beyond anything that had been seen in variety theatre or even from folk comedians like Billy Connolly and Jasper Carrott. Far from following and understanding the rules of joke-telling, as Critchley would have it, they critiqued and reconfigured the rules, or invented new rules of their own, relentlessly challenging established conventions. At the Comic Strip, Sayle asks the audience, 'You are all doing the Open University comedy module, aren't you, by the way?' then imagines them saying to themselves, '"Oh yes, that's *very* funny. I'll laugh at that when I get *home*" [laughter]' (Comic Strip 1981). Here, Sayle throws even the most essential element of comic performance – the audience's laughter – into question.

Similarly, at Pentameters on 9 November 1980, Tony Allen complains that on the recently broadcast *Boom Boom Out Go the Lights*, his act was edited so that it no longer sounded like his usual freewheeling conversational 'raps': 'they didn't – do a rap on the telly, they'd structured it like jokes with punchlines. And I don't do that' (BSUCA). This implies a suspicion of what might be seen as one of the most basic tools of the comedian's trade, the joke itself.

What Allen was objecting to reveals another of alternative comedy's core aims – authenticity. His problem with jokes was that their formulaic nature made them inauthentic, preventing comedians from sharing their honest opinions of the world: 'At the time, the dominant form in stand-up comedy was joke-telling . . . So there was no honesty in it at all' (2016). In place of the 'dishonesty' of conventional joke-telling, many alternative comedians sought to reflect their own experiences in a way that audiences would recognize as authentic, and this was another difference from the stand-up that had immediately preceded them. As Jenny Lecoat puts it: 'We wanted to have something that was structurally different, and that was coming from a different angle. And that showed the world as we recognised it . . . just the experience that we were having in the late '70s, early '80s. Which was not the experience that . . . the Jim Bowens of the world were giving us' (2018).

# CHAPTER 6
## 'ADVANCED SOCIAL THINKERS': PERSONA AND PERSPECTIVE

Sometime in 1980, Tony Allen is performing at the Hemingford Arms in Islington, when he loses his thread and apologizes for his 'bad word-salad'. A punter heckles supportively, trying to help: 'Your adolescence, tell us about your adolescence.' Allen replies, 'My adolescence! Oh no, you can't have that now, there's not enough time.' There are a few laughs and some hubbub, and when he continues to refuse there are shouts of protest from the audience. He digs in: 'No – oh shit, don't start that, oh fuck, what am I –'. Then a different punter, an American, joins the conversation: 'You were talking about not being a stereotype.' He asks her to repeat what she's said, and she elucidates: 'You were talking about not being a stereotype and then it's harder just to be how you *are*' (BSUCA).

This suggests something important about what alternative comedy was and what audiences expected of it. Because many of the comedians eschewed the standard joke, audiences expected them to be telling the truth in what they said about themselves. In Allen's encounter with the two supportive hecklers, this expectation of authenticity becomes gently militant. The first seems to think that by asking him to talk about his adolescence she might be helping him to ad lib great swathes of comic autobiography, and the shouts of protest when he refuses suggest that others in the audience agree. The second seems to be particularly keen to find out who Allen really *is*. His reticence is understandable. Although the audience are clearly being supportive, they seem to want to treat him as a kind of self-revelation jukebox. This might be an extreme example, but it indicates that alternative comedy involved the idea that comedians should open up onstage, express themselves, reveal themselves, share something of their true selves with the audience. This chapter will examine this desire for authentic self-expression and how it relates to such questions as authorship, character, persona and – crucially – the comedian's own worldview.

### 'You didn't borrow stuff'

The idea of self-revelation was tied up with an important ethical principle of alternative comedy – that comedians should devise their own material.

Stealing other people's jokes was taboo (Smith 2009: 187–8; Hannan 2009: 524; *Vox* 1993: 68). William Cook has argued that, 'The establishment of the comic as sole author and rightful owner of his own material is Alternative Comedy's most important achievement' (1994: 6), and that this was more important than its rejection of sexism and racism: '[T]he real revolution was one of authorship, not ethics. Trad[1] comics shared a common reservoir of material. ... Like Buddy Holly or The Beatles, Alternative comics wrote their own material' (2001: 72). The early performers agree that this was an important principle, and that it distinguished them from the working men's club comedians who preceded them. Writing of his time with Threepenny Theatre, Alexei Sayle remembers, '[W]e did not think for a minute that we would not write our own material. It would be one of the ways in which we would distinguish ourselves from the conventional old-style comedians' (2016: 129). Andy de la Tour says that joke theft 'was frowned upon ... You didn't borrow stuff ... because we all realised how difficult it was to write this bloody stuff. And if you start stealing it, you know, you're nowhere' (2018).

That said, this principle was occasionally breached. Generally, comedians did devise the gags and routines they performed onstage, but to suggest that they were the sole authors of every single thing that came out of their mouths would be simplistic. An early article on alternative comedy notes that Tony Allen's Lenny-Bruce-dying-in-a-toilet joke 'seems to be the common property of all comedians who have passed through [the Comedy Store]' (Hughes-Hallett 1980: 74). Allen himself would incorporate lines from various sources into his act, recalling his use (with permission) of a friend's comment about a venue being 'like standing around inside someone's nose', and getting his best laugh of the night with it (2002: 94).

Some comics would buy the odd line from each other. Nigel Planer, for example, acknowledges, 'I paid Arnold Brown a tenner for [a] put-down line' (Planer 2018). When Julian Clary started out, he went to a more traditional source of readymade material, getting a couple of lines from gag sheets bought from a small ad in *The Stage* (Clary 2005: 111). Later, he enlisted Paul Merton to help him write his material (Clary 2005: 192).

Joke theft might have been frowned on, but that doesn't mean it didn't happen. According to Pauline Melville, '[P]eople pinched each other's jokes. And sometimes you could say something funny in the dressing room, just as a kind of chat, and two minutes later, you'd hear it come over the tannoy. Somebody had got it and was using it, you know. So you got to be a bit wary' (2018). Melville sent up this light-fingered tendency in her act. Compèring

### Alternative Comedy

an Alternative Cabaret show at the Greyhound pub in Fulham, she bisociates comedians' desperation for new material with drug addiction:

> Being a comic is a bit like being an addict or a junkie. I mean you've probably realised that we all get desperate for material. And – you know, we, we're scavenging everywhere for jokes. So you go up to one of the others and you say, [hippie voice] 'Oh – er – hey man. Er, can I score a gag off you? [laughter] Erm. Go on, you know I'm really feeling bad, you know I haven't had a gag for three days! [pockets of laughter] I'm having to take all the graffiti off the toilet walls, you know. [a few laughs] I'm really feeling bad!' And er – and then *maybe* one of the others gives you a gag. And then halfway through it, you find it's cut with unfunny stuff. [laughter and applause].'
>
> Alternative Cabaret 1981

Melville performed this routine as herself, but she normally appeared as a character called Edie, and it was in this guise that she would tell the following joke about one of Edie's friends: 'She's had a horrible Christmas, Eileen. She's had a horrible year, really. She's a horrible person. [laughter]' (Alternative Cabaret 1981). Performing at the Elgin on 17 January 1980, Andy de la Tour tells a suspiciously similar gag: 'Margaret Thatcher had a horrible Christmas. She did. [a couple joyless cheers] In fact she had a horrible year. Well, she's a horrible person, in't she? [laughter]' (BSUCA). When I ask him about it, he's quick to confess: '[I]t was Pauline's gag and I shouldn't have done it. I mean it was one of those things, sometimes you just do it. And even as you're saying it, you're thinking, "I really shouldn't do this, it's not my joke"' (2018).

This is by no means a unique case. It's possible to find examples here and there of comedians stealing jokes, sharing lines, or performing routines based on a strikingly similar premise. However, that is not to say that the principle of self-authorship existed more in theory than in practice. In fact, most comedians did write, devise or improvize their own material the vast majority of the time, and using lines that were bought or stolen was comparatively rare. It's significant that de la Tour doesn't just confess to taking Melville's line, he also expresses regret about it after all these years. The principle may not have been adhered to 100 per cent of the time, but the fact that it existed at all made alternative comedy fundamentally different from the stand-up in working men's clubs. As Tony Allen puts it, 'I think people nick things like jokes and lines. You know, I think that happens. Less so where you've got a sort of community of people that have got some sort of agreement that they're doing something different' (2016).

## 'Replacement identity'

Self-revelation is about more than comedians writing their own material. There's also the slippery issue of stage persona. I have previously argued that the stage identity of the comedian should be seen in terms of a *personality spectrum*, with character comedians at one end, comedians who appear to be entirely the same onstage and off at the other, and between them a continuous spectrum of different approaches to persona, each shading into the next (Double 2014: 121–39). At different points in the history of British stand-up, different parts of this spectrum have been more important, but the general direction of travel has been from artifice to authenticity. In the music hall from which patter-based stand-up evolved, performers tended to stress the distance between the grotesque characters they played onstage and their private, offstage selves – and this continued in variety. *The Stage*'s obituary of Max Miller, for example, noted that in contrast with his persona as 'the robust fellow in outrageously coloured and ludicrously baggy plus-fours', offstage he was 'a quiet, still man' (Marriott 1963). In working men's clubs, comedians with exaggerated personas were a minority. Most came on as themselves, presenting themselves as ordinary blokes simply getting up onstage to tell gags. However, the fact that standard jokes made up most of what they said onstage meant that opportunities for self-revelation were limited. Folk comedians like Billy Connolly and Jasper Carrott also came on as themselves, and the fact that they tended to shun standard jokes and delve into autobiography moved things on.

It would seem logical for alternative comedians to continue this trend towards playing increasingly less fictionalized version of themselves onstage. While that was the general trend, in fact there was a range of approaches to the issue of onstage identity. In 1985, Peter Nichols identified three distinct approaches:

> There are those comics, like Dowie and [Tony] Allen, who project much of themselves, the comic platform is their personalised ironic view of the world. Others, in the Sayle mould assume the single comic character closely identifiable, yet distinguishable. The comic as actor appears as the third category. Alternatively speaking Mayall was the first, with Kevin Turvey, offered as a creation in his own right.
>
> *Nichols 1985a*

To summarize, there were comedians who performed 'as themselves', comedians with exaggerated personas, and character comedians.

### Alternative Comedy

Some of the most prominent early alternative comedians adopted clearly defined characters, quite separate from their offstage selves. These characters often had views and opinions that were distinctly different from those of the performer. Pauline Melville, for example, designed the character of Edie to personify elements of left-wing culture that she found silly. Edie is a northern housewife who constantly tries – and fails – to be as alternative as possible. Melville explains, 'I started off as Edie. And I've always felt doing stand-up as Edie was easier and I was more relaxed, and I could be more surreal. Because she always got everything wrong' (2018). Edie was a vehicle for sending up the ridiculousness of the mysticism that was popular on the left. For example, at Pentameters on 16 January 1981, she reacts disapprovingly to the audience's laughter:

> You're not meant to laugh you know, you'll jog yourselves into another astral plane. [laughter] No, that can be very nasty! Mm, that can be very, happened to me once. Suddenly. Whoops! Out of me body. Attached – by a little blue thread, looking down on meself. Floating in the air, looking down on meself. I thought, 'Oh Edie, you must take that nightie to the laundrette.' [laughter].
>
> *BSUCA*

She also gets things wrong by failing to be as radical as she aspires to be. In a later routine, she talks about a trip to the Women's Peace Camp at Greenham Common: 'And all of a sudden, I come face to face with this policeman. So I opened me mouth to say, "Fuck off, Babylon!" [laughter, 5 seconds] And out came the words, "Good afternoon, officer" [laughter]' (*Let the Children Play* 1984).

Although Melville preferred performing as Edie to performing as herself, she recalls that:

> I was always being pushed to do stuff as myself. I think that was because [that was] what the blokes did. They didn't really appear in character as far as I remember. And I did it as myself, and it was fine, and I could get some really good gags and things, but I never had the *flights* that I got with Edie, doing it in a character.
>
> *Melville 2018*

As a character comedian, Melville was in the minority in Alternative Cabaret, but at the Comic Strip characters predominated. Nigel Planer and Peter

Richardson could find themselves playing a range of characters in a single Outer Limits sketch, but Planer also developed a more sustained character that he could use for a solo turn – Neil, the inept, self-effacing folksinger, who became the basis of the character he would play in *The Young Ones*. As with Edie, there's a clear separation between Neil and his creator, but Planer admits that he drew on elements of his own personality to create him, by 'using one's own flaws' (Planer 2018). Recordings from performances at the Comic Strip show that the comedy of Neil is rooted more in character than in gags:

> Hello. Er, huh. [a couple of laughs] Uh. Uh, h-right, I'm g- [quietly plays a chord] I'm gonna do, er – couple o' numbers for you, erm – off my latest, er, demo tape. [laughter] Never mind, they're both pretty short, OK? [laughter] Huh. Er. [laughter] No, they're both pretty bad numbers actually. So, er, what I'm gonna do is I'm gonna do – the worst one first so the second one won't seem quite so bad, OK? [laughter] Right, er – er, this, this first number I'm gonna do is, um – sort of about a big depression, that I had. [laughter] Kind of half an hour ago. [laughter] This is sort of how I felt about it, OK? Er – huh – heh, I probably won't be able to remember the words. [laughter] Never mind, they're really embarrassing anyway. [laughter]
>
> *Comic Strip 1981*

What's hard to capture on paper is the detail of Planer's performance. The awkward pauses, panicked breathing and apologetic chuckles all create tension in the audience, which is punctuated by the punchlines. The first full laugh here is a joke of sorts – Neil announces not that the songs are off his latest record, but merely his latest demo tape – but it wouldn't be funny without the context of the finely-rendered character. Moreover, soon afterwards he gets laughter simply by making incoherent noises: 'Huh. Er.' This laugh is conjured purely from the moment he has built between character and audience, rather than a clearly identifiable gag.

Rik Mayall's poet character – also the basis of his *Young Ones* character – worked in a similar way, using detailed characterization to create an encounter with the audience based on tension and release:

> As you know, we're a group of feminist poets. [laughter] What? W-what's wrong with that? [laughter] Wha-ha! [a few laughs] We'll find out a few things now, won't we? [scattered laughter continues]

Right! Well, er – I'm not one of er, the-the-the comedians. Erm – we, we thought we'd have a little break now. Erm – we're-we're-we're poetry collective. As you can – [to individual punter, change of tone, annoyed and assertive] Shut up, please! [laughter, 9 seconds] We're a p-poetry collective, I thought I'd open up with one of my, er – angriest poems of all, actually. They're – they're all pretty heavy! [An individual punter squeals with laughter, into general audience laughter, 6 seconds, under which Mayall continues] Huh huh, ha ha! Right on! Yes. It's a bit zany here I know, but [laughter reignites] – please be serious OK, right. [laughter surges again].

*Comic Strip 1981*

What stands out here is the quality of the laughter. Mayall creates a character whose attempts to stay in charge of the audience in the face of their laughing refusal to accept his artistic gravitas only generate more laughter. He uses embarrassment as a comic weapon, conjuring up a hilarious gaucheness that brings forth near-constant scattered laughter, regularly coalescing into full laughs. The uncontrolled squeals of individual punters seem to goad even more laughter from the rest of the audience. Significantly, the biggest laugh in this excerpt comes from him telling a laughing punter to shut up. The basic joke of a comedian telling an audience off for laughing was not new – notably, it was a central part of variety comic Frankie Howerd's technique – but Mayall's poet character builds his entire relationship with the audience from it. As the applause marking the end of his first poem dies down, he sarcastically announces, 'It's easy to clap, isn't it? [laughter, 5 seconds] I'm sure it's very funny. [laughter]'. Shortly afterwards, an unwelcome laugh provokes him to fury: '*Oh ha-ha-ha, very funny!!* [laughter with audible squeals]'.

Mayall had other characters based on offbeat relationships with the audience, notably Kevin Turvey. He performed a version of this character at the Comic Strip, and continued to develop it in regular appearances on the TV sketch show *A Kick up the Eighties* and live performances over the next decade. Where the poet was manic and strident, Kevin Turvey was naïve and unassuming. His blinking, wide-eyed delivery was unhurried and coloured with a heavy West Midlands accent, the anecdotes he haltingly told often concerning mundane events, recalled with unnecessary detail. He couldn't tell the audience he had eaten crisps without estimating exactly how many he'd had. His overliteral approach to explaining everything has the Brechtian effect of making even the most taken-for-granted assumptions seem strange and unfamiliar. At the benefit show *An Evening for Nicaragua* in 1983, this is how he explains a statement as simple and straightforward as telling the audience he went downstairs:

> So that's where I went, like, you know, I went down the stairs, right. We got these stairs – in our house, that attaches the first floor – [laughter] er, to the bottom floor. [laughter] No, it's dead convenient, like, well it saves all that trouble of – like, getting out the window and shinning down the drainpipe, you know. [laughter] Breaking into the kitchen window, going in and doing it all in there, [laughter] it's a waste of time. So I used the stairs, anyway. [laughter] As per usual. [laughter].²
> 
> *michtyme3 2006a*

Although both characters were clearly separate from the offstage Mayall, as with Planer's Neil, he saw their origins in his own personality. In 1983, he told the journalist Stephen Pile, '[M]y characters come up from inside. Kevin Turvey comes from seeing myself talk too much and being boring. With the angry poet, I just gave him all the embarrassing qualities I have got. I suppose a lot of the things you find funny are things you don't like about yourself' (Pile 1983: 32–4). However, while the characters might have been rooted in himself, the fact that he adopted fictional identities onstage was important to him. Pile notes, 'If Mayall works in characters, it is partly because he is wary about showing who he really is ... Before any performance he spends 15 minutes ceasing to be himself and working up his replacement identity' (Pile 1983: 34).

With both Planer and Mayall, the detail and depth of their characterization was such that on occasion they were capable of fooling the audience into believing that their characters were real. A 1983 article in *The Face* notes that Kevin Turvey's appearance on *The Russell Harty Show* 'merely confirmed his reality to many viewers', and argues that when Planer performed as Neil at the Comedy Store, 'The audience had a really bad time making up their minds if he meant it' (Taylor 1983: 43). Planer expands on this:

> That's what Rik and I both did in the early days of the Comedy Store. That was a way to get on, was to say, 'We've got a folk singer for you now'... And they're never quite sure. 'Is he really going to be bad?' And Rik with his poet, likewise... you'd think, 'Oo, is he very fragile? Is this guy very, very fragile?' ... Obviously, they then realise, 'This must be

his act.' But there's still that feeling of, 'Oo, is he *really* fragile?' And with Neil . . . early days, it was kind of, 'Oo, is he really just shit?'.

*Planer 2018*

One of the things that made such ambiguity possible was the fact that the audience were expecting to see performers appearing as themselves rather than in character. However, while the audience could be fooled at the Comedy Store, this would not have been the case in shows at the Comic Strip. There, Mayall and Planer appeared as various different characters throughout the evening, thus making it clear that they were not real people but fictional creations. Even so, Mayall would still try to fool the audience, coming on and telling them, 'This is er – this is the real me. Huh. My name's er, Rik, OK?' As the routine continues, it quickly becomes clear that this is not the real him, but an artfully constructed character, a slight variant of the feminist poet (Mayall and Edmondson 1998).

The Comic Strip was unusual in presenting more character comedy than straight stand-up, but as the circuit developed other comedians came along who worked in character, notably Harry Enfield and John Sparkes, not to mention the surreal alter egos adopted by Andrew Bailey in his various acts. However, even the most character-driven Comic Strip acts also sometimes adopted more ambiguous identities onstage. For example, the sketch duo French and Saunders played a whole range of clearly-fictional characters in their various sketches at the Comic Strip, appearing as schoolgirls Cheryl and Lisa working on a 'love project', as members of the painfully left-wing community theatre group 'Red Shoes', and as country and western duo the Farton Sisters. In their funniest Comic Strip sketch, they play two Americans in London, psychobabbling at each other to show how progressive they are, whilst savagely competing over anything from their sex lives to their ancestry. At one point, French's character boasts that her ancestors are 'Scotch': 'Have you heard of the McSondheim tartan? [laughter]' (Comic Strip 1981). However, alongside this cast of comic grotesques, they also developed core personas, which Jennifer Saunders refers to as 'the French and Saunders characters': 'I was the misguided, bossy and generally cross one, and Dawn was the cheeky, subversive upstart' (2014: 97). An early TV appearance gives an idea of how this worked:

French: No I'm sorry, I-I'm sorry, you told me no-one was getting paid for this jig tonight. [laughter] I'm certainly not getting paid.

## Persona and Perspective

| | |
|---|---|
| Saunders: | Well – |
| French: | I'm 27. Yes. |
| Saunders: | Yes. |
| French: | I'm 27. And I'm a bit fed up of being on your comedy YOP scheme, Jennifer. [laughter] I mean when am I gonna get paid, for instance? |
| Saunders: | When you're funny. [laughter] Er – |

*Grimchops 2009*

Here, they are notionally appearing as themselves, however silly their argument may be. Clearly, Saunders hasn't secured French's services via a job creation scheme like the Youth Opportunities Programme (YOP). Nonetheless, they refer to each other as Dawn and Jennifer – their actual first names – and address the reality of the immediate performance situation, dividing their attention between each other and the audience, as each tries to win the audience's approval at the expense of her partner. This dynamic and the contrast in status – Dawn subservient, Jennifer dominant – fit the pattern of a traditional double act. Yet for all the exaggeration and in spite of adhering to an established double act structure, the divide between onstage persona and offstage self is left unclear.

### 'He was me but he wasn't really'

That was also the case with the vast majority of stand-ups who played the alternative cabaret circuit. They adopted personas rather than playing characters, building stage identities out of elements of their own personalities. A persona is an inherently ambiguous thing, leaving the audience uncertain as to exactly how it might correspond to the real person inhabiting it. They may be aware of a certain amount of selection and amplification in the traits and attitudes presented to them, but just how much artifice this involves will differ from comedian to comedian. This was certainly the case in alternative comedy, with some comics adopting personas so exaggerated that, in Peter Nichols's words, they are assuming a 'single comic character', and others so subtle that there was no apparent difference between onstage and offstage identities.

In some cases, comedians found it helpful to maintain a separation between stage persona and private self. Jo Brand initially billed herself as the Sea Monster in order to keep her comedy career a secret from the people she worked with in her day job: 'The reason I did that was actually I was a nurse still, and I didn't want people to see my name in the comedy listings. Because I wanted to see if it worked before telling people that I worked with. So it was just a way of disguising myself, really' (2015).

In other cases, stage persona could feel something that was imposed from outside. Ben Elton recognizes that his appearances as resident comic on *Saturday Live* in 1986 made his reputation as a stand-up, but also pigeonholed him, limiting expectations of him: 'It made my success. I mean it also meant that I would never, ever get away from that first impression, you know, I was going to be set as the anti-Thatch, opinionated . . . shouty guy forever' (2018). However, his persona as a ranting right-on anti-sexist man was also something he could comically exploit, by suddenly shifting to play against type – as he does in a performance recorded at Fat Sam's nightclub in Dundee on 7 July 1987: 'Your average dick – and believe me lads, they're all average – [laughter] Well mine's not, mine's fucking enormous, but yours are – [loud laughter] Oo! And suddenly, the alternative pose drops for a moment and the little bit of Benny Hill in us all jumps out [laughter] onto the stage! Ha ha! Recognise the devil within you and conquer it!' (Elton 1987).

Even when there's no apparent difference between stage persona and offstage self, it's impossible to entirely avoid artifice. As John Hegley points out, the fact that performance is a public act makes it unusual, and being able to bring out the self-assurance of private interactions whilst onstage is part of the challenge:

> It's trying to be as you are in other situations, but the thing is you're not normally talking to a hundred or two hundred people . . . so there has to be a difference. But bringing over that relaxedness or that at ease or spontaneity that you have in other situations is part of it.
>
> *Hegley 2016*

Achieving this kind of ease whilst performing is a central part of the process of developing a persona, but other aspects are more particular to the individual comedian. After starting as a comedian in January 1984, Jeremy Hardy built a young fogeyish persona by exaggerating his middle-class Home Counties background: 'a lot of it was actually quite exaggerated . . . because I wasn't that posh. I'd say my upbringing was sheltered rather than posh. It was suburban Surrey.' As he developed and gained more experience, the distance between his stage persona and offstage self shrank: 'I think over time, I grew into myself. And obviously you change as a person, because being a comedian changes you as a human being dramatically. So two things are going on ... On stage you become more like yourself I think, and in life you become more like your stage self, until they become one' (2018).

Julian Clary developed his Joan Collins Fan Club persona after the costume and props he used for his earlier stage identity – a drag character called Gillian Pie-Face – were stolen from a van. The new persona was much closer to himself, allowing him to 'make an asset of my mannerisms and voice' (2005: 176). Whereas Hardy and Clary decreased the distance between stage persona and private person over time, others went in the opposite direction. Having performed stand-up for a while, Jim Barclay realized he was not enjoying it, and found that wearing a blatantly ridiculous costume allowed him to develop a more unfettered, exaggerated persona:

> I would think ... 'What I need to do is liberate myself in some way' ... The bloke next door to where I lived then ... he had one of those nail-through-the-head things ... and I thought, 'Why don't I just wear that?' And then I put it through a bowler hat, a joke bowler hat, and I thought, 'Well if you wear this ... then you've got to act as if you've got a nail through your head. You can't just walk on and have a nail through your head. What would happen to you if you had a nail through your head? You'd be mad, wouldn't you?' ... And then I put the deely-boppers on, looked in the mirror, I thought, 'This is outrageous. And so this will make me be larger.'
>
> Barclay 2016

Costume also helped Alexei Sayle to discover his own highly exaggerated persona. He found a grey suit in an Oxfam shop, which shrank in such a way as to emphasize his stomach. As he has recorded, 'From the point of view of me wearing my suit out and about socially this was a disaster but as a stage outfit there was something about this ill-fitting mod outfit that really worked' (2016: 197). The suit, combined with his skinhead haircut, gave him an instantly-recognizable look, and also allowed him to joke about his physical size onstage: 'Actually by the, by the, by the way, er, I dunno, er, I dunno if you like the suit, erm. [laughter] Actually, I got it in a shop specializing in clothes for the *fuller* figure, erm. [laughter] Yeah, the shop's called Mr *Fat Bastard!* [laughter, 4 seconds]' (ND).

The aggressiveness of the persona was a response to the fact that many of Sayle's early shows involved conflict situations. His wife Linda argues that 'the persona was partly forged in crowd control', because, 'If the audiences had been sitting there and sipping cocktails and clapping politely, [he] wouldn't have needed to come on and scream at them' (Sayle 2017). Tony Allen has written about how Sayle developed the persona by merging the distinct elements that made up his performances while compering the Comedy Store:

> His only material was a handful of short exquisitely written first person anecdotes about artistic or political arguments he'd had in unlikely settings ... He would present these set-pieces alongside his MCing, which was far less stagey and very abrasive ... He was constantly going in and out of character and in the process of merging the two into the style of an eccentric comedian.
>
> *Allen 2002: 97*

According to Sayle, it was while he was appearing with Allen at the Edinburgh Fringe in 1980 that he finally put these different elements together to create the persona he became known for. After a disappointing performance early in the run, he completely rethought how to present his material:

> I blew my whole act to bits, so instead of going from bit to bit, everything was just part of everything else, like you'd set off a hand grenade in the room. And I ripped the room up that night ... As a solo act that was the night I became more than an MC. Because when I'd been the MC, it was little two or three minute [bits]. That was vital for me. That was when I became me. That was the final step.
>
> *Sayle 2003*

By this stage, there was a clear distinction between Sayle and his persona, but this was not always recognized, as a *Guardian* article reveals: 'Sayle is used to being mistaken for his stand-up stage act, a ranting ball of obscenity and left-wing prejudice in an ill-fitting, torn suit that makes him look fatter and uglier than he really is' (Rosen 1983). Sayle confirms this: 'It's true, people did used to see me in the street and were surprised that I wasn't wearing, like, the three-button mod suit, you know, and the hat, like! Walking around, swearing at people and stuff!' (2015).

For him, the separation was so clear that he refers to the persona in the third person. Yet he still vacillates over exactly how it relates to himself: 'He wasn't me ... I mean, in a sense that's sophistry because of course he was me ... it was a part you were playing, I think.' He expands on this, saying he

## Persona and Perspective

eventually gave up stand-up in 1996 because he found the person restrictive: '[T]he guy in the tight suit was actually a persona. I kind of thought he was me but he wasn't really. He was a comic persona and so in a sense he was very limited because he couldn't talk about my life. You know, my actual existence' (2015). More recently, Sayle has argued that the persona could, in fact, express some of his own worldview, but in a somewhat limited way:

> Obviously, I lived in a tower block and I could see that those houses below were being started to be colonised by the middle classes and I could see the four by fours parked outside and all of that, so ... he-slash-I could do that stuff ... I could do a degree of autobiographical [material] ... It was not so much the material but my attitude to the material, that he couldn't be that nuanced.
>
> Sayle 2017

### 'I review the world'

This is a crucial point. For all the cartoonish exaggeration of Sayle's persona, he could still share his actual opinions and observations of the world, even though this was without much nuance. This notion that comedians should use stand-up to share what Nichols called their 'personalised ironic view of the world' was a key part of alternative comedy's ethos. Performing at the Masonic Lodge at the Edinburgh Fringe in 1982, Tony Allen makes the idea explicit when he declares, 'I'm a comedian, I review the world. That's what I do' (BSUCA).

By defining his job in this way, Allen was expressing a commonly-held view of alternative comedy's project. A magazine article from 1980 states that, 'Comic Strip comedians talk about their own backgrounds, about space invaders, dole queues, sex, drugs and rock 'n' roll' (Hughes-Hallett 1980: 74). In his 1990 show *Why I Stopped Being a Stand Up*, John Dowie told the audience, 'When comedians go on stage they tell the audience, through their jokes, all about themselves. What their likes and dislikes are. What their prejudices are. What kind of personality they have' (1990: n.p.). For William Cook, it was this quality that distinguished altcom from the comedy that preceded it: 'Alternative Comedians dare to direct their humour inwards instead of outwards at an absent minority. They tell tales about themselves, and by extension, their audience' (1994: 15–16).

The idea of comedy as sharing of individual worldview was one of alternative comedy's most important innovations. In America, this had been around since the 1950s, pioneered by Mort Sahl and those who followed in his wake. However, by 1979 Britain had produced little to compare with the sickniks. The views expressed by the standard jokes of the working men's club comedian tended to be lumpen shared assumptions rather than individual perspectives on the world – old-fashioned opinions about the role of women and prejudices against the Irish, Pakistanis, homosexuals, and so on. This is what Cook meant by arguing that the humour was directed outward at an absent minority. The best folk comedians were moving stand-up beyond the standard joke by sharing their perspectives on the world, but there were limits to their observations. Connolly's comedy was rooted in working-class Scottish experience, often focusing on a shared past – by talking about his own childhood, teenage years and early adulthood – and although he did this brilliantly, it meant that he seldom turned his eye onto current trends in popular culture.

By contrast, even the character-based comedy of the Comic Strip critiqued anything from Space Invaders to the mass unemployment of the early Thatcher years. Suddenly, comedians were talking about political events and current trends, in routines referencing youth tribes, drugs, wine bars, Sony Walkmans, Suzuki jeeps and Sainsbury's. The majority of the new stand-ups adopted stage personas that were clearly versions of themselves, and this created a scene in which a multitude of different perspectives on the world could be voiced.

In many cases, these were perspectives that had not been heard in British comedy before. Witness how Tony Allen introduces Alternative Cabaret to the audience at the ADC Theatre in Cambridge in May 1981: 'My name's Tony Allen, er, um – I'm an alternative comedian, and this is Alternative Cabaret. We're a sort of collective of comedians, musicians – dope smokers, dole scroungers, tax evaders, sexual deviants, political extremists, you know. Advanced social thinkers, you know [laughter]' (BSUCA). Even allowing for comic exaggeration, what Allen is suggesting is that the voices the audience will hear will be unconventional ones, from people outside of the mainstream of society. Indeed, the haphazard, uncommercial nature of the early scene meant that many of the performers drawn to it were eccentrics, with unusual perspectives on the world.

Arnold Brown is a good example. Brown explains that his comedy is driven by 'not wanting to be part of a conformist thinking.' He believes that what makes him unique as a comedian is his perspective: 'The only thing that I'm uncertain about is uncertainty. I think it's the ambiguity to everything. That nothing is taken for granted' (2016). This makes for a lightly absurd comic style, full of oblique comments and odd associations. His manner is urbane, his speech flavoured with a soft, warm Glasgow accent, as he gently challenges the Comic Strip audience over his ethnic background:

> I care about these things because I must reveal myself, I'm Scottish. *Why not?* And Jewish. Not sure how to react, are you? [laughter] Liberals, eh? [laughter] Still worried, eh? [laughter] Two racial stereotypes for the price of one, perhaps the best value in the West End today. [laughter] Perhaps not. [a few laughs] People ask me about being Jewish. No they don't. [laughter]
>
> *Comic Strip 1981*

John Hegley is another whose comedy is driven by a unique perspective on the world. Hegley is principally a poet but he also sings songs, and frames the whole act in constant dialogue with the audience, telling them about the items he is about to present, commenting on their reactions, and sometimes telling them off rather in the manner of an eccentric schoolmaster. A review of a benefit gig in 1984 vividly captures the dynamic of the act:

> [H]e has had the good sense to blow his cringing inability out of proportion and turn the embarrassment outwards into the insecurities of the audience. You could almost hear the hot flushes as everyone hung in an appalled limbo, not quite knowing whether this 'poet' was an intentional comedian or not. The line was hilariously thin and John Hegley walked it beautifully.
>
> *Astor 1984*

Hegley explains how his act expresses 'a set of concerns', and that he needs to 'give the concerns a chance', because they are important (2016). This set of concerns includes a highly individual set of comic obsessions. Hegley's songs and poems often focus on dogs, glasses, his father, his brother-in-law, and aspects of his childhood. A performance on a TV chat show gives a good idea of how these obsessions fit together with the relationship he builds with the audience:

> Erm, the first one is another dog poem, this is about, er, dogs and logs. [laughter] Both are very popular at Christmas. But it is not generally considered cruel to abandon a log. [laughter] And dogs are rarely used

as fuel. [laughter] Good. Somebody over there enjoying this particularly. [laughter] Some of these poems are for one person. [brief laughter] And some of them are for *two*. [laughter]

VHS Video Vault 2015

Unlike the WMC comic, uniting the audience by telling jokes at the expense of minorities and outsiders, Hegley himself is the outsider. He confronts the audience with his bespectacled geekiness and the quirkiness of his set of concerns, acknowledging that what he does is not for everybody, and may even just be 'for one person'. Being an outsider also allows him to identify with the minorities who were the butt of WMC jokes. Later in the same performance, he sings a song called 'Glad to Wear Glasses', in which he dreams of a world 'Where everybody's trying on everybody else's glasses. [laughter] Where nobody cares about the colour of your skin. Or the colour of the case your glasses are kept in. [laughter]'.

### 'Remember those articles?'

The principle of creating comedy based on worldview didn't just give a voice to eccentrics and outsiders, it also allowed those who had been on the receiving end of jokes to describe how the world looked from their perspective. In working men's clubs and folk clubs, the comedians had been almost exclusively men, so female comic perspectives were not heard. Even in variety, where women were better represented, female comedians largely avoided describing the challenges they faced in their everyday lives. Alternative comedy has been criticized for its comparative lack of female performers (Cook 1992), but what this fails to acknowledge is the almost complete dearth of women in stand-up immediately beforehand. In fact, there's evidence that women were actively encouraged to take to the stages of the new cabaret venues. Monika Bobinska, who ran the Meccano Club in Islington, says that one of her policies was to 'book more women' (2015), and Maria McErlane confirms that she was 'very pro-that' (2018). Indeed, a number of female performers talk about how much they were encouraged by promoters on the circuit (Eclair 2018; Lecoat 2018; McErlane 2018; Melville 2018). That said, Jo Brand points out a number of structural problems with the circuit that were discouraging to women (2019).

Ultimately though, even if female comics were still a minority in alternative comedy, the fact that it opened up a space for them to share their worldview made it very different from earlier British comedy. Performing in an Alternative Cabaret show at the Elgin on 27 March 1980, Maggie Steed shares her put-downs for men making unwanted sexual advances, and goes on to discuss the downside of using the contraceptive pill. She describes the aftereffects of hurriedly taking one last thing at night, having forgotten to take it earlier in the day:

> So you wake up in the morning, look at the packet, what do you find? Ha ha ha ha! You've taken next Wednesday's! [murmur of laughter] And today's Thursday! And it's gonna leave a whole week you're gonna spend taking *yesterday's* pills – today. [laughter] And you get to the weekend, you get pissed a couple of times – and come Tuesday, you've got *five pills*. [laughter] Staring at you in the face, accusingly. [laughter] So you take them out, you know, and – grind 'em up [laughter] – and you have 'em on your toast for breakfast. [laughter]
>
> *BSUCA*

Steed only did stand-up for a short time, but other women emerged who would become major figures in the scene by articulating distinctly female perspectives. One of these, Jenny Lecoat, made getting her own back on sexist men a core part of her act. A review of a CAST New Variety show at the Cricklewood Hotel from January 1984 describes how, 'Feminist comedienne and songwriter Jenny Lecoat got things off to a good, aggressive start with some verbal attacks on a few of the men who have passed through her life' (Rush 1984). Looking back, Lecoat self-effacingly questions her early reputation as an aggressively feminist comedian:

> This thing about being a feminist comic, I mean certainly that's what I called myself. And I've always referred to myself as a feminist and I still would . . . But in terms of my act, I mean all I was really doing was taking the piss out of men. It wasn't really that smart . . . It was a lot more attitude, and a lot less philosophy than perhaps . . . I would have liked to have thought at the time. I think there was an awful lot of sticking two fingers up at a world which our mothers had suffered.
>
> *Lecoat 2018*

Many of her routines expressed a certain basic feminism. Appearing on *Saturday Live* in 1987, she addresses the issue of weight:

Are there any women here obsessed with their weight? A few. The rest of you are all [waves a hippie V-sign, and puts on right-on voice] *really happy about your bodies, OK*. [laughter] No I – I just ask 'cos I'm obsessed with mine. I know that logically I'm not really fat. But I'm obsessed with it 'cos when I was twelve years old – I used to read – *Jackie* magazine. [laughter] Remember those articles? 'Feeling fat, girls? Try this simple test. Just slip yourself down between the wall and the radiator. [laughter into applause] If you can't do it – you're a fat bitch.' [laughter]

Saturday Live: The Best of Series Two *2008*

There's an important similarity between this and Steed's routine. In both cases, the comedian takes a private experience – using contraceptive pills or worrying about weight – and shares it in a public context. The audience are invited to relate to the experience described, the men momentarily invited to see the world from a female perspective, the women perhaps recognizing the truth of the description in their own lives. Sometimes this recognition becomes tangible. When Lecoat asks, 'Remember those articles?' a couple of female voices can be heard replying, 'Yes!' This kind of sharing of female experience had not been heard in British stand-up before alternative comedy emerged.

In the same way, alternative cabaret opened the door for out gay comedians like Julian Clary, Simon Fanshawe, Claire Dowie and Bernard Padden to share their individual perspectives on the world. For Clary, being gay was just part of what made him feel like an outsider, and his act allowed him to overturn the normal order of things: 'I deliberately set out to create my own world where I was the norm and the audience were the outsiders. What's more, they were to feel privileged to get a glimpse of my superior environment' (2005: 176–7). He would pick out aggressive-looking, apparently straight men from the audience and assert his dominance over them. On *Saturday Live* in 1987, he's drawn towards a beefy man in a checked shirt: 'Oo Good Lord, you're very close, aren't you, in a – particularly unpleasant shirt that you didn't manage to iron. [laughter]'. He tweaks at the man's quiff: 'This man, er – this man dyes his roots black, look. [laughter]'. His shiny rubber top, studded necklet and heavy make-up would make Clary an outsider in other contexts, but while he holds the microphone, he's able to critique the punter's much more conventionally masculine look and make it seem ridiculous. Later, he questions the punter's masculinity more bluntly: 'I want you to shut up now and act like a man. [laughter] Or don't you do impressions? Erm – [outraged laughter]' (*Saturday Live: The Best of Series Two* 2008).

## 'Public declaration of self'

What all of this draws out is that there is something fundamentally political about basing comedy on a worldview. As Pauline Melville points out, alternative comedy often went beyond purely personal perspectives: '[I]t wasn't just everything that was looked at from an individual my-point-of-view. We were all Marxists. We had a very well worked-out way of looking at the world ... And it's not just a personal observation. It's a political analysis, really' (2018).

That said, not all of the more openly political acts shared a Marxist perspective. Notably, Tony Allen had a worked-out way of looking at the world, but from an anarchist viewpoint. An early article on him notes that, 'His manner now is not so much jokes and gags, as having a slant on a view of the world. Sex life, relationships, the contradictions between the theory and practice of an anarchist/lefty.' It also quotes him on how the people from the Ladbroke Grove squatting scene have influenced him: 'I reproduce a lot of their lifestyle on stage, and I think that's political in itself' (Brazil 1979). This happens in a routine from his very first stand-up performance, at Ovalhouse in Kennington on 2 April 1979:

> The drug squad – in Portobello Road. Police intelligence. Those two words are mutually exclusive. [laughter] The drug squad in Portobello Road. Plain clothes. They've got khaki anoraks, navy shirts, denim jeans, and sensible boots. [laughter] And they're sidling up to Rastafarians – and they go, 'Er, hi man. Erm. Could you tell me where I can *score* some *reefers*?' [laughter] And they wanna pay 1966 prices, as well. But that's an improvement, because up until November they were wearing kaftans and beads. [laughter]
>
> BSUCA

Here, an established form of authority – the police force – becomes ridiculous when described from the perspective of the anarchist squatting subculture. The jokes grow out of their inability to fit in with the group they are trying to infiltrate, getting the clothing and language hilariously wrong, and generally being hopelessly out of date. As with Clary's comic attacks on conventionally masculine men, the established order is turned upside down. This routine laughs in the face of the popular press's portrayal of squatting culture in the 1970s. Not only are the police laughable in their failure to imitate the norms of the alternative society of Portobello Road, there's also the suggestion that they are racist, targeting Rastafarians as likely drug dealers. This routine stayed in Allen's repertoire for a while, and as it developed he added extra gags, which placed the critique of the police into a broader political context. In his 1981 performance at the ADC Theatre, the routine continues:

> That's all bollocks, actually, that's just a joke. Don't look like that at all. They look just like me and you. In fact, they look more like me and you than me and you, it's a bit scary. [laughter] What I wanna know is – where is the cop on the beat – when it comes to arresting the *real* criminals? I mean, the *real* criminals. 'Well. I was, er, walking in a northeasterly direction, in the boardroom of Amalgamated Conglomerates – er, when I noticed the accused and several other persons unknown making a dubious decision as to the economic future of Latin America. Well – [laughter] I cautioned him, arrested him, and bunged him in the back o' the Transit. [laughter] That's when he hit his head.' Doesn't happen, does it? [laughter][3]
>
> BSUCA

After a gag which suggests that police infiltration is, in fact, more sinister than inept, Allen goes on to question the nature of what is seen as crime, when multinational corporations can wreak untold damage on Third World countries with impunity.

Although alternative comedians took a whole range of approaches to the thorny issue of onstage identity – from fully-fledged character to barely detectable persona – what the new wave of comedy achieved was to put the idea of self-expression centre stage. They firmly established the principle that comedians should write their own material rather than buying or stealing it. Even character pieces and highly exaggerated personas could reflect direct personal experience. The job of stand-up comedy shifted from being about telling impersonal standard jokes to reviewing the world from an individual perspective. A range of different viewpoints came into stand-up for the first time, allowing audiences to hear about anything from the pressures felt by ordinary women to the personal revelations of an anarchist squatter. Establishing the principle that stand-up could be based on personal perspective was fundamentally important to the development of the form in the UK. As Mark Thomas puts it: 'Freedom of expression is one of the truest things and forms of identity we have. It creates us. Expressing who we are. That's what art is ... It expresses who we are. And that ... public declaration of self is an incredible thing' (2018).

# CHAPTER 7
'COMEDY OF DIRECT CONFRONTATION': RELATING TO AUDIENCES

The audience for the opening night of the Comedy Store on 19 May 1979 must have been quite noteworthy, because reviewers of that show do tend to mention them. In *Punch*, Alan Brien dedicates around a quarter of his review to the crowd, mentioning the 'deafening whispers of the conversationalists in the rear seats', and confessing:

> I kept being riveted by the customers (admittedly they weren't paying and had been lavishly laced with free champagne) who looked like a caricature crowd out of *Mad* magazine ... Their reactions, favourable or unfavourable, were random, mindless and mechanical. It seemed to me I was in the drying room of an android factory. Perhaps Peter Rosengard should stop worrying about auditioning his entertainers and begin auditioning his patrons.
>
> *Brien 1979: 927*

The impression is of a barely human audience – like cartoons or androids – and rather an unruly one, drunk on free champagne, reacting mindlessly and talking while the comedians are onstage. As we have seen, Tom Tickell's *Guardian* review gives the same impression, with the audience getting drunker as the show progressed and 'baying for each act to end almost before it had begun'. In *Performance Magazine*, Steve Thorne takes a more balanced view, describing the atmosphere as 'pleasant' and an audience which was 'neither inhibited nor out for blood' (1979).

Reviews like these originated one popular view of the alternative comedy audience – that they were uninhibited and prone to rowdiness. An article from 1981 contrasts the new scene with the passivity of television: 'It is the comedy of direct confrontation, a million miles away from the safety nest of the boob tube ... that makes the [Comic] Strip and [Alternative] Cabaret such exciting propositions' (Norman 1981: 13). The Comedy Store had a particular reputation for rambunctiousness, but the alternative comedy audience in general were known for answering back. In the *Time Out London Student Guide* in 1987, Malcolm Hay argues that, 'Even at its worst, [the circuit] can provide the sort of spectator sport – like the tussle between a performer and a persistent heckler – that makes a visit to cabaret such a distinctive experience' (80). Carol Sarler makes a similar point in an article for *London Daily News*:

> A large part of the pleasure comes from the sense of dialogue between audience and performer. Although the gong is no longer used, venues tend to be small enough to allow for interaction: a joke in bad taste will be heckled. Unlike a trip to the theatre, where you buy your ticket and sit passively to receive what's given, with cabaret you can actually say: 'No, this is unacceptable to me.' Some performers enjoy a good heckle, some don't – but all of them take note to adapt their act accordingly.
>
> Sarler 1987: 32

Pauline Melville contrasts the audiences she encountered in cabaret with quiet, well-behaved theatre audiences:

> I'd been doing a lot of stand-up and I went back to do a show with Joint Stock. An ordinary play, a Balzac adaptation. And when I came on, I thought there was nobody there. Because I'd forgotten how reverential theatre audiences are. And how noisy the cabaret gigs were – with people heckling and cash registers going and glasses clinking and all that.
>
> Melville 2018

The other prevailing view of the alternative cabaret audience is that it was dominated by – or even exclusively made up of – the right-on, politically sensitive, anti-Thatcher Left. Sarler's article talks about 'the trendy, generally middle-class, liberal, would-be "socially aware" bulk of the cabaret audience'. Sarler was writing as a fan of the circuit, but a scathing *Stage* editorial from around the same time describes the audience in similar but sneerier terms: 'university and polytechnic graduates, small "l" liberals, *Guardian* readers, Thatcher-haters, supporters of all manner of "caring" causes both in this country and overseas – in other words the middle class at that early stage in their lives before they are honest enough to admit that they actually belong to it' (*Stage* 1988).

### Alternative Comedy

Comedians who played the circuit in the 1980s tend to paint the audience in similar colours. According to Bernard Padden, 'The demographic ... particularly for the Earth Exchange, was *Guardian* readership. Kind of liberal left. I'd say that was ... reflected throughout most of the comedy places I played' (2017). Jeremy Hardy agreed: 'Probably in a lot of the clubs in the mid to late '80s, people were liberal-left, I would say. Or certainly the people who were vocal' (2018). In 1990, looking back from a less distant vantage point, Jenny Lecoat recalled, '[I]t tended to be very much PLUs, you know, People Like Us, it was sort of people from about twenty to forty, pretty much middle class, lefty, pretty much of the same opinions, same sentiments' (1990).

Put these two views together, and the alternative comedy audience becomes a middle-class left-wing crowd, prone to shouting things at the acts, particularly if they hear something they find politically unacceptable. Although there may be a degree of truth in this, it is of course something of a caricature, and doesn't allow for the possibility that alternative cabaret might have attracted different types of audience in different venues. This seems to have been the case in the early days of the circuit, to the extent that Jim Barclay even talked about it onstage. At the ADC Theatre in 1981, he explains, 'You see when you're a stand-up comedian, you've only got three audiences. You're an *alternative* comedian, you've got three audiences to play to.' He goes on to describe these three audiences. First, there's 'The anarcho-syndicalist Kropotkin tendency o' Ladbroke Grove. [laughter]', presumably a reference to the punters at venues like the Elgin. He continues, 'And then there's you lot', and mocks the very audience he's talking to: '*Your* idea of political action – is to sign – apologetically – in invisible ink [laughter] – the Vegetarians Against the Juggernauts petition. [laughter and applause]'. Finally, he describes 'the last lot you can play to' as 'the Plaistow branch o' the British Movement – in a talent contest – in the Truncheon Arms on a Monday night [laughter]' (BSUCA).

In this chapter, I'll try to go beyond simple caricatures of the alternative comedy audience, using recordings to look in detail at how people actually behaved in particular shows, and how comedians discovered complex ways of relating to their audiences.

### Tony Allen compères the Comedy Store

The early Comedy Store audience has an almost mythological image, thanks partly to the florid turns of phrase banged out on journalists' typewriters. In the *Observer Magazine*, Richard North wrote about comedians being 'put to the test by a merciless audience' (1980: 26) and in the *Sunday Times*, Gordon Burn described them as 'mostly young and looking as if they had been selected from one of the artier rock shows', recording that they 'started off unkind, and did not get any kinder' (1980). Steve Absalom waxed particularly lyrical in *The Stage*:

> Throughout the ages the biggest box office hits have always been those which traded on man's inhumanity to man. Roman arenas were packed out when the Christians came to town, the Spanish were just crazy about the rack and 20th century Britain invented fringe theatre. Not to be outdone, London came up with something which beats the lot – the Comedy Store in darkest Soho.
>
> Absalom 1981

He was watching a show compèred by Tony Allen, and he notes that, 'His job, and it must be an exhausting one, is to prevent the "gong-happy wallys" (his term) in the audience from taking over, and it is due to his own talent as a comedian that we get through the evening without a riot.'

As it happens, the British Stand-Up Comedy Archive contains a complete recording of a night at the Comedy Store with Allen compèring. The running order of the show is as follows:

1. Jim Barclay
2. The Greatest Show on Legs
3. John Revell (AKA Nick Revell)
4. Arthur Mendacious Brain (AKA Tony Green)
5. John Hegley
6. Pamela Stephenson
7. Paul Goodman and Ian Russell
8. Pamela Stephenson
9. 'Stig' (audience spot)
10. 'Martin' (audience spot)
11. The Greatest Show on Legs

The tapes are undated but references made by the acts suggest the show probably took place around September 1980.[1] By listening to the recording, it's possible to get beyond journalistic hyperbole, and properly examine both the audience's behaviour, and the strategies performers used to try and control it.

At the very start of the show, Allen enters to scattered applause, half-hearted cheering, and a couple of whistles. It's not the unified response of a well-trained and compliant audience. Some of them are still talking loudly among themselves as he starts speaking: 'Good evening. That's a nice friendly audience, everyone talking to each other, yeah-huh. And we've – sorry about the delay, we've had a gas cylinder blown out whatever that means, "A gas cylinder's blown out!"' A male punter shouts churlishly: 'Liar!' Allen retorts, 'No really, d'you think I want us to be here all night?' This innocuous comment provokes the first shouts of 'Gong!', less than thirty seconds after Allen has taken the stage. It will be the first of many, shouted throughout the night, sometimes individually, sometimes *en masse*, sometimes playfully, sometimes savagely.

Allen treats the first 'Gong!' as more of a chore than a threat: 'Now – let's calm down, no but, this – for people that don't know, this is a nice, mellow little club, and we have a – bit of satire and general comedy, you know, it's beautiful. Erm – what happens is, there, we – we got a whole bunch of comedians go on –'. He stops, noticing that a punter has been la-la-ing a little playground taunt style tune, and comments: 'Calm down, calm down.' 'Don't believe it!' shouts somebody. It's not clear exactly what he doesn't believe, but that doesn't seem to be the point. Allen continues, getting scattered laughter with a crack about the Comedy Store's décor, and explaining the format of the evening, breaking off to deal with the fact that some punters are still conversing among themselves: 'You'll have to stop talking otherwise the people around you won't hear, I know *you* don't wanna particularly hear, but you know, it's just one of those little things.' Then he explains the gong to the uninitiated:

> Now, there's a dubious device of a gong. Now I've got a headache tonight, right, so I'm not gonna use it unless I really have to, I find it a bit of a dubious device anyway. And – you'll hear the locals and the regulars shouting out 'gong' occasionally but I'd ignore them. And if you – if somebody's going on far too long, a bit like I'm going on now, and you really get – [playful shouts of 'gong' start up] Erm, you think to yourself, what – you know, that's a hard job that guy's doing, you know, and then you think, 'I'll give him another five minutes.'

BSUCA

He starts an anecdote about a recent gig with Alternative Cabaret, but is interrupted by various punters making no effort to hide the fact that they're calling out to each other about delivering drinks to their friends. A distinctly posh voice shouts 'Liz!', then brays, 'Over there, coming over this way!' Allen imitates him mockingly, and after more yelling, picks out another of the shouters: 'If you could see the state of this character over here. [laughter with some clapping and yelling] How can you get so pissed at these prices, man? [laughter]'. Eventually, he manages to get to the end of his anecdote with the Lenny-Bruce-dying-in-a-toilet joke, and by this point he has galvanized the audience enough to get proper, unified laughs. Having achieved this, he introduces the first act.

A few things that stand out about Allen's opening spot. First, like Alan Brien's description of the first-night audience in *Punch*, the comments the punters shout on this occasion appear to be random and mindless. This is not the unified hostility suggested by the Christians-and-lions analogy, but much more haphazard behaviour. The interjections come from individual punters here and there, and don't seem to be motivated by any consistent logic. One might be pointlessly accusing Allen of lying, the next la-la-ing a tune, and a third shamelessly calling out to his friend. Throughout the evening, the audience's behaviour continues in much the same mindlessly random fashion regardless of who's onstage. They often talk loudly among themselves, and individuals throw in a perplexing variety of comments. The nearest they come to unity is shouting 'Gong!' together, but even this is somewhat arbitrary and sporadic. Hubbub, chaotic noise, and calls of 'Gong!' easily outnumber full-bodied laughs.

This chimes with what performers remember about the audience in the early days of the Store. Those who compèred it talk about not just the audience's hostility, but also their unpredictability – partly a result of the fact that people went to the venue for a variety of reasons. Jim Barclay remembers Japanese businessmen wanting to see the strip show being misdirected to the Comedy Store instead (2016). Ben Elton recalls:

[T]he licensing laws were totally different then, so this was one place where you could get a late night drink. It was expensive ... which made the punters angry ... [T]here would always be at least a quarter of the audience, often more, who were there because it was somewhere to get a drink, drunken lads out ... And that's where I developed my shouting ... I had some really quite subtle good material, but you couldn't afford to play it subtly. You just had to give the impression that you were ... angry and shouty and full of yourself. None of which I am ... it was a very, very, very tough time appearing at and particularly compèring, and having to try and create an atmosphere where some acts could at least have a chance ... It was my job to make the evening not descend into complete and utter bedlam. It was horrible, absolutely horrible.

*Elton 2018*

Tony Allen describes the audience as 'polarized' between friends of the performers 'wishing their mates well' and 'people who are just sort of going there for a late night drink', adding that the gong made things worse: 'I think it stopped performers being subtle ... I wanted to see people be subtle ... But that's the wrong audience to be doing it to, really. And so to give them a gong ... as well as a gutful of beer is probably, you know, [the] wrong thing to do' (HistComPod 2017a). Elton disliked the gong too: 'Obviously a gong show encourages witless heckling. You know, I think a gong show is stupid. I mean it couldn't possibly be more anti-comedy ... It was just vandalism. I mean always the quiet acts, always the women ... would just be battered' (2018).

Throughout the recorded show, Allen adopts a number of strategies to minimize the gong's vandalistic effects. Before finishing his opening spot, he warns that those who shout for the gong might get a taste of their own medicine: 'Incidentally, for – for people who get a bit gong-happy – right – there is a – there is a spot in the second half where we actually drag you out of the audience if you have been a persistent gonger. Right? [laughter and general rowdiness]'. Later, before introducing John Revell[2] as a new act, he warns, 'We've got a little bit of a rule. There's no gonging first timers.' He deigns to use the gong for the first time when Arthur Mendacious Brain is on, as the baying becomes particularly vocal, but ignores the calls of 'gong!' while John Hegley is doing his act – probably because Hegley was one of the people he wanted to see being subtle.

Even at this early stage, Hegley's material is playful, whimsical, and geeky, deftly manipulating words and images in a distinctive style for which he would become well-known. Indeed, the three songs he performs – 'Armadillo', 'I feel like a suitcase' and 'Amoeba' – are early versions of poems that would stay in his repertoire and appear in published volumes (Hegley 1997: 16–17, 24–5; Hegley 1990: 90). However, the merits of his act don't protect him from audience onslaught. The first shout of 'Gong!' comes as soon as he steps onto the stage, and he's barely wished the audience good evening before somebody shouts 'Get off!' After a brief preamble, he starts singing 'Armadillo'.

Shouts of 'Gong!' ring out over the opening chords and he has to compete with a rising tide of abuse throughout most of the song.

Looking back on his early performances at the Store, he remembers: 'You just went in and you did your best. I wasn't armed with a lot of the things that came later.' The recording reveals that he didn't yet possess the performance skills that would make him such a star of the circuit later in the decade. In this show, his persona is shrilly defensive, lacking the vulnerable charm of his later work and his ability to keep potential miscreants under control by telling them off like a world-weary schoolmaster. He explains:

> It was hard … It was nerve-racking … You knew that you were going into a conflict situation. But I wanted to do it, I wanted to get it right.… Maybe there is something instinctive in it … Because you were trying to survive, maybe you had to learn fast. And you had to learn in an instinctive way. Maybe it was a certain animal element to it.
>
> *Hegley 2016*

His survival instinct seems to come into play in the second number, when he tries to get them to join in the chorus. He says he will sing 'I feel like a' and he wants them to shout back 'Suitcase!' Predictably, when he gets to the first chorus, any shouts of 'Suitcase!' are utterly drowned out by punters bellowing 'Gong!' He tries to take control of the situation by orchestrating the crowd's barracking: 'Right now, I want, let's hear it now, let's hear the "Suitcase!"s and let's hear those "Gong!"s as well, let's have those "Gong!"s nice and loud, and let's hear those "Suitcase!"s.' The crowd bays incoherently, but he goes back into the chorus anyway: 'I feel like a – [audience: "GONG!"] Now let's hear those suitcases a bit louder, "I FEEL LIKE A!" [shouts of "GONG!" and one or two of "SUITCASE!"] D'you think the gongs are louder?' As compère, Allen refuses to bow to the crowd, answering, 'No, the suitcases have got it, I think. [laughter and some clapping]'.

Hegley finishes the song, and gets off to a comparatively generous round of applause, but Allen calls him back: 'He's got a lovely song, I wanted him to do it. [punter: "Amoeba, Amoeba, yeah."] Yeah, d'you wanna hear "Amoeba, Amoeba", it's beautiful actually. [one or two people say "Yeah"] John, they want you back to do "Amoeba"! [Punter: "yeah!"] Yeah, let's do it!' Hegley starts his encore with a nice impromptu gag, suggesting the song will involve exactly the same call-and-response as the previous one, but with the audience shouting 'Amoeba!' instead of 'Suitcase!' – and he's rewarded with no more than scattered laughter for this. However, the audience refrain from yelling as he sings the song. They join in with the chorus, and even hail the ending with cheering and applause.

It feels like a match won on points, and only with the intervention of the referee. The audience laugh when Allen declares the suitcases have won, the gag being that he is conspicuously refusing to acknowledge their wishes as expressed in their hollering. What we can hear in the recording is an example of Allen's efforts to curate the emerging movement, helping to turn the Comedy Store into a truly alternative venue by favouring certain acts. After Hegley has finished, he also deploys another strategy to subdue the gongers: 'Actually, I must warn you, you keep gonging, right – I mean, we'll have no comedians left and you'll all go home in twenty-five minutes, right. And you do four quid. So you've wasted four quid anyway.'

The recording of this show suggests that the early Comedy Store audience was as chaotic as it was hostile, with background chatter more ubiquitous than laughter or even shouts of 'Gong!' It also offers clear evidence that this was not a crowd uniformly made up of the liberal Left, and that any non-sexist, non-racist policy that may have existed at this stage was far from strictly observed. The barracking that frequently erupts has a distinct football terrace tone, dominated by male voices, suggesting that much of the abuse hurled at the stage was fuelled by testosterone. The only woman on the bill is Pamela Stephenson, a television star and occasional visitor to the alternative circuit. Her fame does nothing to deter witless male hecklers. She's barely finished her opening song when a man shouts, 'Show everyone your tits!' and a few male punters laugh. She responds, 'Hang on, hang on. Is the gentleman trying to say something to me?' Another man tries a different tack, patronizing her rather than objectifying her: 'Carry on dear, you're all right with me.' After some more back-and-forth, a man shouts, 'More like this and you'll be happy.' She regains control by saying, 'Thank you. Have that boy washed and brought to my tent. [laughter, some applause and a shout of "Woo!"]'. The fact that Stephenson experiences such obnoxious sexist behaviour here supports Elton's point about women being a particular target for an audience battering.

Alongside the sexism, racism also rears its ugly head. The second audience spot is filled by a drunk-sounding punter called Martin, who stays onstage for over ten minutes – despite increasing audience hostility. In fact, the show descends into such bedlam while he is on that at one point Allen has to join him onstage to wrest back a modicum of control, getting laughs by impatiently recapping the joke Martin is trying to tell but has lost the thread of. Before this intervention, Martin interrupts his own rambling, poorly told gag to tell the type of racist joke that flourished on the working men's club circuit. He asks, 'Any Pakistanis in?' Several punters shout, 'Yes!' probably more to be difficult than to provide an accurate declaration of their ethnicity. Martin says something indecipherable then goes into his gag: 'What's the difference between a Pakistani and a Polo mint? People like Polos, don' they?'[3] There's the sound of what could be a couple of people laughing before a woman shouts, 'Gong!' and others join in enthusiastically. It's impossible to tell whether they disapprove of the knuckleheaded bigotry or simply the poor quality of the gag, but the audience can't have been entirely non-racist given that Martin himself is a punter.

## 'What can I really say to flatten that bloke?'

The Comedy Store may have attracted a haphazard and hostile audience, but according to Elton, 'It was really only the Comedy Store that was like that. Nowhere else was like that' (2018). Recordings in BSUCA of early shows in a range of venues – including the Elgin, the Hemingford Arms, Pentameters, and further afield at the Edinburgh Fringe – suggest that the chaotic belligerence of the Comedy Store was indeed rare. However, even the more genteel alternative cabaret venues involved a dialogue between audience and performer, as drunken or unpredictably hostile punters could infiltrate even the best-behaved crowds. Appearing with Andy de la Tour at Pentameters on 9 November 1980, Tony Allen is in the middle of a joke when a male punter starts repeatedly shouting, 'More! More! More!' for no apparent reason. There's a bit of hubbub before Allen steps in: 'Look, you're not paid, I know, you're not paid to sit here and do jokes. Well I'm not paid here to listen to your fucking rubbish either, all right? [some laughter and applause] Amyl nitrate and pig tranquilisers. [laughter] Do not mix drugs, I mean it's bad for you, right? [laughter]'. The heckler starts shouting again, and Allen imitates him mockingly: 'Yuh yuh yuh yuh yuh!' The heckler shouts, 'I just drink beer!' Allen snaps back: 'You just drink beer. You've drunk far too fucking much of it! [laughter] Honestly, I wouldn't be sitting there 'cos you'll be throwing up doner kebabs and peanuts over everybody [laughter, 8 seconds]' (BSUCA).

This incident comes over as an actual conversation between performer and punter, rather than an exchange of standard heckles and prepared put-downs. Allen listens to what the heckler says, and uses it back against him. There are different levels of sophistication to this, from simply mocking mimicry to colourfully fleshing out the simple idea that the punter is inebriated, conjecturing over his particular choice of drugs and the likely contents of his vomit. Throughout the entire exchange, Allen sounds authoritative and distinctly unrattled, and getting a laugh that lasts a full eight seconds makes him the clear winner. Shortly afterwards, he's able to continue with his joke uninterrupted – at least for the time being.

Hecklers continued to shout out even at the quieter gigs throughout the 1980s. Jim Barclay had a standard device for dealing them, which involved taking Michael Kilgarriff's book *Make 'Em Roar: A Comedian's Handbook* (1979) onstage with him. Barclay explains: '[Y]ou'd say, "I've got *Make 'Em Roar, the comedian's handbook.*" Which bought me time to think. I wasn't looking through the book, I was thinking, "What can I really say to flatten that bloke?"' (2018). He brings it out at the ADC Theatre in 1981, when a punter starts randomly making a popping sound with his mouth:

> This book 'ere – see this. *Make 'Em Roar! The comedian's handbook.* Now in 'ere – there are twenty seven put-downs – to deal with every single kind o' heckle. First of all you get latecomers. Earlycomers. And then people that go [popping noise]. [quiet laughter, 5 seconds] I don't believe in Darwin's theory but looking at you I'm not so sure. [laughter, 8 seconds] I knew you'd get that one. [brief laughter]
>
> BSUCA

As well as buying him thinking time, the device of bringing the book onto the stage is comically subversive. There's an unwritten assumption that comedians should deal with hecklers by being – or appearing to be – spontaneous, putting them down with a quick-witted, off-the-cuff response. Reading put-downs from a book conspicuously bursts this bubble. There's also the nice gag of pretending that the specific situation he's dealing with, no matter how uncommon, is covered in the book – which establishes complicity with the audience as they realize he's pulling their leg. That said, the Darwin-based gag he uses to put the heckler down so effectively is actually taken directly from page 19 of the book.

Coming up with strategies for dealing with hecklers was part of the communal learning process that was going on in the early days of alternative comedy. There was no older generation of performers in the scene to learn this essential skill from, so they invented their own techniques and learned from each other. Similarly, alternative comedians also had to learn a range of other skills for interacting with audiences. The common stand-up technique

## Relating to Audiences

of 'crowd work' – engaging a few punters near the front in conversation – was largely unknown in the early alternative scene. Paul Merton recalls that this was learnt from visiting American comics: 'You'd get an American come on and . . . start chatting to the people in the audience, "Where are you from?" I mean nobody, in the very early days, ever asked anybody in the audience where they were from' (2018).

While they might not have talked to punters in exactly this way, they did find various ways of making their relationship with the audience more interactive. Jim Barclay includes some simple audience participation in his set at the ADC Theatre:

> We'll all be wacky and zany. See this? The Wacky and Zany Song. [quiet laughter] 'W and Z!/ W and Z!/ Bright yellow tights/ And a nail through the 'ead!' Got that? [quiet laughter] It's a winner, innit, eh? [laughter, 5 seconds] Wacky and zany! Right! Now, 'cos you lot down 'ere – you paid more, you upper class bollockses! [laughter] *You* – will only 'ave the 'Bright yellow tights'. My friends up the back there – they can have the punchline. 'Nail through the 'ead.' [quiet laughter] Right? Here we go then. 'W and Z!/ W and Z!' [audience: 'Bright yellow tights/ And a nail through the 'ead!'] Great! Fan-tastic! [laughter] What a bunch of wallies! [laughter, 4 seconds].
> 
> BSUCA

The idea of playing to the different sections of the auditorium harks back to variety theatre, but pitching the people in the cheap seats against the posher ones in the more expensive ones is an effective ploy, allowing Barclay to make a reference to class that fits nicely with his self-proclaimed Marxist-Leninist stance. Making the audience join in with such an inane ditty draws them into the stupidity of his comic world, and the deliberate perversity of then ribbing them for going along with him helps to build a playfully cheeky relationship with them.

A less interactive technique involved the comedian conjecturing about the private reactions of people in the audience to the material. On his second solo national tour in Autumn 1987, Ben Elton included a routine in which he recommends talking after sex: 'You don't just roll over and start farting. [laughter, 6 seconds]'. Having got the laugh, he pretends to pick out a couple from the audience who have apparently had a very particular reaction to the gag: 'I don't know, I may be wrong, but I think I may have touched a nerve there. [laughter] Possibly broken up a fledgling relationship over 'ere. [quieter laughter, which reignites]'. He then imagines one of the couple saying to the other: 'You *do* that! [laughter] You do, you do that, you should listen to him, some of his stuff's quite good, you do that! [louder laughter] Fart-fart-fart, that's you! [laughter] You don't hear it because you're asleep, but I'm the one that has to listen! [laughter]' (1988).

Imagining audience reactions in this way again builds complicity, because it acknowledges a particular kind of interaction between performer and audience. By pretending to peel the lid off the top of individual punters' heads and voice what they are thinking, Elton is reminding the audience that they are not just passive recipients of the gags, but are actively interpreting them. However, sometimes alternative comedians aimed for a less benign kind of interaction with their audience.

### 'Dent the prejudices of the audience'

In 1987, Tony Lidington pointed out that one of the things that linked alternative cabaret to punk was that, 'Many acts, especially comedy acts, directly confront – even affront – the audience in an attempt to provoke a response' (116). This is confirmed by the numerous reviewers who talk about audiences flocking to see alternative comedians making fun of people just like them. In 1984, Jim Barclay told *The Sunday Times*, 'What I try to do ... is subvert the technique of the Jim Davidson school of comics. You dent the prejudices of the audience rather than confirm them.' He went on to make it clear that although he was a left-wing comedian, left-wingers in the audience would not be exempt from ridicule: 'I'm a debunker of the Dave Sparts, too' (Williams 1984) – Dave Spart being a *Private Eye* character parodying left-wing dogmatism. Recognizing that alternative cabaret audiences tended to be dominated by left-wingers, it became common to do what Alexei Sayle refers to as 'mocking the idiocies of the Left' (2015).

Video footage of Barclay playing the St Matthew's Community Centre in Brixton in 1980 shows him mocking the audience both directly and indirectly. His first ploy is to address the immediate circumstances of the gig:

> Right, as you've – probably gathered – here, at the St Matthews Community Centre. You know, there's one thing I love doing – community centres. Because you can be one hundred percent certain you won't be playing to anybody who belongs to the community. [laughter] D'you know what? I arrived tonight – and I counted –

twenty-seven Citroen Deux Chevaux. [laughter] All with 'Nuclear Power Nein Danke' stickers all over them. [laughter into smattering of applause, five seconds] What I'm waiting for – what I'm waiting for is the sticker that says 'Petrol Fumes from Deux Chevaux Nein Danke', you know. [laughter].

BSUCA

By telling the audience they're not part of the community, Barclay is implying that they're not authentically working-class, but just well-meaning middle-class liberal do-gooders. He ribs them some more by suggesting they all drive a type of car popular with middle-class left-wingers, adorned with a sticker that was popular among the same group. They laugh, recognizing that they're exactly the kind of people who would drive a car like that. The final line is more challenging, suggesting that although they might be against nuclear power, by driving a petrol-driven car they're contributing to pollution and thus not entirely free from blame.

His second and less direct ploy is to parody left-wing subculture, for example describing a party at a particularly right-on household:

Little terraced house in Barnes, brilliant. Pretty, pretty railings. And on the – on the garden gate, it's got, 'Beware of the dog'. And I looked again, that's crossed out. And underneath, it says, 'Please be kind to our dog – as he's trying to come to terms with his own naturally male aggressive tendencies.' [laughter 6 seconds, over which he continues] So – so – I rang the bell. [laughter ripples back into life] And – and this – this ten-year-old kid answered the door you see, so I said, er – 'Hello, what's your name then?' He says, 'Wotan!' [laughter] I said, 'Oh yeah.' I said, 'Er. What d'you get for Christmas then?' He said, 'My parents don't recognise the patriarchal myth figures imposed on capitalism to preserve the status quo.' [laughter].

BSUCA

Much of the comedy of Pauline Melville's character Edie worked in a similar way. The juxtaposition of Edie's down-to-earth northernness with left-wing dogma – and even the *faux pas* she made around it – humorously question the excesses of the Left. In a 1981 routine, Edie's husband Derek tells her he wants an open marriage: 'He said, "Edie, monogamy is finished. Monogamy is over." I said, "Yes Derek." He said – he said, "Monogamy is the reproductive core of capitalism." I said, "Yes Derek." [laughter] He said, "We must smash the family!" I said, "Smash *your* family, yes! [laughter] Smash my family, no!" [laughter]' (Alternative Cabaret 1981). Melville often focused on the woolly mysticism that thrived among certain sections of the Left. Playing Pentameters with Alternative Cabaret on 18 January 1981, she tells the audience: 'Oh no, well you see I've studied these things. You know, because I've studied, er – Zen Buddhism. You know, the ones with anorexia nirvana. [laughter] Isn't it wonderful how you all laugh at the same time. [laughter] Are you all Aquarians? [laughter and some clapping, 7 seconds]' (BSUCA)

All of this challenges the habits and thinking of the Left, suggesting that questioning absolutely everything about the status quo – including Christmas and beware of the dog signs – might end up being a bit silly, and that challenges to the nuclear family might be easier in theory than practice. It could be argued that this is just gentle joshing among friends, joking about the community of the Left from within by playing on references that this type of audience will instantly recognize. However, it's clear that mocking the idiocies of the Left sometimes cut deep. An early article about Alternative Cabaret notes that they were 'sharp ... at spotting political sympathies in their audience', and gave examples of recent shows where their gags offended particular factions: 'Recently they knew some Communist Party of GB (Marxist-Leninist) were present, and a string of Albania jokes followed[4] – the comrades walked out in regimented protest. Another time, a CP audience were hugely amused by some well-tailored Trotsky cracks till the subject suddenly turned to Stalinism and suddenly it was not so funny' (Brazil 1979).

The habit of challenging audiences continued through the 1980s. Appearing in a TV programme filmed at Jongleurs in 1988, Mark Steel plays on the wealthy and fashionable image of the area where the show is taking place – and perhaps on the venue's reputation for attracting an audience of yuppies – by suggesting that the people he's talking to might not be as politically progressive as they would like to think: 'This here is being, er, filmed in, in Battersea. Erm, one of the trendier bits, now, of South London, erm. This is one of the places where voting Tory is like wanking, really. [a few laughs] 'Cos everyone does it and no-one admits to it [laughter and applause]' (*Cabaret at the Jongleurs* 1988a). Similarly, appearing on a different edition of the same show, Felix Dexter nods to the elephant in the room by ironically commenting on the fact that he's a black comic playing to a conspicuously white audience: 'By the way, what's really nice about – er, this evening is to see so many West Indians in the audience, and it's really good, you know, sort of – [laughter]' (*Cabaret at the Jongleurs* 1988b).

### 'Frontal assault'

Such challenges were an important part of alternative comedy, but they might not quite constitute the kind of confrontation – or even affront – that Lidington talks about. However, there were comedians who would offer a more robust challenge, refusing to accept the essentially benign performer-audience relationship that was long established in popular entertainment, and instead adopting a more punk approach. In 1986, *Cabaret News* – a typed four-page newsletter photocopied onto a single folded sheet of A4 – included an article about Tony Allen, asking: '[T]ell me of another comedian who could order an audience of cabaret lovers not to applaud him when he left the stage because he wasn't happy with his set, and have that same audience remaining mutely passive in an alt cab equivalent of one minutes silence', and adding, 'For many cabaret devotees, Tony Allen is the master' (BSUCA). By instructing the audience at the Pied Bull not to applaud at the end of the act, Allen was asking them to breach a long-established convention, and challenging them to reject such ritualized responses. The fact that they went along with him suggests he wielded considerable command over them and that they saw his challenge as serious.

Two first-generation alternative comedians developed a particular reputation for challenging audiences: Alexei Sayle and Keith Allen. It has often been said of and by Sayle that what distinguished him from most other comedians was that he had no desire to be liked by the audience. As early as 1983, he told *The Guardian*, 'I don't want the adulation of 1500 strangers ... Most comedians do, which I think is really pervy ... And if you want to be loved by the maximum number of people, then by and large its [sic] easier to be a Nazi, like most comedians are' (Rosen 1983). Sayle rejected the cosy rapport that other comedians aimed for, in favour of a more combative approach. He explains: 'I used to encourage rowdiness to a degree, really. I mean the whole performance was kind of inflammatory, wasn't it? And then I'd often turn on them if they were having too good a time. Eccentric modus operandi ... I'd be horrible to them' (Sayle 2017).

His habit of confronting the audience didn't go unnoticed by critics. A glowing review in *The Times* of the Comic Strip at the Venue in 1981 notes that Sayle's 'obscenity and ferocity indicate that mere satire has been abandoned in favour of frontal assault' (Appleyard 1981b). The *London Review of Books* vividly captured the effect he had as compère of the Comic Strip at the Raymond Revuebar: 'Sayle's posture is manically contemptuous, his rhythm a hysterical crescendo of obscenity with spat-out satirical asides.

## Alternative Comedy

Both the stance and the timing are near-perfect, and within seconds he has the audience agape. Most of them, it seemed, had never been called *cunts* before' (Hamilton 1981).

Getting ready to introduce the first act at the Comic Strip, Sayle establishes the attitude he's going to take to the audience, addressing them in a manner which is anything but convivial: 'Let's have a big, warm Comic Strip welcome – yeah, let's have a big, warm Comic Strip welcome! [laughter] No, not yet you fuckfaces, you know what I mean?? [laughter] This is a People's Collective, you do what I fuckin' tell you, all right?? [laughter]' (Comic Strip 1981). He uses a similar level of abusive language in warning hecklers what they can expect from him: 'As you know, I know lots of bitter, witty instant repartee like, "Why don't you fuck off, you cunt??" but er – [laughter]' (Sayle 1998). Later, in his solo touring show, he explains how he wants the audience to react to him in no uncertain terms: 'I'm, er, I'm a Marxist comedian, erm. I'm non-sexist, non-racist, erm. So if you don't laugh at me, you're a fuckin' Nazi shitbag, all right? [laughter]' (Sayle ND).

In common with many of his contemporaries, despite being on the Left, he didn't want to develop to cosy a relationship with left-wingers in the audience: 'I didn't want to confirm the opinions of the people in the audience ... rather I wanted to challenge and mock them' (2016: 130). For example, one of his early gags savagely targeted the kind of well-meaning member of the caring profession who might have been attracted to an alternative comedy show: 'I'm er – I'm actually very glad you could come tonight, because er, this gig is actually in aid of charity, erm. It's in aid of a charity called Help a London Child – Kill a Social Worker [laughter]' (Comic Strip 1981).

It was his use of language that caused the most unease in that section of his audience. It wasn't just that he was obscene and aggressive, but also that he chose to use a word which some on the Left believed was inherently misogynist – the word 'cunt'. In *The Female Eunuch*, Germaine Greer had argued, 'Part of the modesty about the female genitalia stems from actual distaste. The worst name anyone can be called is *cunt*' (1991: 44). By the 1980s, the idea that saying 'cunt' was misogynist was well established. A book on sexual slang published in 1984 argued that it is 'a term of abuse which reflects the deep fear and hatred of the female by the male in our culture', but also noted that, 'In reaction, since the late seventies, some feminists have attempted to "reclaim" the word' (McConville and Shearlaw 1984: 45–6). In 1991, Jo Brand – who also chose to use the word in her act – acknowledged both of these positions: 'It's such an awful word, so tied up with misogyny.

## Relating to Audiences

There's a case for keeping it unsaid, for retaining one word that still has so much power, but also a case for using it because it then becomes less shocking and the taboo is broken down' (Chateau 1991). Sayle has recalled how what he refers to as 'The Great Cunt Question' became 'a central kind of ideological debate': 'We used to do a lot of radical venues, and people would come backstage afterwards and say 'Look, Alexei, we really liked the act, but ...' I became more and more of a resolute cunt-ist, really. I got more and more hard-line' (Barber 1991: 14).

Recordings of his act confirm just how hard-line he was. It was absolutely peppered with the word, the tendency reaching its peak in a routine called 'Say Hello Mr Sweary', in which he takes foul language to the point of utter absurdity, hurling out great strings of obscenities in a Cockney accent. This is a mere snippet:

> René Descartes, 'e's another one, i'n' 'e, eh? Eh? René Des-fucking-cunt-cartes, eh? [laughter] René Des-fucking-cunt-shit-piss-wank-fuck-cartes, René Cunt-cartes, fucking-cunt-wank-shit-piss-fuck-cunt-bollocks, René Cartes, fucking cunt! [laughter] René Fucking-cunt-cartes-shit-piss-Descartes-fucking-cunt, René Cartes, fucking-cunt-fucking-cunt-fucking-cunt, shit-piss-wank-fuck-cunt-bollocks-give-it-a-portion-wanker. [laughter] René fucking conju- [somebody squeals with laughter] Fucking-cunt-fucking-cunt-shit-piss-wank, conjugate that you cunt, je cunt, il cunt, cuntez vous? [laughter] Quelle cunt, if you'll pardon my French. [laughter]
>
> *Sayle 1982*

It's worth noting the volume of both laughter and 'cunt's here. I've tried to accurately transcribe where the laughs come, but in fact the laughter rumbles away under most of his speech. Meanwhile, he manages to say the word 'cunt' a total of nineteen times in just thirty seconds.

So why was Sayle so committed to breaking the left-wing taboo on the word so excessively? There's a clue to this in his graphic novel, *Geoffrey the Tube Train and the Fat Comedian*, in a scene that imagines him provoking the ire of a politically correct audience in a London comedy club for saying 'cunt'. In a voiceover between frames, Sayle interprets the audience's anger: 'This tribe put a lot of store in words. If you said the wrong words it was bad magic. They became very cross' (Sayle and Zarate 1987: n.p.). What this suggests is that Sayle found the Left to be too fixated on language, with a quasi-superstitious belief in the 'bad magic' of words. When I ask him about why he persisted with using the word onstage, he explains he used the word because, 'It was just very powerful. And also, it was always important to me to push back against the orthodoxies not just of the Right, but of the Left as well. So if it was inflaming to certain parts of my audience, then *good*' (2019).

More generally, no matter how left-wing they may be, comedians tend to resist restriction, often finding funny ways to subvert any attempt to regulate what they say onstage. As Mary Douglas pointed out, a joke represents 'a victorious tilting of uncontrol against control' and a 'triumph of intimacy over formality, of unofficial values over official ones' (1999: 152). Alternative cabaret in particular prized free expression. As the Meccano Club's Monika Bobinska puts it, alternative comedy was 'a kind of space for a bit of independence and uniqueness and freedom and all those things' (2015). Alternative comedians might have taken a voluntary ethical stance – explicitly rejecting sexist and racist gags – but they still valued their right to speak freely and chafed when people told them what they could and couldn't say. Even Ben Elton – who had a reputation for being particularly politically correct, Simon Hoggart once calling him 'horribly priggish' (1992) – mocked potential censorious criticisms of his material:

> The other day I was up the Old Priest's Hole. Which is a pub, incidentally, not an archaic criminal offence. [laughter] There's always a few liberals wondering whether to laugh at that one. [laughter] Was that gay-bashing or was that left-wing? They can't be sure. [laughter] Ask your lecturers in the morning, they'll sort it out for you, [laughter] ha ha ha.
>
> *Elton 1987*

What Elton's concerned about here is that his gag blending an anal sex innuendo with a satirical comment about the fact that sex between men was once illegal might be seen as homophobic. Such an interpretation would be uncharitable given the context of the rest of Elton's meticulously egalitarian act, but the fact that he raises the issue suggests a wariness of an overly-serious interpretation of gags, and comic defiance in the face of it.

### 'On the brink of violence'

Where Sayle challenged the audience with obscenity and ferocity, Keith Allen presented a different kind of confrontation. Although his delivery was calmer and colder than Sayle's, those who saw his stand-up suggest that it could inspire fear as well as laughter. An *Observer* article describes a performance at the Comedy Store:

> His style is to seem to be on the brink of violence, brooking no criticism from the audience, outstaring them with a look from his roll-around popout eyes ... A heckler doesn't like the act. After fidgeting towards a fire-extinguisher, Allen assaults the man with his own beer. The rest of us laugh away, obedient and not a little fearful. Comedy becomes nightmare on a light rein.
>
> North 1980: 28

Maggie Steed confesses: 'I can remember being terrified of Keith Allen. But ... he was completely brilliant ... He was just very surprising and anarchic. And quite dangerous' (2018). In Tony Allen's view, 'Keith's act was the closest thing I've ever seen to the shamanic quality that I strived for and would continue to strive for ... It was a situationist manifesto from the barricades – actualised' (2002: 104). Jim Barclay believes that what Keith Allen did was rooted in the moment of performance:

> All of us, even Lexei, would be, on certain nights, completely intimidated ... Your mouth goes dry. And you just think, 'I don't know what to do now ... All I can do is get off. And I've lost.' Keith always refused, he would go on for another hour if he had to. So he was remarkable and he had resilience coming out of every pore of his body ... But I couldn't actually put my finger on what it was that made him electric. It's certainly not on any recorded thing, you had to be there to see what he had.
>
> Barclay 2016

To give just one example of his act's resistance to the camera and the microphone, Allen has described his appearance on *Boom Boom Out Go the Lights* as 'fucking terrible', arguing that, 'My style of comedy didn't translate onto TV, which just couldn't capture the edginess of my performance' (K. Allen 2007: 243). Nonetheless, there's a hint of his love of confrontation when he addresses 'all those grovelling, cretinous, *moronic* comics out there in Noddyland', staring straight into the camera silently for three seconds before announcing, 'That was the sound of me earning ten quid.' He thumbs his nose and blows a raspberry, as the audience break into laughter, then applause (*Boom Boom Out Go the Lights* 1980).

Written accounts from the time give a better idea of Allen's style. Like so many others, part of what he did was to challenge the audience's beliefs. An article from 1982 recalls how he 'once ordered his audience into a five minute silence "for Poland" and then observed "don't like the Poles much meself"' (Petty 1982) – this being in the context of widespread left-wing support for the Solidarity trade union's challenge to Poland's authoritarian communist regime.

In 1981, Allen told a journalist that his motivation for challenging the audience 'was annoyance at people's inability to actually do something and really feel something about *anything*. I find most people so tepid. Admittedly it's not always their fault. You live in a society that's designed to make you like that. But what fucks me off more than anything is that loss of spirit'. The journalist argued that the 'greatest virtue' of Allen's act was 'an emotional level so intense that it breaks stage conventions: whatever is happening is for real' (Harron 1981a). What this suggests is that Allen's stand-up was absolutely centred in the direct encounter between performer and audience, and the immediate reality of the performance situation. For example, Allen would often subject punters who displeased him to mild physical attack. A letter to Jim Barclay from Goldsmiths College Students' Union dated 31 October 1979, complains about 'very dangerous behaviour' from some of the performers in Alternative Cabaret's show at the Millard Building on Tuesday 23rd:

> I was shocked to hear that one member of your act actually let off a $CO_2$ fire extinguisher in the faces of two members of the audience. I realise that the act did recieve [*sic*] a hostile reception, however, it is a totally unprofessional attitude on your behalf when you stoop to merely swearing at your audience, attempting to attract their attention by smashing a crate of empty bottles from our bar on stage, and then reverting to acts of violence likely to cause very serious injury to members of the audience . . . Your services will not be required by this college in the future.
>
> *BSUCA*

The fire extinguisher and the broken fruit juice bottle brandished to threaten hecklers were both Allen's handiwork. This was par for the course. According to Alexei Sayle, 'Fire extinguisher was often his weapon of choice' (Sayle 2017), and he was also known to hurl beer or ashtrays at the audience (K. Allen 2007: 230; Peters 2013: 7). Allen has even recalled what happened after he threatened the audience at the Royal College of Art with a set of darts, and one heckler refused to be quiet: 'No sooner had he said whatever it was he said than the audience came to know I was a man of my word. If he hadn't ducked there's every chance I would have spent part of the eighties inside charged with malicious wounding' (K. Allen 2007: 207).

## 'There's no norms'

All of the evidence – recordings, written accounts, the recollections of performers – suggests that there's some truth in the alternative comedy audience's reputation for being unruly and full of left-wingers. What this fails to recognize, though, is that audiences also varied. At the Comedy Store they were chaotic and difficult, at Pentameters polite and sometimes reserved, perhaps with the odd nuisance heckler. Alternative cabaret tended to appeal to a left-wing audience, but the recording of the Comedy Store in 1980 shows that punters there were far from politically correct, with their sexist heckling and punters telling racist jokes.

Although audiences could be hostile, the aggression flowed both ways. Alexei Sayle argues that, '[I]f anything it was the comics attacking the audience rather than the other way around. I remember Keith Allen. There was some hecklers and he started throwing darts at [them]. For a while ... none of us could figure out whether that was going too far!' (2015). It might seem ridiculous to even entertain the idea that throwing darts at the audience might be legitimate, but what this suggests is that the rules and conventions governing relationships between performer and audience were up in the air. The reinvention of stand-up meant that the interaction between stage and auditorium were being actively renegotiated, with both performers and audience having to invent and learn new norms of behaviour at comedy gigs. Jenny Eclair believes that audiences simply 'didn't know how to behave' (2018). It certainly sounds like that was the case with the chitter-chattering, randomly-interjecting, 'Gong!'-yelling audience in the early Comedy Store recording.

It also seems to have been the case at the Tunnel club. Its proprietor Malcolm Hardee wrote of 'its "hard" audience who didn't suffer fools gladly and easily resorted to heckling' (1996: 50), and performers recall them in the most colourful terms. Mark Thomas remembers playing there as 'a bloodied rite of passage' (2018). Steve Gribbin describes how the mere prospect of a Tunnel gig made him 'feel sick with worry. When I knew it was in the book ... I couldn't relax, I was thinking about it all week, or all month' (2018).

## Alternative Comedy

Maria McErlane recollects how the Tunnel audience 'would hum you off ... rather than heckle you, they would start a gentle hum at the back which would get louder and louder and louder, which was really eerie and horrible and evil' (2018). JJ Waller had the eggs he was going to juggle smashed on his head (Waller 2016), and the Long and the Short of It had glass ashtrays hurled at them (Crick 2018). The Tunnel's eventual demise was hastened by an incident in which the double act Clarence & Joy Pickles had various objects thrown at them and Babs Sutton (AKA Joy) had her spectacles broken by a flying glass (Hardee 1996: 153).

Off the Kerb's Joe Norris has his own take on how the Tunnel became so wild and lawless:

> It got the reputation, so the reputation fed off of it. I think when things are in their infancy, there are no standards, there's no norms. So what we would now expect now is, 'Surely you can't get away with this. This isn't right.' No-one knew how to run a club in those days, so it would be pretty anarchic .... it's self-perpetuating, isn't it? Like, one day people are talking about this club that is all a bit chaotic, and then obviously it becomes a lot more chaotic down the line, because of what's gone on in the past.
>
> *Norris 2018*

What started, then, as an audience being aggressive because they didn't know how to behave grew into a new norm, in which bad behaviour was seen as desirable, even necessary.

By the same token, comedians were learning how to interact with audiences, and experimenting with new – and often rather confrontational – ways of doing so. As the scene developed, inevitably new norms were established for performers too. However, for some this settling down meant a shutting down of possibilities. In particular, the establishing of new norms governing the audience made Keith Allen lose interest in the scene. Partly this was because of the increasingly left-wing audience. An account of a performance at Andy de la Tour's Comedy Cabaret at the Boulevard Theatre reveals that Allen 'smiled and explained that he had given up alternative comedy because it was full of wimpy liberals – the audience laughed in agreement – "and the people who applauded just proved my point"' (Harron 1981a). Another reason was, as he explained to *The Face*: '[I]t annoys me, people coming expecting me to be dangerous; I can feel *that* in an audience. I fuckin' hate that ... There's no surprise' (Kohn 1981: 45).

# CHAPTER 8
# 'I TELL JOKES WHICH PRECIPITATE THE DOWNFALL OF CAPITALIST SOCIETY': POLITICS

Onstage, Jim Barclay was quite the revolutionary. He starts his set at the ADC Theatre, Cambridge on 29 May 1981 in the guise of some kind of left-wing demagogue, addressing the audience in cod-Spanish and listing the types of people who might be present: '*Comarades! Marxistos, socialistes, liberales, anarcho-syndicales, e spartacistos!*' This continues for a while, before he lapses back into English, announcing shortly afterwards: 'Well, as you've gathered from what you've seen so far of my act, I'm the Marxist-Leninist comedian.' There's a wave of uncertain laughter, lasting four seconds. He continues: 'And I tell jokes which precipitate the downfall of capitalist society.' This provokes a five-second flutter of even more uncertain laughter (BSUCA).

Barclay wasn't the only one to joke about comedy bringing about radical change. Sharing a bill with him at the Hemingford Arms in 1980, Tony Allen tells the audience about how he has just witnessed what happened as the sound of Barclay's cod-Spanish spoof revolutionary speech drifted out of the windows into the street:

> I just walked outside, it was *great*, you should've been there. It was like er, the gate, the windows were open, and Jim was doing his sort of erm, *Marxistas dadadada*, and it was going all the way down Hemingford Road, and all down, [laughter] there was all these people looking up, going, 'It is the revolu- yes, it's happening!' [laughter].
>
> *BSUCA*

The first point to make here is that these are *jokes*. The Hemingford Arms show was just a comedy show, so it's *funny* that passers-by overhearing Barclay might have mistaken his cod speech for the start of a revolution. The very concept of a 'Marxist-Leninist comedian' is *funny*, not least because before alternative comedy the very idea of an explicitly left-wing comedian was practically unheard of in Britain. In Eric Midwinter's survey of British comedy, *Make 'Em Laugh* – published in 1979, the very year the Comedy Store opened – he starkly declares: 'It would be difficult to conceive of . . . a Marxist comedian treading the boards of one of the private theatre circuits, not just because the management would object, but because the audiences would feel uncomfortable' (15).

Similarly, when Barclay claims his jokes will precipitate the downfall of capitalist society, he's not intending the audience to take him seriously. He explains the thinking behind this comic ploy:

> My most comforting thing I discovered was you have to subvert yourself. Initially. And then you can subvert everything else. Including the audience. My key to that was to say, 'I'm up here to tell jokes which precipitate the downfall of capitalism and bring an end to tyranny and injustice wherever it rears its ugly head.' That's an impossible thing. I've already taken the rug out from under my own feet. Which in a way lays everything else up for grabs. And you're saying to the audience, 'Nothing is sacrosanct here . . . I'm just giving you my take on what I think is most evil, most worthy of debunking, most hypocritical. This is just my take. You can take it or leave it, but this is what I think.' And that is very liberating.
>
> *Barclay 2016*

Barclay believed that making himself ridiculous with ludicrously overblown claims for the political efficacy of his gags was the basis of his comic licence, creating a space in which he could confront the audience with comedy that expressed his radical beliefs.

So even though telling the audience that he was a capitalism-overthrowing Marxist-Leninist was clearly a joke, it did, in a sense, reflect his actual politics and his hopes for his act.[1] He explains, 'I didn't really want to be a comedian who just made people laugh, ever . . . What's the point in doing that?' (2016). Pauline Melville makes a similar point: 'Being a stand-up would have been of no interest to me whatsoever. But finding a frame in which I could say certain things that were dangerous or provocative or challenging – that's why I was doing it' (2018). Both were interested in stand-up as a form of radical political expression – and possibly one that might have potential to create change.

What's striking about both Barclay's and Allen's jokes is that they play on the ambiguity of radical political comedy. The uncertainty of the laughter at

Barclay's claim that his jokes will bring down capitalism suggests that they are not sure exactly how serious he is being. Allen's anecdote about the people passing by the Hemingford Arms suggests that although revolutionary comedy is not the same as an actual revolution, it might briefly be mistaken for one. Two important questions arise from this. First, just how radical were the politics of alternative comedy? And second, did alternative comedy have any tangible political effect?

## 'Thatcher didn't matter'

In order to answer these questions, it's important to see past the myths that have built up around alternative comedy. One of the most popular perceptions is that it yielded, as Gavin Schaffer puts it, 'a myriad of hostile jokes about Thatcher and her government' (2016: 376). This idea was well established by the late 1980s, when Julie Burchill dismissed alternative comedy with her scabrous line: 'just substitute "Mrs Thatcher" for "mother-in-law" and you'll get a laugh – don't worry about being funny' (1987). It's even been claimed that there was something hypocritically sexist in the way that alternative comedians attacked Margaret Thatcher: 'Cracking jokes about prime ministers is the proper job of stand-up comedy, but this Comedy Store Aunt Sally was condemned with bilious savagery conspicuously absent from equivalent quips about her male ministers, using terms like bitch or cow that often degenerated into blatant misogyny' (Cook 2001: 102).

However, many performers who were actually involved in the scene dispute this perception. According to Tony Allen, 'Thatcher didn't matter. Until the Falklands War, really' (2016). Alexei Sayle agrees that Thatcher 'didn't at first figure that much in the routines of even the left-wing Alternative Cabaret comics' (2016: 187). Mark Steel, who emerged slightly later, argues, 'There's a sort of myth that it was all anti-Thatcher and so on. And that was a very, very small part of it' (2018). Jeremy Hardy, another later act, expanded on this idea: 'The great myth is it was all people who were ranting about Thatcher, and it really wasn't … Ben Elton is the person that people think everyone was like. You know, he was loud and brash and shouty. But even Ben, a lot of his stuff wasn't about politics. A lot of it was … shouty, angry observational stuff' (2018).

Elton himself agrees, arguing not only that Thatcher jokes have been exaggerated, but also that alternative comedy was far less political than it is remembered in the popular imagination:

> [T]here weren't as many political comedians as the myth has it. I mean I used to think I was a sort of one-person cliché because most acts didn't do actual political content ... but they were political in as much as they were definitely, self-consciously non-sexist and non-racist. And they tended to sympathise with ... the Left, so they would tend to do benefits ... So the idea of the left-wing comedian is true and not true ... Certainly Rik and Ade, and Jen and Dawn, and the Outer Limits – they weren't political. Down the level of success a bit, Alternative Cabaret was definitely political.
>
> Elton 2018

Others agree. Andy de la Tour, for example, writes, 'It's a common myth that the early days of the so-called 'alternative comedy' scene in Britain were dominated by angry young left-wing comics. There were quite a lot of us who fitted that bill, more or less, but many who didn't and that's no criticism' (2013: 18).

Recordings of performances support the comedians' perception. Trawling through tens of hours' worth of recordings made for broadcasting, commercial release or for the performers' own private use, it becomes clear that overtly political material is far from ubiquitous, and jokes about Thatcher herself are quite rare. Of the handful I have found – by performers like Alexei Sayle, Pauline Melville, Andy de la Tour, Ian Saville and Ben Elton – I've not found a single example using the word 'bitch' or 'cow', and nor have I managed to find one which is 'blatantly misogynist' in the way Cook describes.

The jokes I have found may be abusive but the bile aimed at Thatcher is linked with her actions rather than her identity as a woman. For example, in an early TV appearance on the short-lived late night show *OTT*, Alexei Sayle performs a short routine about the pomposity of naming his country *Great Britain* ('I mean nobody says, "Bloody Brilliant France", do they? [laughter] Or "Not Bad Italy". [laughter]'), and concludes with a comic jibe about Thatcher: 'I mean it can't be *that* great, you know, three million unemployed and with the country being run by a lunatic, you know. [brief laughter breaks into cheering and applause]' (michtyme 3 2006b). The clear implication is that part of what makes her a 'lunatic' is that she's presiding over mass unemployment.

Similarly, after she had a minor operation on her right hand in 1986, Ben Elton joked: '*The tendons! In her hand! Were constricting! And drawing in the fingers! TO FORM A CLAAAWWW!!!* [laughter] And the doctors tried to reverse this! You cannot undo what God is doing! First the claw! Then the horns! Then the FORKED TAIL! [brief laughter into applause and whistles]'. Suggesting that Thatcher was metamorphosing into Satan is abusive, but Elton directly links the attack to a comment on her actions – specifically, the apparent hypocrisy of choosing to have her operation in a private hospital: 'Every general election she *swears* – she will not touch the National Health Service – and she keeps her word – when she has an operation, she does it in a private hospital! Now I respect that! [brief applause] The single most glorious institution this country will *ever* produce, and the Prime Minister won't touch it' (Elton 1988).

Another common perception of alternative comedy is that however political it was, it was politically ineffective. Asked in 1982 whether he thought his act might have a political effect, Alexei Sayle replied: 'No, not really ... As to it having any effect, it's like any artistic effort, when you get out of the theatre you're back in the world of crap ... I know you can't change anything by doing a comedy act' (Taylor 1982b:19). When I ask him about comedy's potential to create change, at a public event in 2015, he quotes Peter Cook's line about wanting 1960s satire venue The Establishment 'to replicate those cabaret clubs in the Weimar Republic which'd done so much to stop the rise of Hitler'. Other comics share his scepticism. In 1996, Mark Steel wrote, 'There is only one reasonable answer when someone asks whether you can change people's minds through comedy? Of course not' (159). Similarly, in 2009, Arthur Smith wrote, 'I am not persuaded that the routines of a small number of obscure comics troubled Conservative Party "think-tanks" for long' (158). Some academics who have written about alternative comedy agree. Notably, Gavin Schaffer argues that, 'Despite the best efforts of radical, first-generation alternative comedians, Thatcher's political project continued apace as Britain's left struggled to articulate an alternative' (2016: 397).

Scepticism about the political effectiveness of alternative comedy is often tied up with the criticism that it was merely preaching to the converted. This idea was well established even in the 1980s. For example, a *Times* article published in 1985 wryly notes that, 'Many of the "right on" comedians are trying to raise laughs and consciousness among an already "right on", mainly middle-class audience. (If you're "right on", you read *City Limits*, eat lentils and worry about heterosexism.)' (Davies and Janes 1985). Part of Schaffer's scepticism is that, 'If the alternative comedians were not preaching to the converted, which they often were, the chances of changing views or outlooks through jokes were seemingly very small indeed' (2016: 385).

However, scratching the surface of this kind of argument reveals some surprisingly shaky thinking. The accusation of preaching to the converted assumes that the only way that political comedy – or political art in general – could be effective is if it changes minds. In fact, there are a number of different ways it might have an effect apart from bringing about 180-degree Damascene conversions in its audiences. Moreover, there's an all-or-nothing quality to Schaffer's suggestion that alternative comedians' failure to bring down the Thatcher government is proof that they had no effect whatsoever. In fact, between zero and toppling the government there's a whole range of possibilities.

## 'You can't be racist and you can't be sexist'

When I mention the accusation that alternative comedy had no effect to Roland Muldoon, he immediately replies, 'I think it did have a lot of effect ... I think first of all it was a major combat to sexism at the time ... And we had a policy that we would never put on a bill without a female act in it ... So here was comedy with an agenda which said you can't be racist and you can't be sexist' (2018). Coming at the end of the 1970s, a decade that frothed with comedy that was brazenly – sometimes viciously – sexist and racist, for the first alternative comedians to choose to impose an ethical code of conduct on themselves was a radical change in itself. In his article on the Comic Strip in the *London Review of Books*, Ian Hamilton was struck by the contradiction between the new comedy's general willingness to offend its audience and its specific rejection of sexist and racist prejudice: '[T]he swearwords ... inject meat and venom, an illusion of anything-goes rebelliousness: if you can say *that*, then surely nothing's sacred. It is only after the show is over that you register what *hasn't* been treated with contempt. Women's lib, gay pride, black power' (1981).

As with the principle that comedians should write their own material, the non-sexist non-racist rule was an aspiration rather than an infallible law. Undoubtedly, there were exceptions, when comedians used material that might justly have been accused of being sexist or racist. For example, Lee Cornes, who performed at the first night of the Comedy Store, has confessed that, 'I was doing very dodgy stuff, as I'm continually reminded by Tony Allen ... I did a very racist sketch as a Japanese who couldn't speak English very well ... that sticks in my mind because I'm embarrassed by it now' (Wilmut and Rosengard 1989: 81). The important thing about such examples is that they are rare, exceptions to a rule that was far more often adhered to.

The fact that Cornes looks back on his routine with embarrassment shows how seriously the avoidance of sexism and racism was taken, as does the fact that he was continually reminded of the breach by Tony Allen.

It wasn't just the performers who took the embargo seriously. Audiences could be vociferous in objecting to anything said onstage that they found politically offensive. Jennifer Saunders has recalled a show at the Drill Hall in which French and Saunders were 'hissed throughout our set for showing women in a negative light' (2014: 59). Somebody shouted 'Racist!' at Arthur Smith when he put on a Jamaican accent for an imitation of a Rastafarian reciting Wordsworth: 'I wouldn't do it now – but at the time the thought that I'd said something offensive to a right-on audience was scary' (Cook 1994: 223). Different performers have different perspectives on this kind of audience behaviour. For Jenny Lecoat, it was an exciting expression of a kind of political idealism. She remembers the Crown and Castle as a particular hotbed for the militantly right-on, recalling a show in which Roy Hutchins had to stop his act 'because a kind of a debate had broken out in the audience ... it was just a very political debate about whether what he'd said was acceptable in terms of a feminist perspective'. She reflects, 'It sounds kind of hilarious now, but for someone who'd grown up in Jersey with no politics in my family ... I thought it was fantastic' (2018).

Others take a more jaded view. For Jeremy Hardy, 'There was a policing mentality at one time which was probably not helpful ... It was being policed by people going around saying ... "You can't say this and you can't say that." Instead of saying, "Have you thought about why you're saying that and what effect it might have?"' (2018). Mark Hurst remembers how challenging the audiences at CAST New Variety gigs could be: '[I]t was tricky, because you did get that forensic pulling apart, especially by feminists, inverted commas ... You did just sometimes get ... people sat there waiting to just pick up on anything. And it did get on your nerves a bit because sometimes it was just completely wrong' (2018). For Mark Steel, the censoriousness of left-wing audiences could be hypocritical, concentrating on sexism and racism whilst ignoring or even perpetuating class prejudice: 'The overtly political nature of some of the clubs that grew up was actually quite snobbish. There was sort of assumption that if you were from a working-class background, you were a typical sexist racist' (2018).

This helps to explain a gag from Steel's early set, quoted in a 1985 *Guardian* article, in which he pointed out that 'you can really confuse Islington trendies by announcing you're bringing to supper someone who worships a fascist dictator and thinks all women are whores – horrified faces all round – and then turn up with a Rastafarian.' The joke plays on the idea that Islington trendies would be made to feel uncomfortably conflicted by encountering views they would normally abhor in a member of a Jamaican religious sect. Steel told the journalist: 'The only reason I say things like that is because I get so furious at people who come along and only want their own views confirmed. Sometimes it's even tempting to say things you don't believe just to get them going' (Shearman 1985).

This kind of combative approach to audience censoriousness reached its peak with the Glaswegian comedian and magician Jerry Sadowitz, whose incendiary approach is encapsulated in his most celebrated gag: 'Nelson Mandela, what a cunt! [laughter] Terry Waite, fuckin' bastard! [brief laughter] I dunno, you lend some people a fiver, you never see them again [laughter]' (Sadowitz 1988). This was precisely designed to be as offensive as possible to the kind of left-wing audiences who came to watch alternative cabaret. The most infamous part of the joke is its opening line – technically only the set-up. Originally, the gag consisted of this alone. Sadowitz opened his act with it after a backstage discussion about the most offensive thing he could possibly say onstage led Nick Revell to suggest it to him (Cook 2001: 301; Smith 2009: 189). The concentration of elements calculated to offend the alternative cabaret audience is impressive in a line that contains just five words. Not only does it denigrate Mandela, a figure viewed with saintly reverence by many on the left, it does so using a word which many deemed to be unacceptably misogynist in its own right. As Tony Allen put it, 'Only the naughtiest kid in the world shouts that out. Especially in the mid-eighties with most comedians avoiding a discussion of sexist/racist language and when Mandela was still in prison and half the Student Union bars in the country bore his name' (2002: 142).

Arguably, some of Sadowitz's material spilled over from provocative to straightforwardly sexist or racist, but this doesn't mean that alternative comedy's non-sexist non-racist rule was ineffective. On the contrary, much of his comedy only makes sense in the context of an audience who not only accepted the rule, but also felt they had the right to police it. Without this content, the line about Mandela being a cunt would lack the incongruity needed to get a laugh.

### 'Entertainment with a left-wing agenda'

The idea that alternative comedy was largely made up of anti-Thatcher jokes may have been highly exaggerated, but that doesn't mean that its political radicalism was entirely mythical. While many acts lacked any overtly political content, there were others who – like Barclay – believed that comedy could express radical beliefs. Nick Revell argues: 'I think it's really important to stress how you did feel you were part of a counterculture ... And the acute issues at the time, union busting, cruise missiles, riots on the streets. There was a lot of real, serious, hardcore issues that just informed everybody's attitude' (2017).

It's important to stress that this new brand of entertainment did not have an entirely unified agenda. Performers subscribed to a range of different, sometimes contradictory radical beliefs. For example, Jenny Lecoat referred to herself as a feminist comic: 'I've always referred to myself as a feminist and I still would because ... for me it's very simple. I don't think anyone thinks that unequal wages or female circumcision or rape are great things' (2018). By contrast, privately Alexei Sayle was more sceptical about feminism, seeing it as 'reformist' because it was 'trying to attack the symptom rather than the cause', but would not criticize it onstage because, 'I can't very well say "I'm having a go at feminism, but from a supportive left-wing point of view"' (Rosen 1983).

Similarly, while comics like Sayle and Pauline Melville see themselves as Marxists, Tony Allen is an anarchist who identifies with a different political tribe. At the Elgin on 10 April 1980, he tells the audience: 'I hate fucking *Marxists!* As far as I'm concerned, the British road to socialism, right, is like the Harrow Road, you know, like *loooong* and *narrow* and *drab* – with a lot of police! [cheering and applause] You know. And you get to the end and it's very bourgeois, you know what I mean? [laughter and applause]' (BSUCA) To him, there's a crucial difference between socialists and anarchists:

> The thing about the anarchos, they're doing it *now*. So the revolution starts now, this moment. Whereas the others, you've got to wait for half the population of the earth to agree to it ... To me it was very important, the squatting culture and all the anarchist politics that went with it, as opposed to the socialist politics, which I ... thought was the devil's work.
>
> *Allen 2016*

Sayle took a different view of the anarchist squatting culture: 'It was very influential on Tony ... it's not something I was particularly sympathetic to' (Sayle 2017). Such differences start to challenge the idea that alternative comedy was doing something as simple as preaching to the converted, begging the question: converted to *what*? Feminism? Marxism? Anarchism?

## Alternative Comedy

However, the fact that self-described feminists, Marxists and anarchists were performing stand-up was in itself a radical departure. Eric Midwinter argued that a Marxist comedian would be difficult to conceive of partly because he saw comedy as essentially conservative: 'Comedians stay within the restraints of the state and its generally accepted norms: they rail a little at its institutions ... but it is affectionate sniping, and of menace to those institutions there is none' (1979: 15). This kind of analysis is still relatively common. For example, Simon Critchley argues that, 'Most humour ... simply seeks to reinforce consensus and in no way seeks to criticize the established order or change the situation in which we find ourselves ... much humour seeks to confirm the status quo either by denigrating a certain sector of society ... or by laughing at the alleged stupidity of a social outsider' (2002: 11–12). Such descriptions cannot easily be applied to alternative comedy, whose non-racist ethos made laughing at social outsiders far less likely. Moreover, it's easy to find examples of alternative comedians going beyond affectionate sniping and seeking to criticize the established order.

In amongst his high-octane ranting and cartoonish absurdism, Alexei Sayle included various routines about the social conflicts churned up by the early years of Thatcherism. In one, he describes the area of London he's living in to make caustic quips about poverty in the face of mass unemployment:

> At the moment *in* Stoke Newington, actually there's a big '60s revival going on. There's whole families trying to live on eight quid a week! [laughter] And now there's a big '30s thing as well, you know. I mean you're nobody unless you've got malnutrition, you know what I mean? [laughter] Absolutely fantastic, you know. Whole shops in the high street selling nothing but them lovely leg irons. [makes noise, pulls face and wobbles body to illustrate] [laughter]
>
> *Sayle ND*

For several years, Jim Barclay included a routine in his set that satirized the enormous cost of Trident nuclear submarines. In the version performed at the Comedy Store in September 1980, he imagines 'a little girl who lives at number 10, Downing Street, Westminster, SW1' writing in to the wish-granting TV programme *Jim'll Fix It* to ask for a replacement for Polaris submarines:

> 'My friend Jimmy says he has some new submarines called Trident, which he says will knock seven tons of shit out of 'em! [quiet laughter] Jimmy says we can have these Tridents at a bargain rate of five thousand million quid, including the VAT.' Now she goes on to say, 'Unfortunately, my pocket money does not go very far, so can you fix it for me? Good luck and best wishes, Mags Thatcher, aged 62.'
>
> BSUCA

Here 'Jimmy' is a reference not to Jimmy Savile,[2] the presenter of the TV programme, but to the American President Jimmy Carter, whose government was brokering the deal. The routine continues with Savile making a charity appeal to the audience at home:

> Now – we've done a little bit of calculation in the studio, and we've worked it out, that if every family digs in their pockets and comes up with a meagre sum, of four hundred quid – we could provide Margaret Thatcher with the submarines. Oh yes! And already – we have five thousand schoolchildren in Dorset – who have agreed to go without their school dinners for the rest of their school careers. [laughter, 6 seconds, under which:] Wonderful! What a gesture! And – yes – here. [laughter ends] Another – five – twenty-five kidney patients have agreed to melt down their kidney machines in order to provide the metal for the nuclear submarines! [laughter, 5 seconds].
>
> BSUCA

This blackly comic idea, in which weapons of death are funded only by sacrifices made at the cost of life-giving services like school dinners or kidney machines, savagely sends up the public spending priorities of the Thatcher government. It also echoes other criticisms of Thatcherism at the time, particularly the trope of missiles being prioritized over kidney machines. In March 1980, the Jam's single 'Going Underground' included the line 'You'll see kidney machines replaced by rockets and guns', and in May the same year left-wing Labour MP Tony Benn made a speech in which he declared, 'To cut down on money for kidney machines and spend five billion on a new Polaris submarine, that is wrong' (Atkinson 1984: 104). What's striking about Barclay's routine is not only that it's a radical attack on the Thatcher government, but also that it's well researched. Like Benn, he correctly names the successor to Polaris as Trident, and the figure of 'five thousand million quid' was indeed the cost of the new missile system (Fairhall 1980).

As the Falklands War divided the nation, alternative comedy quickly became part of the opposition to the prevailing mood. According to Arthur Smith, 'the Comedy Store was one of the few public places where you could escape the outpourings of jingoism' (2009: 157), and Jim Barclay recalls, 'I was at the Comedy Store the night that four different acts turned up with tins of corned beef, because Thatcher had authorized the Falklands invasion. Four different comics had jokes about tins of corned beef coming from the Argentine' (2016).

In his Edinburgh show at the Masonic Lodge in 1982, Tony Allen includes a routine about the Falklands that comically upends the logic of war:

> When it first started I was lying in bed listening to the World Service, right. And er, they just said something about scrap dealers in Saint Geor- in South Georgia. And this – Tory MP came on and they were interviewing him, he said, 'Yes, er – Argentinia [*sic*] – actually owes British banks, er – three billion pound.' I thought, 'Yeah. Problem. Fair enough. Probably international thing with monetary [indecipherable]. Probably true.' And then that suddenly got reduced – when the troops started to move. And then it was, 'Yes, they owe us three billion!' Hm. *Us?* Eh, three billion? Oo! Sixty million of us. Three billion! [laughter] [indecipherable] That's fifty quid each! [laughter] And then when *we* won and I didn't get my fifty quid! [laughter].
>
> BSUCA

Again, this is well researched. The amount Argentina owed to British banks was reported at various different levels, but one of the figures given was 'just under $3 billion' (Rodgers 1982). More importantly, the joke undercuts the propaganda implying that the interests of banks are the same as the interests of the general population, so that the money owed to them is portrayed as the money owed to 'us'.

Joking about the Falklands was not without its risks. Pauline Melville recalls: 'I'd been doing stuff about the military. And when the Falklands War started … the whole atmosphere changed, and nothing worked. Nobody laughed … often I felt when I was doing stand-up that I had a sort of radar connection with the state of the nation, and what people were thinking … I do remember suddenly realising that the audience had become, overnight, patriotic' (2018). On the other hand, Falklands material could whip up passionate discussion among audiences. Jim Barclay has recalled performing a show with Tony Allen at Huddersfield Polytechnic, with an audience of left-wing students and more conservative punters who went there for the evening classes: 'At the end of the show there was this debate, pockets of debate all over the audience … and that evening did more in terms of polemic than all the 7–84 shows with bands and so on. We disappeared down the M1 and they were still arguing' (Wilmut and Rosengard 1989: 45).

As with Allen's gag about the financial aspects of the Falklands War, the best political material could get under the skin of an issue and see it in a new way. When three Labour MPs – Allan Roberts, Ron Brown and Bob Litherhand – went on a 'fact-finding tour' of Afghanistan in January 1981 – shortly after the Soviet invasion – they were roundly condemned as 'stooges of the Russians' (White 1981). At Pentameters on 18 January, Pauline Melville, in the guise of Edie, reverses the logic of the story:

> Because as a matter of fact, I, I heard that there was two Afghanistani MPs coming over here on a fact-finding mission. [laughter] Yes, no, I did, no you see you're all laughing. But it's absolutely true, they were coming over – to find out for themselves as unbiased observers – the facts of capitalism. Well the trouble was – that erm – you know, their faces are bit dark. You know, darker than ours, and of course – they didn't get beyond Heathrow, did they? They're in the detention camp out there. [a few laughs] Bit sad really, because now they'll never know what capitalism's like. [laughter into applause, 7 seconds. Another burst of laughter, 3 seconds].
>
> BSUCA

Thus, a story about Labour MPs' complicity with Soviet propaganda becomes an occasion to examine the imperfections of capitalism, in particular racism in the immigration service. Edie's naivety is used as a precision tool, her lack of nous in direct contrast with Melville's cleverness in constructing the kind of ironic punchline that forces the audience to make the connection for themselves.

### 'Sick political satire'

Routines that questioned Thatcherite economic policy, nuclear weapons, the Falklands War, or racism in the immigration service don't seem to fit

### Alternative Comedy

Midwinter's or Critchley's descriptions. They neither stay within the generally accepted norms of the state, nor do they seek to confirm the status quo. However, none went further outside accepted norms and challenged the status quo more than Andy de la Tour's routines about Northern Ireland.

To appreciate de la Tour's daring, it's important to remember how republican terrorist groups like the IRA and the INLA were seen in the 1970s. The rigidly upheld view of them found in almost all public discourse was that their violence was a product of wickedness, criminality or psychopathy. Any deviation from this was fiercely condemned. In October 1981, Ken Livingstone – Labour leader of GLC – told the Cambridge Tory Reform Group that the IRA 'are not criminals or lunatics running about. That is to misunderstand them . . . If they were just criminals and psychopaths they could be crushed. But they have a motive force which they think is good' (*Times* 1981). Shortly afterwards, the *Daily Mail* reported that, 'Red Ken Livingstone's support for the IRA left him facing a revolt last night from within his own Left-Wing group' (*Daily Mail* 1981). Similarly, when he played host to the mother of one of the IRA hunger strikers from the Maze prison, a *Daily Express* editorial fumed, 'It is sickening and disgusting that the majority leader of Britain's capital city should be giving encouragement and publicity to the enemies of this country' (*Daily Express* 1981).

Emotions ran particularly high in the aftermath of terrorist incidents, and in 1979 republican paramilitaries committed two of their most high-profile murders. On 30 March, Conservative MP Airey Neave – a close associate of Margaret Thatcher – was killed when a bomb planted in his car by the INLA went off as his was driving out of the House of Commons underground car park. Labour Prime Minister Jim Callaghan said, 'I am shocked and appalled by the cowardly murder', and Thatcher herself told a TV interviewer, 'Some devil has got him' (Harrison and Passmore 1979: 2). SDLP MP Gerry Fitt declared, 'This further act of terrible and callous murder horrifies everyone – except the psychopaths of the IRA', and the Liberal leader David Steel stressed Neave's status as a Second World War veteran: 'To my generation he was also a war hero because of his exploits at Colditz' (Gill 1979: 2).

Then, in August, an IRA bomb killed Lord Mountbatten, a relative of the Queen, as he sailed his boat from Mullaghmore harbour in County Sligo. The Queen was reported to be 'deeply shocked' (Hampson 1979), and Thatcher stated that the IRA deserved 'the condemnation and contempt of people of goodwill everywhere' (*Daily Mail* 1979). The *Daily Express* ran a front page headline that read 'THESE EVIL BASTARDS' for an article that called Mountbatten 'one of the greatest men of the century' and said he had died on 'Britain's blackest day in Ireland for a decade' (*Daily Express* 1979).

Such was the national mood when, on 27 March 1980, Andy de la Tour told the audience at the Elgin about why Thatcher had been having such a horrible year:

> No, the reason, the reason why she's pissed off is 'cos all her best friends keep, get blown up, you know what I mean, like – Mountbatten. Ha ha! [laughter] Ha ha ha ha! Oh dear! He had dandruff you know, they found his head and shoulders on the beach. [laughter] Airey Neave. Poor old Airey Neave, eh? He got down a sheer cliff face at Colditz, couldn't get up a twenty foot ramp in Westminster. [laughter]
>
> BSUCA

The laughter at this last joke is followed by the sound of somebody giving an 'oooh' of disapproval, which de la Tour picks up on: 'Wuuuurr, innit sick political satire? Wuuurr!' Then there's some not-entirely-sincere hissing from the audience, which de la Tour imitates back at them. This gag was part of de la Tour's repertoire for some time, and was generally seen as sick or controversial. A review of Alternative Cabaret's 1981 Edinburgh show called de la Tour 'probably the funniest comic in the Assembly Rooms' but acknowledged that 'Some would retch' at his Airey Neave gag (Kravitz 1981). On 29 May 1981, de la Tour told the audience at the ADC Theatre, Cambridge about the floor manager's reaction when he told the gag while being filmed for the second edition of *Boom Boom Out Go the Lights*: 'And he comes up to me and he says, "Mm, er, Andy, er, Nigel *loved* the gag, we'll have to cut it, not enough time." [laughter]' (BSUCA). Tony Allen has recalled a night at the Comedy Store when de la Tour's Ireland material led to such a violent dispute in the audience that the police had to be called (2002: 105).

Looking back, de la Tour is self-critical about the Mountbatten gag, saying 'it's apolitical.' By contrast, he defends the Neave joke: 'The point about my comment about Airey Neave is that I'm contrasting his image as a war hero with his real political function ... as basically a diehard anti-republican and close ally and mentor of the new Prime Minister. So I like to think that my comment about Airey Neave has some context, has some substance to it' (2018). At the Elgin gig, he directly follows the Neave gag with a more explicitly political critique of the situation in Ulster, complaining that 'they never talk about the *war* in Ireland, right. They always call it something else, to play it down'. This establishes an effective satirical premise, in which he asks '[C]an you imagine – how the BBC broadcast would've sounded like during World War Two if they'd treated *those* events the same way they treat Northern Ireland?' He then delivers a spoof BBC news broadcast reporting well-known events from the Second World War while incorporating the tropes of coverage of the Troubles, for example: 'Two bombs went off today in the predominantly Japanese towns of Hiroshima and Nagasaki. [laughter] No-one has yet claimed responsibility. [laughter]'³

In February 1980 – shortly before this Elgin show – de la Tour was invited to perform at republican clubs in Northern Ireland, having been approached at the Comedy Store by an Irish political activist, Roisin McDonough. The trip was significant enough to be reported in the newspaper *An Phoblacht/Republican News*, which said of de la Tour's Neave gag, 'In Britain such a joke provokes a clear responce [*sic*] because it shock-assaults the audience's sense of "good taste"' (Delaney 1980). In Belfast, however, the gag ceased to be sick and became something quite different. At a club called the Markets, the audience show no hint of disapproval: 'No, but I think Margaret Thatcher did have a horrible year, didn't she? Mountbatten. [cheering and applause, 5 seconds] Airey Neave. [cheering] Poor old Airey Neave, eh, he got down a sheer cliff face at Colditz but he couldn't get up a twenty foot ramp at Westminster, could he? [laughter into applause, 8 seconds]'. Here, the cheering that greets the mention of Mountbatten and Neave suggests that their deaths are not seen as terrorist murders but as victories over the enemy. The punchline is not sick but triumphant, getting not hissing but applause.

Such responses might suggest that de la Tour's opinions perfectly aligned with those of the Irish republicans in the audience, but in fact while being sympathetic to the republican cause, he did not support terrorist violence: '[T]he point I'm making ... wasn't the mainstream opinion ... in Britain ... IRA actions were just viewed as terrorist and as criminality ... But I was trying to make it slightly subtler than that ... I was trying to say, "We have to view these things in the context of war. But that doesn't mean that I personally endorse the actions." Now that's a fine line to walk' (2018). Even to view the Troubles as a war situation rather than the result of wicked or psychopathic criminality was politically beyond the pale in the early 1980s, as seen in the reaction to Ken Livingstone. Both the hisses that greeted the Neave gag in London and the cheers it provoked in Belfast suggest that de la Tour was venturing far outside generally accepted norms.

## 'A plethora of benefit concerts'

As well as expanding the range of political opinions expressed in stand-up, alternative comedy also involved itself more directly in politics. From very early on, acts from the alternative cabaret circuit performed for a range of left-wing causes. Here are just a few examples. In May 1980, Andy de la Tour, Maggie Steed, and Alexei Sayle appeared at a benefit cabaret for Equity Left Alliance at the Albany Empire (*Stage* 1980c). In November 1981, Alexei Sayle appeared in a concert at the Rainbow alongside bands like Madness and The Members, for Jobs for Youth (Harron 1981b). In February 1982, Tony Allen, JJ Waller, and a band called ABA went on a ten-date No Nukes cabaret tour in aid of Sussex Alliance for Nuclear Disarmament (*NME* 1982). In February 1983, Andy de la Tour organized *An Evening for Nicaragua* at the Shaftesbury Theatre, in support of the left-wing Sandinista government – a cause célèbre for the British Left at the time. The bill included Alexei Sayle, Pauline Melville and Benjamin Zephaniah, as well as less political acts like Rik Mayall (Harron 1983).

There were two political causes in particular that galvanized performers in the alternative cabaret scene. The miners' strike of 1984–5 inspired all kinds of activities. There were collections for the miners every week in CAST's New Variety venues. Alexei Sayle, Jim Barclay, Jenny Lecoat and the Flying Pickets appeared in the 300 Days Miners Benefit Concert at the Piccadilly Theatre on Sunday 6 January 1985. Alternative comedians even went outside the normal limits of their circuit, travelling out to pit communities to perform for the miners themselves. For Linda Smith – who started as a stand-up in the 1980s alternative cabaret scene before becoming well-known on Radio 4 – performing in her double act Token Women on the *Pit Stop Tour* in 1985 was a significant moment in the formation of her act (HistComPod 2017c). Performing to audiences of miners was a long way from the liberal-Left metropolitan enclave – which alternative comedy has often been portrayed as – and not without its challenges. Mark Steel remembers playing a miners' welfare club in Shirebrook:

> [I]t was three or four acts from the comedy circuit. It was packed, this welfare club, of miners and their families. And they'd never seen anything like this. And they didn't know whether to laugh or whatever ... and sometimes you would feel like you were dying, but it was just that they were sitting there going ... 'Where's the joke?' But they weren't hostile, they were just genuinely confused.
>
> *Steel 2018*

### Alternative Comedy

It was an important moment for Pauline Melville when she performed for miners at Armthorpe colliery in Doncaster, because of what she was able to say to them politically and how they responded:

> That was amazing ... The guy that was introducing me ... said, 'I just want to warn you, love ... This is the club that made Bernard Manning weep.' ... It was rather wonderful actually, because I'd had the idea of linking police brutality with the SUS laws and stop and search with the miners, and they'd never made that connection. And I knew that they suddenly saw the similarity.
>
> *Melville 2018*

A joke that made the link between the police's treatment of the miners and the experience of the black community being disproportionately targeted by the stop and search policy would have been a radical departure for a working men's club audience more used to packaged gags about Irishmen or Pakistanis.

Perhaps the most significant miners support event took place towards the end of the strike, on 11 February 1985. A large poster advertising this is headed 'ALL OUT FOR THE MAGNIFICENT MINERS', and reveals that a number of key players in the alternative cabaret scene were among the organizers, including CAST New Variety, Crown & Castle Cabaret, and Off the Kerb Productions (BSUCA). There were two parts to the event. In the evening, there was a benefit gig at Islington Town Hall, with Frank Chickens, Jenny Lecoat, Ben Elton, Pookiesnackenburger, Pauline Melville, John Dowie, Benjamin Zephaniah and Rik Mayall.

More remarkably, throughout the day of the show, a huge array of alternative cabaret performers picketed outside Neasden Power Station, entertaining as they did so. Among the names listed on the poster are Jim Barclay, the Brown Paper Bag Brothers, Otiz Cannelloni, Andy Cunningham, Dusty & Dick, Jeremy Hardy, Roy Hutchins, the Joeys, Mark Miwurdz, Oscar McLennan, Bernard Padden, Podomovski, Porky the Poet, the Popticians, Maggie Steed, Ian Saville, Vicious Boys, Wild Girls, and Pete Zero, as well as some of the acts from the evening show. Footage from the event shows Brian Mulligan of Skint Video, in a toy police cap, saying, 'Good afternoon, it's nice to see so many plain clothes officers attending today,' to scattered laughter, before the musical comedy duo launch into their parody of 'The Laughing Policeman' – a jibe at police brutality in the strike (TonyGemail 2010). Roland Muldoon, who was instrumental in setting the event up, claims, 'The most amazing thing about it was the only time the pickets closed any power station down, in the whole of the miners' strike ... because the police were faced with Ra-Ra Zoo or pickets of jugglers or people like that, they didn't think they could beat us up, I think!' (2018).

The other crucial cause was nuclear disarmament. The 1980s saw a significant ramping up in the Cold War, with a surge in membership for the Campaign for Nuclear Disarmament reflecting genuine fears that nuclear war might become a reality. Anti-nuclear campaigning became extremely important to the Left, and alternative comedy played its part in this. For example, in June 1984, the Labour Party and *New Socialist* magazine staged *A Night for a Nuclear Free Europe* at the 2,500-capacity Wembley Conference Centre, with a bill that included Pookiesnackenburger, Mac McDonald, Nigel Planer, Ben Elton and Rik Mayall. Jim Barclay not only performed his stand-up act, but also featured in two other items listed in the programme: as one of three 'Pre-curtain up and interval entertainers' in the guise of Wonder Wally the alien; and officiating over an 'Interval Competition' (BSUCA). After the event, Barclay received a letter of thanks, dated 9 August, from the then-leader of the Labour Party, Neil Kinnock – who had also appeared. What Kinnock says in it suggests that he believed that this type of show had the potential to make a genuine contribution to campaigning:

> I wish to thank you for your splendid contribution to Labour's Night for a Nuclear Free Europe at Wembley ... I think that we have really hit on a winning formula for political entertainment which can appeal to a far larger audience than the usual political meeting. It was also extremely satisfying to outdo the Conservative' [*sic*] Wembley effort last year![4] The results of the European Elections show that, with an exciting and imaginative campaign, Labour can make real advances in winning people's support.
>
> BSUCA

### 'Oh, you're preaching to the converted'

The benefit shows that alternative comedians performed at are tangible proof that they did have some political effect, however small. The money raised to support, say, the miners' strike was in itself a real and tangible contribution to their struggle, even though – of course – it wasn't enough to make the kind of decisive difference that might have allowed them to triumph. However, with some events, the primary aim was not to raise money but to change minds, and this is something that Labour politicians like Neil Kinnock clearly believed in.

So why was it that comedians like Alexei Sayle, Mark Steel and Arthur Smith were so much more cynical about its potential for change? The idealistic Ben Elton points out, 'It's a human desire to undermine principle ... people on the left have to talk about principle, whereas people on the right can laughingly dismiss it, and in a way almost look cool' (2018). While Sayle, Steel and Smith are not remotely on the right, Elton may have touched on something important here, and it relates to a point George Orwell made in his classic essay, 'The Art of Donald McGill':

> I never read the proclamations of generals before battle, the speeches of führers and prime ministers, the solidarity songs of public schools and left-wing political parties, national anthems, Temperance tracts, papal encyclicals and sermons against gambling and contraception, without seeming to hear in the background a chorus of raspberries from all the millions of common men to whom these high sentiments make no appeal.
>
> *Orwell 1965: 153*

Orwell's point is that high-minded talk always risks being greeted with raspberries, and that is something comedians generally try to avoid, being creatures of irreverence, allergic to accusations of pomposity. Cook's line about Weimar cabarets doing so much to prevent the rise of Hitler is a great gag, but it doesn't resolve the issue of whether or not comedy can have an effect.

The accusation of preaching to the converted is often taken as a knockout punch, a QED from which there is no comeback. Yet as Sophie Quirk has pointed out, it can be an effective ploy for comedians to perform to an audience of politically like-minded people: 'By laughing, cheering and applauding together, the faithful affirm and develop their own notions of propriety. This may or may not translate into activism, but ... coming together to verify what this community collectively thinks and feels, is bound to affect the way these individuals function in society' (2016: 258).

A number of comedians acknowledge the idea that coming together to laugh can strengthen conviction, even if it doesn't change minds. Mark Steel now acknowledges that alternative comedy 'has had impact. Not a critical one. You're not going to change people's minds through a joke or a song or something but you can embolden people' (2018). Ian Saville makes a similar point: '[O]ne of the important things that was happening was that you were giving people a bit more hope and ... getting them to enjoy themselves while they were doing this work. Which makes it more likely that they'll carry on doing it' (2018). Jeremy Hardy expands on the idea, unpicking the logic of the preaching-to-the-converted accusation by examining the phrase's origins:

> People say, 'Oh, you're preaching to the converted,' and you think, 'Did you listen to what you just said? Don't you realise the whole history of organised religion is getting the converted into one space and preaching to them? So that you motivate them and keep them onside. And give them the thing that they want, that keeps them going, which is why that they converted to you in the first place.'
>
> *Hardy 2018*

Even the pleasingly cynical Alexei Sayle acknowledged this kind of effect once he got big enough to tour nationally and play to audiences beyond the London cabaret circuit. In 1982, he told *The Face* magazine: 'All that stuff about trendies and social workers and wimpy middle-class consumerism – when it's done to a largely working class audience and especially one outside of London, it generates real solidarity' (Taylor 1982b: 19). What is generating solidarity if not an effect?

Jenny Lecoat turns the accusation on its head, applying it to the kind of comedy that altcom sought to replace: 'What's interesting is that nobody ever says that Roy "Chubby" Brown is preaching to the converted. Or that Jim Davidson is preaching to the converted' (2018). This is an important point, because many on the Left who might be cynical about alternative comedy's effectiveness would be less willing to argue that, say, racist comedy has no effect because it's merely preaching to the converted. The philosopher Michael Philips has argued that racist comedy's ability to confirm racist feelings is at least as important as its likeliness to spread racist beliefs:

> [I]nsofar as racist humor constitutes an assault on members of an ethnic group, it joins together those who participate – both performers and audience – in a community of feeling against that group. By appreciating such humor together, we take common joy in putting them down, e.g., in turning them into objects of scorn or contempt or into beings not to be taken seriously ... Our mutual participation in

this through shared laughter legitimizes this way of feeling about them.

Philips 1984: 90

To transpose Philips' argument, by telling jokes that articulated radical opinions, alternative comedians legitimized the way the audience felt about the issues. For Andy de la Tour, the accusation of preaching to the converted is a 'false criticism', because:

> It's never used about dominant or mainstream culture, which *de facto*, by definition, preaches to the converted, if you like. So that any new cultural movement – comedy or painting or cinema – that galvanises, that mobilises those people who endorse the ideas, that's seen as a threat. And the way of trying to overcome that threat ... is by saying, 'Oh, these people are ineffective. They're just preaching to the converted.'

De la Tour 2018

In any case, there are examples where alternative comedians were not just playing to audiences of the converted. Pauline Melville acknowledges that she was preaching to the converted when she played venues like the Elgin or the Half Moon Theatre, but at the Comedy Store, 'I think it was a much more generalized audience who came in off the street from anywhere ... [and] when I went to the Comic Strip, that didn't feel so much like preaching to the converted' (2018). For Ian Saville, Jongleurs was the venue where a left-wing audience couldn't be guaranteed: 'I didn't only play to the Labour Party people ... or SWP or whatever. I did also play that sort of venue and sometimes, I recall once or twice where it didn't go so well, but there were quite a few times where I went down really, really well' (2018).

A *Time Out* article vividly describes the effect Sayle had on audiences by 1985: 'Fame has caught Alexei Sayle ... whisked him away from the forums of aficionados, and into the land of the 1500 seater packed with post-crackerjack pubescents, straining at his every fulmination ... And his tirade ... leaps from topic to topic, inflaming his audience and uniting them in a common disparagement' (Nichols 1985b). This suggests that once he was famous enough to tour big venues, instead of performing for 'aficionados' – the sympathetic left-wing audiences of the alternative cabaret circuit – he was playing to teenagers, and 'uniting' them in shared dislike of the targets of his comic invective. Again, this suggests that he was doing something rather more than preaching to the converted.

Like Sayle, Ben Elton found himself encountering different kinds of audiences once he began to tour nationally, and he even joked onstage about how the politics of his act went down in different towns. Appearing in Dundee in 1987, he tells the audience: 'It's funny, when you move round the country, you see the different reaction, up here I get a nice big cheer. Time I get to Manchester, it's still a round of applause. When I get to Brighton, they're goose-stepping up the stage [laughter] beating the fuck out of me. [into applause and whistling]' (Elton 1987). It also seems unlikely that he was preaching to the converted when Phil McIntyre took him out to perform to young, working-class audiences in Ibiza in the mid-1980s.

Sometimes, playing to the non-converted could yield surprising results. Performing outside Neasden Power Station in 1985, Jim Barclay found he was getting laughs not just from his fellow pickets, but also from the police officers who were there to maintain order – even when he was joking about deaths in police custody. Jeremy Hardy, who was less political and more cynical at the start of his career, recalled this incident to *The Guardian*, asking, 'And why were they lapping it up? Because no one takes comedy seriously. All you can change with comedy is comedy itself' (Shearman 1985). Looking back in 2018, he recalled, 'Jim was upset by that and he said to me, he said, "Well – what do you except the police to do? Of course they laughed at me because they're watching me, they're there. And they're going to look like idiots if they look cross." And I thought, "Yeah, fair play Jim, I hadn't thought of that"' (2018).

### 'Everything that happens has an effect'

By 2018, Hardy acknowledged that alternative comedy might have had some kind of political effect, carefully arguing that, 'It's impossible to say that anything has no impact. I mean everything that happens has an effect and there's all sorts of different things in the mix, and it's a combination of things. It's not "What effect does comedy have?" it's "What effect does comedy have at this time when all these other things are happening?"' (2018). Others argue that comedy can change minds, because it can affect perceptions. As Nick Revell puts it:

> One of the effects of any art form is to make you think about what you're engaging with and perhaps change your perspective, your opinion, or the way you look at something. Whether it's the way you

look at light on a pond, or the way you look at policemen walking down the street, it's all part of changing your ... critical attitude to something.

*Revell 2017*

Tangible examples of this include the arguments that Tony Allen and Jim Barclay whipped up with their Falklands material among the students and locals at Huddersfield Polytechnic, or Pauline Melville telling an audience of white coal miners that their experience with the police was like that of black people being plagued by the racist use of stop-and-search policies. To give another example, during his first flush of fame as a stand-up, Ben Elton had a routine about the coyly euphemistic tone struck by the first adverts for sanitary products that were starting to appear on British television. His satirical point was to attack sexist taboos surrounding menstruation:

> And over the voiceover comes – 'Ladies – do *you* – have a secret?' [laughter, over which:] AAARRGH!! *Half the population of the world does it every month, what's so fucking secret about that??* [laughter into applause, cheering, whistling] I tell yer – we'd have a lot less of this po-faced   let's-not-talk-about-it-let's-keep-it-in-a-closet-let's-make-it   – embarrassing-for-young-girls-when-it-first-happens-to-them   if   it was *men* – what had periods! Oh yeah! Then it'd be a subject for after dinner conversation! [laughter] [Posh, self-satisfied voice: ] 'It was a marvellous sunny afternoon. [laughter] I'd just strolled out to bat and would you believe it, my period started!' [laughter, some applause and whistling] Yeah!

*Elton 1987*

Looking back, he recalls:

> When I did my routine 'if men had periods' on the first series of *Saturday Live* ... I really believed that was an important routine. I think that had a genuine effect. Within months ... you know, suddenly, people did talk about menstruation ... Please don't make this look like I'm claiming some kind of credit. But there's no doubt that there was something going on. And I was really one of the people at the heart of it.

*Elton 2018*

He couches what he says carefully – possibly wary of an Orwellian chorus of raspberries – but he also offers anecdotal evidence of the effect his *Saturday Live* performances had on the audience: 'I'm proud that I used to get a lot of letters from women, and funnily enough, single mums ... it was amazing how many single mums would write in and say, "You spoke for me"' (2018).

Ultimately, the effect a comedy routine might have had on the thoughts, feelings and beliefs of any individual punter is unknowable. As Max Atkinson wrote in a study of political oratory, written at around this time, '[T]here is no way of getting inside people's heads in order to discover what goes on there in response to different verbal formats' (1984: 158). However, it's worth noting that while the alternative comedians themselves may not have believed they could have any political effect, there were politicians who did not share this scepticism, including the Leader of the Opposition. The GLC had enough faith in the propaganda value of alternative cabaret to fund tours supporting political causes. It put £30,000 into the *Nuclear Bunker Party* tour in 1983 – featuring acts like Pauline Melville, David Rappaport, Benjamin Zephaniah and the Oblivion Boys – Tony Banks seeing this as 'first and foremost a weapon of propaganda' (Petty 1983). Indeed, the GLC's faith in alternative cabaret as a political weapon directly contributed to the growth of the circuit, when it funded the anti-abolition *Live 32 Borough Touring Show* in 1984. It's also worth noting that while Britain remained Conservative throughout alternative comedy's first decade, London – where the scene was mostly based – elected a radical Labour council, which remained a thorn in Thatcher's side until her government abolished it.

While it may be impossible to prove any tangible political effect, what's certainly true is that alternative comedy brought about a seismic shift in British stand-up. In 1985, when Jeremy Hardy said, 'All you can change with comedy is comedy itself', the word 'all' suggests that changing comedy was something small and insignificant. In fact, British stand-up was changed fundamentally, from being a form based on a common stock of standard jokes based on a small set of ingrained prejudices, to a medium of self-authored material, which disdained sexism and racism and allowed the expression of radical left-wing opinions. It's true that many performers lacked much in the way of openly political material, but it was entirely new for stand-ups to make jokes against nuclear weapons or the Falklands War, and – particularly – challenge mainstream opinion about Northern Ireland. As Andy de la Tour puts it, 'The value of the new comedy as we were doing it is that although the ideas behind our comedy were ideas that were being more and more broadly accepted, the important thing is that audiences had never heard it in the form of stand-up comedy. That's the important thing. It's the medium which is the radical act' (2018).

It seems implausible that such a seismic shift in as popular a form as stand-up comedy had no effect whatsoever – even if its precise effect is unknowable. Barclay may have failed in his mission to 'precipitate the downfall of capitalist society' with his jokes, but he still believes in the political potential of comedy: 'I think in some ways, if you are seriously interested in upsetting the applecart, stand-up comedy's actually one of those few refuges where you can go to do that. And I mean I don't necessarily subscribe to art for art's sake ... I don't understand why you do it if you're not trying to change hearts and minds' (2016).

# PART THREE
LEGACY OF ALTERNATIVE COMEDY

# CHAPTER 9
# ALTERNATIVE COMEDY NOW

In 1989, alternative comedy turned ten. It was a decade since the birth of the Comedy Store and Alternative Cabaret. The event was marked by a flurry of press articles – Malcolm Hay in *Time Out*, John Connor in *City Limits*, Jay Rayner in *The Observer* – and the first book to record the history of the movement, Roger Wilmut's *Didn't You Kill My Mother-in-Law?*[1] What the press coverage reveals is how established certain key narratives had become among both the performers who worked in the scene and the critics who covered it.

The first of these was how big alternative comedy had grown. Rayner noted that the circuit had become 'an established part of London's nightlife', estimating that there were more than fifty regular comedy nights in the capital and over 5,000 punters attending shows every Friday and Saturday night (1989: 18). Hay asked himself what shape the scene was in after ten years, answering, 'Well, there's a lot more of it, for a start. More clubs, more performers, more punters and more critical attention ... every year there's more evidence of expansion' (1989). There's perhaps no more potent symbol of alternative comedy's increasing commercialism than the fact that the Comedy Store's tenth birthday festival was sponsored by Whitbread's brewery (*Stage* 1989). Alternative comedy's success led some to argue that the word 'alternative' was becoming redundant (McCoid 1989).

The second was that as the scene had grown, it had lost its radical edge. As Jay Rayner put it, 'Much of [the] political radicalism has ... disappeared' (1989: 19). Arnold Brown felt that 'the whole atmosphere is less exciting and far more commercially orientated – a lot of the danger has gone out of it' (Hay 1989). Pauline Melville recalled, 'I left when the madness went. The content used to be so much more savage and attacking. Everyone had things they wanted to kick at' (Connor 1989: 17). Keith Allen took a particularly hard-line approach, claiming, 'For me it was over after six months – it was very much like punk' (Connor 1989: 16).

In 1989, I was starting to do open mike spots in the London alternative cabaret scene, where the idea that the circuit was 'selling out' or losing its edge was widely discussed. I found the same when I interviewed comedians for my PhD. Jeremy Hardy told me, 'I used to love it, but I don't like it any more because it's ... bland, samey, indifferent people with nothing to say, just doing the same sort of subjects' (Hardy 1989). For Felix Dexter, the decline in radicalism was a direct result of increasing professionalism:

> A lot of people have got a career structure about comedy, and they're thinking almost from the first time they go on stage about their future career in comedy ... What prompted [alternative comedy] was that people were genuinely interested in performing differently, and making some kind of social comment. That's all gone now, and people's main concern is about getting on telly.
>
> *Dexter 1990*

An important variant of this argument was that improvements in the general standard of performance had been matched with increasing conformity and a lack of experimentation. Looking back on the early days, Arthur Smith recalled, 'It was wilder. Many of the acts weren't that good. The overall standard is higher now. But the striking difference is that people were much more experimental then' (Hay 1989).

Not everybody shared this point of view. David Baddiel, then comparatively new to the circuit, argued that the idea of increasing professionalism robbing the circuit of its original danger was a 'dangerously reactionary stance' (1989). Similarly, Jenny Lecoat told me, 'I mean there's a lot of stuff talked about, oh, the good old radical political days, and the fact that everything's got very bland, I don't think that's actually true' (1990). That said, with the benefit of nearly thirty more years of hindsight, she now argues, 'I certainly think in many ways it was more interesting and forward-thinking and perhaps a bit more exciting than what's going on at the moment' (2018).

The key narratives about the state of alternative comedy in 1989 – growing commercial success, increasing professionalism, decreasing radicalism – have continued to dominate how we look back on the movement today. So it's useful to use them as a focus for examining what the movement's legacy actually is.

### 'A career structure about comedy'

Perhaps the most straightforward aspect of alternative comedy's legacy is that it established an infrastructure that's still the basis of the UK's live comedy circuit today. Although comedy clubs come and go, the current circuit can trace its origins back to the performers and venues that emerged in the 1980s. Indeed, some of the clubs started in that decade are still part of the circuit. Downstairs at the King's Head in Crouch End was started by Peter Grahame and Huw Thomas as early as 1981 – when it was known as Comedy in the Cellar. The Banana Cabaret started at the Bedford in Balham in November 1983. The Bearcat has been running at the Turk's Head in Twickenham since 1985. The Joker in Southend and the Comedy Cellar (originally the Friday Alternative) at South Hill Park Arts Centre in Bracknell were both set up in 1986. Ivor Dembina, whose Pranksters organization helped to establish the alternative cabaret circuit, is still part of London's comedy scene today. Still a working comic, he's been running the Hampstead Comedy Club since 1994, and argues: 'If you came to my club . . . and watched the show, you will see something that in a very unsentimental and totally un-nostalgic way is in some way a representation of what I think is the best lessons that were learnt over the years from those early days' (2018).

However, whereas the scene in the 1980s was made up of little more than a series of small, pub-based clubs, today such venues are just the bottom level of a comedy industry whose titanic scale would have been unimaginable when Malcolm Hay was writing about the ongoing expansion of the circuit in 1989. The most successful comedians progress from pub gigs to television, theatre tours, perhaps even arena shows. Live comedy has changed from a DIY scene with enthusiast entrepreneurs paying the comedians in 'folding blue ones' (Williams 1984), to a situation where one of the biggest stand-ups on today's circuit, Michael McIntyre, was reported in 2013 to have earned over £21 million in the previous two years (Trueman 2013). Arena comedy stalwart McIntyre is represented by Off the Kerb – the agency which, in the heady days of the 1980s, Addison Cresswell ran from his flat. Clearly, comedy has become a career, and for some an extraordinarily lucrative one.

On the other hand, some aspects of today's highly professionalized comedy scene are proving less profitable, even costly, for many comics – notably the Edinburgh Fringe. In 1989, Carol Sarler noted in *The Guardian* that, 'Ten years ago the Edinburgh fringe programme contained virtually no cabaret. Now, reflecting the mushrooming of the craft throughout the year, we have well over 100 shows.' Two years later, another *Guardian* article noted that comedians 'are frequently accused of squeezing new theatre out', because they were cheaper to put on (Coles 1991). However, another article claimed that 'most comedians either lose money, or just about break even' (Murray 1990). These are trends that have only increased in the decades since then. The complaint that comedians are taking over the Fringe at the expense of theatre companies continues to resurface every few years, well into this century. Meanwhile, comedians who go to Edinburgh increasingly risk incurring significant debts. In 2002, Brian Logan reported that comedians can come away from the Fringe with debts of £8,000 or £9,000, having to spend the entire year performing gigs to pay it off. Ten years later, Stewart Lee put the situation starkly: '[T]he cycle of Fringe debt makes loyal slaves of artists, perhaps paying off their loss by working for their management's own subsidiary production and promotion companies' (Lee 2012). Professionalization has clearly taken things a long way from the situation in 1983, when Rik Mayall, Ben Elton and Andy de la Tour were each able to take home £2,387.82 for their Edinburgh run.

Some of the performers who started out in the early days of alternative comedy now have offspring who are working as comedians in today's circuit. Mark Steel's son Elliot Steel and Kevin Day's son Ed Night are both stand-ups, Jennifer Saunders and Ade Edmondson's daughter Beattie Edmondson is part of the sketch trio Birthday Girls, and Jim Barclay's daughter Ellie Gibson is half of the double act Scummy Mummies, as well as doing solo stand-up. Comparing the experiences of these second generation performers with those of their parents gives a good idea of how live comedy has changed since the 1980s. Thinking about his son Elliot's experiences, Mark Steel argues that today's circuit allows comedians to develop more quickly:

> The sort of professionalism that they have, that took me years... They write stuff all the time... when I was doing the circuit, if you wrote a new ten minutes in six months, people were going, 'I can't believe the amount of new stuff you can get through!' Whereas now they're expected to have a whole new 20 minutes every three or four months.
>
> *Steel 2018*

Kevin Day believes that while opportunities for new acts have proliferated, the nature of these opportunities has changed:

> [E]very second gig is a new-act night or it's a competition or somewhere you have to bring two friends and buy two drinks. So there are more opportunities for new people to try comedy out, but then far fewer opportunities for them to move on. I mean the big difference from our days [is] that you did open spots on the main bill, basically.

## Alternative Comedy Now

So you were on with Jeremy Hardy and Paul Merton and Kit Hollerbach, you just happened to be on doing five minutes.

*Day 2018*

This is a crucial difference. Playing a new-act night where every act on the bill is an unpaid newcomer is a very different proposition from appearing alongside professional comedians. When I did my first open spot on the London circuit, at Screaming Blue Murder in Hampton Wick in the spring of 1989, I was the only unpaid act on a bill compèred by Eddie Izzard, featuring established London acts like Sheila Hyde and Lee Evans. This gave me the chance to play to a proper comedy audience, meet and get advice from professional acts, and – after I had gone down well enough – an offer of a paid booking next time I appeared there.

By contrast, today's comedians expect to work new-act nights for much longer before they start getting paid. In 2014, Ellie Gibson was interviewed about doing her first hundred gigs as a stand-up, and confessed: 'I still feel like an imposter. I added up all the money I've made and it works out at about a pound a gig' (Stuart 2014). This is in spite of the fact that stand-up is something she was exposed to from an early age: 'I grew up in the 80s ... watching stand-up. They mainly dragged me to CND gigs and miners' strike things ... So I grew up watching it, but I never really thought about doing it until after I'd had children'. She's rueful when I ask her about being the daughter of one of the pioneers of alternative comedy: 'I mean it's no kind of advantage, to be quite honest. I wish it was. It hasn't got me anywhere' (Gibson 2016).

Another important aspect of professionalization is that the ethos of self-authorship in stand-up has been subtly eroded. Nowadays, well-known TV comedians who once played the circuit employ uncredited writers to help them develop material for appearances on panel shows or live tours of big theatres and arenas. This trend is barely discussed in public discourse, but older generations of comedians look askance at it. Robin Ince writes wryly about the 'big name comedians who seem to deliver personal opinion/autobiographical stand up ... armed by [a] coterie of sometimes poorly paid and forcibly anonymous writers' (2014), and Stewart Lee bemoans the practice of 'using conspicuously uncredited and poorly paid writers to generate profitable stadium-filling laugh content for the TV viewer market' (2015).

The evidence suggests, then, that the trend of increasing commercial success and professionalization noted by journalists in 1989 has continued to grow on a scale that has transformed the live comedy scene, making it not only bigger but also more prone to the kind of practices associated with neoliberal capitalism.

### 'No right-wing comedians at all'

In spite of the narrative that alternative comedy quickly ditched its early political radicalism, another important legacy is that it shifted British stand-up to the left. Before the emergence of the new scene in the 1980s, stand-up comedians tended to be implicitly or explicitly right-wing. There was a long tradition of comedians supporting the Conservative Party, from the music hall comic George Robey embracing Conservatism as part of a desire to show off his offstage middle-class respectability (Cheshire 1974: 76), to stand-ups like Les Dawson, Bob Monkhouse and Jimmy Tarbuck contributing to Tory rallies for the General Elections in 1979 and 1983 (Hill and Lochhead 1979: 4; Porter 1983). Beyond this, working men's club comedians tended to use material that espoused reactionary values, particularly in their preference for racist and sexist gags. However, by 1989, Charles Spencer, who had followed the alternative cabaret scene from its early days, was arguing that, 'Jokes about mothers-in-law and Pakis are an endangered species. The alternative has become the norm' (Bradshaw and Spencer 1989).

The following year, two things happened that suggested just how far attitudes had shifted. In February, *The Stage* announced that the holiday company Thompson was changing the entertainment policy in its resorts, booking its acts through Jongleurs to ensure 'that the entertainment is non sexist and non-racist' (*Stage* 1990). Then in June, the well-known television comedian Les Dennis – who had started his career in working men's clubs – told the *Radio Times* that he admired Alexei Sayle and Ben Elton and would no longer do sexist or racist material (Guttridge 1990).

It would be a bold claim to argue that sexism and racism has completely disappeared from British stand-up, and Jeremy Hardy has pointed out that in today's comedy circuit 'you'll hear pretty repugnant stuff. Which you wouldn't have done in the '80s, because people would have just not booked you again or the audience wouldn't have stood for it' (2018). That said, it would be difficult to find any young stand-up today delivering the kind of nakedly racist gags that circulated in working men's clubs in the 1970s and 1980s. Nobody on the comedy circuit is likely to tell the one about Pakistanis being melted down to make rubber bullets, for example. Even beyond the comedy clubs, tastes have changed, pushing comics like Jim Davidson and

Roy 'Chubby' Brown to the fringes. Looking back to his experiences of performing in northern WMCs in support of striking miners, Mark Steel reflects:

> Somewhere along the line it must have changed, because you know, now if you went to Shirebrook, or to ex-pit villages, and you ask anybody under 50 who their favourite comic is, they would say people who are familiar with our world. You know, they would say [Michael] McIntyre or Micky Flanagan or something ... I mean a few of them might say 'Chubby' Brown I suppose, but even that would be the older ones.
>
> *Steel 2018*

Although the political element of alternative comedy might have been exaggerated, it certainly opened up the possibility of comedians expressing radical views in their material. The widespread belief that the early radicalism quickly disappeared was already established by 1985, when *The Guardian* published an article about the current state of the scene. In it, Colin Shearman argues that, 'Most ... second wave performers have abandoned the hard-hitting political satire of the early days for something much more mainstream and accessible.' He gives Jeremy Hardy as an example, describing his act as being 'based entirely on the unpolitical problems of being middle-class'. He also quotes Hardy's somewhat jaded view of political comedy: 'For a while it was very exciting that people actually came out and slagged off the Tories and their policies ... But then the fact that it wasn't always necessarily funny palled a bit' (Shearman 1985).

Interestingly, a video of Hardy performing at the Zap Club in Brighton on 26 January 1985 suggests that his act was not quite as 'unpolitical' as this article – published just four months later – claims. Despite his polite, middle-class persona, he makes some surprisingly cutting comments about such subjects as police brutality and racism: 'Given time, there could be blind police officers with – dark visors and guide Alsatians and – long white truncheons to [mimes beating people with truncheons] feel their way down the street. [laughter] 'Cos when you're blind everything's black, isn't it, so *they* enjoy themselves [laughter and some clapping, 6 seconds]' (BSUCA).

In spite of Hardy's early cynicism about political comedy, he recently acknowledged that his act became more radical over time: 'I think I increasingly decided to become political ... By the early '90s, I thought that what I was doing was important ... and that I was using my platform well. As

## Alternative Comedy

a satirist, that I was using it in a good way. And that that was important that I did that. Which certainly wasn't what I thought when I started' (2018). Until a few months before his death in February 2019, Hardy was one of a number of political comedians from the alternative scene of the 1980s still active on the current comedy circuit. Others include Mark Thomas and Mark Steel, and they are part of a long line of political comedians that stretches from then until now, including later performers like Robert Newman, Stewart Lee, Josie Long, Bridget Christie and Frankie Boyle. While being an overtly political comedian may be the exception rather than the rule, it has become normal for comics to appear in benefit gigs for liberal causes. It's also not unusual for comedians not labelled as political to make satirical comments – Eddie Izzard criticizing American gun laws, for example, or Bill Bailey making jokes at the expense of Swiss banks that handled Nazi gold.

All of this has led to the widespread belief that there are now no right-wing comedians (Logan 2013; Blackall 2013; Duffin and Ensor 2013). In 2016, the controversialist Rod Liddle recalled the fact that most of the comedians of his childhood were Tories, and boldly claimed that, 'Today there are no right-wing comedians at all ... Even the ones who pretend to be a tiny bit right wing ... are as achingly PC as the rest of the crew.' This is factually untrue, as there are a small number of overtly right-wing British stand-ups – Geoff Norcott is a Conservative, for example, and both Lee Hurst and Andrew Lawrence have expressed sympathy for the United Kingdom Independence Party. However, the fact that the right-wing comedian is such a rare beast is an indication of just how far alternative comedy shifted British stand-up.

### 'Fuck Jongleurs'

As for the narrative of decline in artistic radicalism, this reflects actual tangible changes in the circuit since its 1980s infancy. The fact that the early scene was usually referred to as 'cabaret' rather than 'comedy' reflects the sheer variety of acts it played host to. However, by the early 1990s increasing professionalization led to creeping homogenization. In a 1991 *City Limits* article, Kim Davis noted, '[W]ith a few exceptions like poet and poptician [John] Hegley, it's hundreds of male stand-ups that line up for stardom ... The bull-market in simple punchlines encourages uniformity' (16). Mark Thomas recalls how poets, street performers and crazy eccentrics were sloughed off in favour of male stand-ups: 'There's a whittling down ... into comedy as a stand-up, individual form' (2015a). Having run Downstairs at the King's Head since 1981, Peter Grahame is well-placed to observe the changes the circuit has been through since then. He explains how the nature of bills has changed:

> In the early days ... you'd have at least one music act, probably straight music. At least one what you would loosely term as a spesh act, you know, a clown or a mime or magic or whatever. And that would then be straight-ish, or more down the sort of street entertainer, theatre route. And then maybe two or three what we would now regard as stand-ups, but it was very rough at the edges around then. I mean I now see all these people, products of stand-up courses and evening classes and whatever, who are very slick in terms of being able to look the look and take microphones out without banging themselves on the nose, but [have] got nothing to say. It was much more content and risk-taking, I think, then than there is now.
>
> *Grahame 2018*

For many, nothing symbolized the homogenization of comedy more than the success of Jongleurs. Established in 1983, by 2000 Jongleurs had grown to a chain of eight clubs, which was sold to Regent Inns for over £7 million (Chortle 2017). It grew from there, but by 2009 its parent company Regent Inns went into administration and closed five clubs (Kettle 2009). Jongleurs struggled on in various forms for a few more years before finally closing all its clubs in 2017 (Chortle 2017). Nonetheless, even while it was thriving, Jongleurs was not well liked by comedians. As Tim Arthur wrote in 2010, 'For certain comics Jongleurs became synonymous with the corporatization of alternative comedy. Drunken hordes of stags and hens demanded a coarse and lowest-common-denominator form of comedy which was essentially seen as a return to the bad old days of the working men's clubs.'

In response, a new comedy scene began to emerge in reaction against what Jongleurs was seen to represent. It started to become noticed by the wider world when Tim Jonze wrote an article about what he called 'DIY comedy', made up of performers like Josie Long, Isy Suttie and the sketch group Pappy's Fun Club, and nights like Robin Ince's Book Club and Terry Saunders' Laughter in Odd Places (2007). Robin Ince made the connection between Jongleurs and DIY comedy explicit: 'One of the best things about

### Alternative Comedy

Jongleurs is that as it became bigger and bigger, people started to kick against it ... It's almost through Jongleurs that a new alternative scene started' (Kettle 2009). In 2005, Josie Long collected an award from the comedy website Chortle with the words 'Fuck Jongleurs' written on her arm. Looking back on this time, she recalls:

> I think there were a group of us. And I do think what we were trying to do was open up more space on the circuit. 'Cos when I first started, it was like, 'You need to do the clubs! You're dying at the clubs! You must be doing it wrong!' Whereas, now it does feel like there's so much more diversity and I feel like it was partly down to people ten years ago trying really hard to force it a little bit and create more space.
>
> *HistComPod 2017d*

Jonze characterized Long – and by extension the whole scene – by praising her 'enthusiasm', 'homemade props', and 'shonky amateur charms', arguing that she is 'the refreshing antidote to slick, male-dominated mainstream comedy'.

Broderick Chow pointed out the similarities between the DIY and alternative comedy, arguing, 'Both alternative comedy and emergent DIY comedy oppose a dominant culture of mainstream comedy that reduces or constrains comedians according to how their work may be consumed or disseminated' (2008: 123–4). Stewart Lee – who started out in the alternative comedy scene of the late 1980s – makes the same connection: 'If the phrase hadn't lost its meaning once already, you could almost say we were witnessing the birth of a new Alternative Comedy, in opposition to the crowd-pleasing composite that the Alternative Comedy of old had become' (2010: 36). Given the chance to curate a comedy show for Comedy Central broadcast in 2013 and 2014 – presenting the kind of acts he saw as being in opposition to this 'crowd-pleasing composite' – he chose a name for it that directly referenced the scene he had started out in: *The Alternative Comedy Experience*. Similarly, when a younger group of performers led by John-Luke Roberts and Thom Tuck started a regular comedy night dedicated to the pursuit of 'noble failure' in 2011, they chose a name that referenced the 1980s scene in a delightfully tongue-in-cheek way: the Alternative Comedy Memorial Society.[2]

In a sense, the DIY scene and the re-emergence of the term 'alternative comedy' reflect the same kind of contrast Arthur Smith expressed when he told Malcolm Hay in 1989 that although the standard of performance had improved, the wilder and more experimental elements had disappeared. On the one hand, there's the slick, professional, crowd-pleasing world of the Jongleurs-style 'mainstream' club. On the other, there's the DIY 'alternative' venue, which celebrates looseness, enthusiasm and the homemade – and even deems failure to be noble.

### 'The hairs did stand up on the back of your neck'

As 1979 recedes ever further into the past, the urge to celebrate and memorialize alternative comedy continues as strongly as ever. In addition to the perennial television and radio documentaries about it, the last decade has seen a number of live events showcasing the stars of the 1980s scene. On 29 May 2011, Stewart Lee curated *At Last! The 1981 Show* at the Royal Festival Hall featuring, among others, stand-ups like Alexei Sayle, Arthur Smith, Norman Lovett, and Arnold Brown, and more cabaret-oriented acts like Nigel Planer (playing both Neil the folksinger and his actor character Nicholas Craig), the Greatest Show on Legs, Frank Chickens, and Andrew Bailey's Lenin act. One of the most remarkable acts on the bill was Pauline Melville, who had not performed stand-up for decades, yet still managed to create a genuine frisson with a series of gags comparing Osama bin Laden with Jesus: 'People say Jesus didn't kill three thousand people. But Jesus was only 33 when he died, bin Laden was 54 – so who knows what Jesus would have been capable of if he'd lived longer.'[3] Alexei Sayle enjoyed performing in the show so much that it inspired him to return to stand-up, after years away from it working as a respected author of short stories and novels. He appeared at the Soho Theatre in January 2012 to work on new material – supported by performers like Bridget Christie and Josie Long – and returned there the following year with an hour-long solo show, followed by an Edinburgh run and a 22-date national tour.

Other shows have celebrated landmark birthdays of comedians who are now reaching ages that might be described as venerable. On 21 November 2016, the Comedy Store hosted *Arnold Brown's Birthday Bash*, marking Brown's eightieth birthday with a show featuring 1980s veterans like Paul Merton, John Hegley, Jeremy Hardy, Nick Revell and Norman Lovett, alongside alternative comedians of today like Bridget Christie and Sara Pascoe, and performers like Stewart Lee who bridges the gap between the generations. Jim Barclay's seventieth was marked with *Barclay's Birthday Cabaret*, a benefit for War on Want held at the Ivy House Community Pub on 23 May 2017. Jeremy Hardy, Steve Gribbin and Ian Saville appeared on a bill compèred by Barclay, which also featured his daughter's double act the Scummy Mummies.

What's striking about these examples is how many of them are intergenerational, if not biologically (Ellie Gibson) then artistically (Bridget Christie, Josie Long). This suggests a conscious continuity between the alternative comedy pioneers of the 1980s and the comedians of today who are seen as alternatives to the commercial comedy club. Indeed, in early 2013 Alexei Sayle wrote of performers like Josie Long, Bridget Christie, and Tony Law: 'I think of them as my true children, and I hope they will accept their old, estranged dad back into the family home' (2013).

It's worth asking why alternative comedy continues to be celebrated and memorialized after all these years, and why it continues to capture the imagination of younger performers. Of course, the most immediate answer is that it represents such a pivotal moment in British comedy, with almost the entirety of today's live scene springing forth from it. However, it might also be that it also symbolizes something very attractive: the extraordinary creative and political freedom that an anarchic, loosely organized scene can offer.

At a time when comedians start out by doing months or years of unpaid new-act nights before they start to get paid, and work for years before doing their first solo hour at the Fringe – which might well leave them with massive debts – it's easy to see how appealing the loose, anarchic 1980s circuit might look. This is perhaps why one of the arguments has been so enduring: that decreasing political and artistic radicalism was matched by an improvement in the standard achieved by most comedians in terms of the craft skills of stand-up. The idea that the original alternative comedians were interesting but incompetent by today's standards could be comforting, the loss of freedom and innovation counterbalanced by an increase in skill.

Nonetheless, while early recordings confirm that acts sometimes struggled to get consistent laughs, the idea that all of the early pioneers were less competent than comedians today is a simplification. Off the Kerb's Joe Norris recalls seeing the double act Skint Video playing to university audiences of 400–500 and hearing laughter which was 'just as loud as it might be today in some arenas' (2018). Perhaps the best example of somebody who combined expert skill in the craft of stand-up comedy with radical politics and wild inventiveness was Alexei Sayle. Watching and listening to live recordings shows that his technical skills were impressive, whether dealing with hecklers, commenting on his own mistakes, or getting the kind of regular big laughs enjoyed by today's best acts. However, his craft skill was

## Alternative Comedy Now

matched by the wildness of his comic imagination – whether calling the audience 'fuckfaces', yelling 'Bib-bib-bib-bib-bib-bib-bib-bib-bib!', making acerbic jokes about poverty in Stoke Newington under Thatcher, recalling a teenage dancer at a Liverpool club asking him if he was Bertolt Brecht, or imagining a working men's club comic slagging Lenny Bruce off for failing to tell racist jokes.

What's remarkable is that he achieved this without the grind of professionalism that characterizes the current comedy circuit. Sayle became an extraordinary stand-up without what amounts to a long, unpaid apprenticeship, without the relentless competition that grows from a saturated market, and without being honed by the complex professional superstructure that has grown up since he started. Indeed, he became a comedy star at a speed that would seem absurd on today's circuit. He played his first Edinburgh Fringe just over a year after starting at the Comedy Store, and two years after that he released a stand-up album and toured nationally as a solo act. This, ultimately, is why the first alternative comedians are still remembered so well. They reinvented British stand-up comedy whilst barely knowing what they were doing, discovering for themselves how it worked, driven by a combination of passion and sheer self-belief.

# NOTES

### Chapter 2

1. Sometimes referred to as Cliff Shaw.
2. A duo which contained Stuart Turner, who later became a successful solo comedian under the name Oscar McLennan.
3. Using the Bank of England's inflation calculator.
4. Throughout the book, figures in square brackets indicate the 2018 value using the Bank of England's UK inflation calculator.

### Chapter 3

1. Merton is listed here as Paul Martin. He only adopted the stage name Merton in January 1987.
2. Tony Allen, Clive Anderson, Jim Barclay, Arnold Brown, Lee Cornes, Steve Dixon, John Dowie, Ben Elton, Simon Fanshawe, Roy Hutchins, Jenny Lecoat, Norman Lovett, Oscar McLennan, Pauline Melville, Paul Merton, Nick Revell, Mark Steel, Andy de la Tour.
3. Tim Bat, Phil Herbert, Mac McDonald, Karl Mellor, Daniel Rovai, Lynn (AKA Lyn) Thomas, Captain JJ Waller.
4. Christians from Outer Space, French and Saunders, the Oblivion Boys, Wild Girls.
5. John Hegley, Pete Zero, Benjamin Zephaniah. It's worth noting that these categories are not always straightforward. For example, I've counted John Hegley and Pete Zero as poets even though both also performed songs, and Hegley had some experience of street performance.
6. These being, respectively, Ronnie Golden, Bob Flag, Chris Barrie, Andrew Bailey, the Mivvys, the Joeys, Ian Puleston-Davies, Ian Kelly and David Rappaport.
7. According to one source, the name was spelt Witzend.
8. Better known as Dave Cohen.
9. At this stage, Felix Dexter was still billed simply as 'Felix', or sometimes even 'Dexter Felix'.

# Notes

## Chapter 5

1. Deely-boppers were a kind of novelty headgear popular at the time, made up of a plastic headband with two springs attached, each of which had plastic shapes stuck to the end, creating the impression of the kind of antennae seen on an insect or a cartoon alien.
2. A number of different performances of this routine were recorded, with small variations. Not all of them include a contraceptive gooseberry bush.
3. Magritte the Mind Reading Rat was one of several acts performed in alternative cabaret by the puppeteer Andy Cunningham.
4. The YouTube clip labels the clip as having appeared on *Friday Night Live*, but TV listings reveal that McAleer actually appeared on *Saturday Live* on 28 February 1987.
5. There are a few variant spellings of the name Podomovski, but when I asked Bailey which was the correct one, he said he is happy with any spelling.

## Chapter 6

1. Cook uses the term 'trad comics' to refer to comedians who worked the 'mainstream circuit', which was essentially the working men's club circuit.
2. The Brechtian quality is not surprising, given that there's an echo here of Brecht's friend and occasional collaborator Karl Valentin, the German Kabarett comedian – particularly his routine 'Das Aquarium', which contains a similarly overliteral explanation of the concept of stairs.
3. Allen included a less developed version of the Amalgamated Conglomerates gag in his debut set at Ovalhouse, but it was separate from the drug squad routine, coming later in the act.

## Chapter 7

1. The biggest clue is that Jim Barclay refers to the Thames Telethon happening 'next week'. This was broadcast on 2 October 1980, so it seems likely that this show happened in late September.
2. AKA Nick Revell.
3. 'People like Polo' was a well-known advertising slogan at the time.
4. The Communist Party of Britain (Marxist-Leninist) was a left-wing faction whose main distinguishing feature was their inexplicable admiration for Enver Hoxha, the brutal dictator of Albania. Alexei Sayle was an ex-member of the CPB(M-L) when he joined Alternative Cabaret, so he knew whereof he joked.

# Notes

## Chapter 8

1. I should point out that Barclay was more a radical socialist than a Marxist-Leninist, but 'Marxist-Leninist' sounded funnier when juxtaposed with the word 'comedian'.
2. Today, the meaning of this joke would be undermined by the fact that since Savile's death it has been revealed that he was a dangerous sexual predator. By ironic coincidence, in another version of Barclay's routine, the letter from Thatcher was imagined in the context of a Telethon hosted by Rolf Harris, who has now also been revealed as a sexual predator.
3. The key to understanding these gags is recognizing the habitual language of news reports, which spoke of 'predominantly Catholic' or 'predominantly Protestant' areas, and reported that no terrorist groups had 'claimed responsibility'.
4. On 5 June 1983, the Conservative Party held the Wembley Youth Rally at the same venue, which became notorious for an appearance from the TV and radio comedian Kenny Everett, who made such supposedly funny comments as 'Let's bomb Russia!'

## Chapter 9

1. The book is credited to Roger Wilmut and Peter Rosengard, but in fact Rosengard only wrote the introduction, a delightfully evocative personal account of the beginnings of the Comedy Store.
2. For a detailed account of the origins of this name, see Quirk (2018: 81).
3. I transcribed this joke from memory when making notes on the show a couple of days after seeing it.

# REFERENCES

Absalom, Steve (1981), 'Man's inhumanity to man', *The Stage*, 28 May: 5.
Alexander, Andrew (1982), 'They won't be able to stop her now', *Daily Mail*, 24 May: 6.
Allen, Keith (2007), *Grow Up*, London: Ebury Press.
Allen, Tony (1988), interview with Oliver Double, Madhouse Comedy Club, Rotherham, 30 September.
Allen, Tony (2002), *Attitude: Wanna Make Something Of It?*, Glastonbury: Gothic Image.
Allen, Tony (2016), in conversation with Oliver Double, Aphra Theatre, Canterbury, 9 May.
Allen, Tony (2019), in *Pioneers of Alternative Comedy in Conversation*, Gulbenkian, 3 May.
Alternative Cabaret (1981), *Alternative Cabaret* [LP], UK: Original Records.
*An Audience with Jasper Carrott* (1978), LWT, 10 February.
Appleyard, Bryan (1981a), 'How to play Stalin for laughs', *The Times*, 26 October: 6.
Appleyard, Bryan (1981b), 'Cultural savagery', *The Times*, 18 September: 9.
Arthur, Tim (2010), 'Comedy – Is it the end for Jongleurs?', *Time Out*, 14 January: 52.
Astor, Peter (1984), 'Right to Read Benefit: London LSE', *New Musical Express*, 18 February: 39.
Atkinson, Max (1984), *Our Masters' Voices*, London: Methuen.
Baddiel, David (1989), 'Demystification corner', *Comedy Pages*, Issue 1, May: 17.
Bailey, Andrew (2018), interview with Oliver Double, London N1, 24 April.
Barber, Lynn (1991), 'Offstage it's not so funny', *Independent on Sunday* (Review section), 29 September: 14–15.
Barclay/Brimstone/Capstick/Harding (1974), *There Was This Bloke* [LP], UK: Rubber Records.
Barclay, Jim (1990), interview with Oliver Double, Rub a Dub Club, Sydenham, 1 February.
Barclay, Jim (2016), interview with Oliver Double, Crofton Park, 16 May.
Barrow, Tony (1985), 'Do you know the one about the mother-in-law? . . . It's still making them laugh', *The Stage*, 29 August: 8.
Beckett, Andy (2016), *Promised You a Miracle: Why 1980–82 Made Modern Britain*, London: Penguin.
Billington, Michael (1982), 'Sexual angst in full swing', *The Guardian*, 19 March: 11.
Blackall, Luke (2013), 'Can you have a right laugh?', *The Independent*, 13 March: 28.
Bobinska, Monika (2015), interview with Oliver Double, University of Kent, Canterbury.

## References

*Boom Boom Out Go the Lights* (1980) [TV], BBC2, 14 October.
Bradshaw, Peter and Charles Spencer (1989), 'Why did the alternatives lose their bite?', *The Daily Telegraph Student Extra*, Summer: 12.
Brand, Jo (2015), *Talking Comedy* (live interview with Oliver Double), Assembly Rooms, Edinburgh, 19 August.
Brand, Jo (2019), *Linda Smith Lecture*, Gulbenkian Theatre, 1 May.
Brazil, David (1979), 'How to talk dirty and get arrested', *The Leveller*, no. 33, December: 14.
Brecht, Bertolt (1964), *Brecht on Theatre* (ed. and trans. John Willett), London: Methuen.
Brien, Alan (1979), 'Metropolis', *Punch*, 30 May: 926–7.
BritishComedyGuide (2016), 'Alexei Sayle talks to Stewart Lee', https://www.youtube.com/watch?v=lLsJu7rqs8o (accessed 19 February 2018).
Brown, Arnold (2016), interview with Oliver Double, King's Place Café, London N1, 26 July.
BSUCA, various items from the British Stand-Up Comedy Archive.
Burchill, Julie (1987), 'Why I hate students', *National Student Monthly*, October: 9.
Burn, Gordon (1980), 'After they all get dressed ...', *The Sunday Times*, 27 January: 13.
*Cabaret at the Jongleurs* (1988a) [TV], BBC2, 25 February.
*Cabaret at the Jongleurs* (1988b) [TV], BBC2, 7 April.
Callan, Paul (1979), 'Heard the one about ad-man Phil who became Vernon Vomit the punk comic?', *Daily Mirror*, 23 November: 16–17.
Carlisle, Anne (1987), 'Practical solutions: Making art work: The artist & the Enterprise Allowance Scheme', *Circa Art Magazine*, March–April: 21–3.
Chateau, France (1991), 'Language most foul', *The Guardian*, 3 October: 19.
Cheshire, David (1974), *Music Hall in Britain*, Newton Abbot: David & Charles.
Chortle (2017), 'Jongleurs clubs all close', https://www.chortle.co.uk/news/2017/10/17/38176/jongleurs_clubs_all_close, 17 October (accessed 22 November 2018).
Chow, Broderick D V (2008) 'Situations, happenings, gatherings, laughter: Emergent British stand-up comedy in sociopolitical context', *Theatre Symposium*, 16 (1): 121–33.
Church, Michael (1981), 'The Comic Strip: Boulevard Theatre', *The Times*, 14 February: 8.
Clary, Julian (2005), *A Young Man's Passage*, London: Ebury Press.
Coles, Joanna (1991), 'A tale of emptier houses, emptier pockets', *The Guardian*, 29 August: 26.
Comic Strip, The (1981), *The Comic Strip* [LP], UK: Springtime Records.
Connolly, Billy (1972), *Live!* [LP] UK: Transatlantic Records.
Connolly, Billy (1974a), *Solo Concert* [LP], UK: Transatlantic Records.
Connolly, Billy (1974b), *Cop Yer Whack for This* [LP] UK: Polydor.
Connolly, Billy (1975), *Get Right Intae Him* [LP] UK: Polydor.
Connolly, Billy (1979), *Riotous Assembly* [LP] UK: Polydor.
Connor, John (1989), 'Laughs in Store', *City Limits*, 4–11 May: 16–17.
Connor, John (1990), *Comics: A Decade of Comedy at the Assembly Rooms*, London: Papermac.

# References

Conway, Robert and David McGillivray (eds.) (1988), *1988 British Alternative Theatre Directory*, London: Conway McGillivray.
Cook, Peter and Dudley Moore (1976), *Derek and Clive (Live)* [LP], UK: Island Records.
Cook, William (1992), 'Learning to dish the dirt: Why are there so few women comics on the alternative circuit?' *The Guardian*, 27 August: 31.
Cook, William (1993), 'Comedy: Red Grape Cabaret, Hemel Hempstead', *The Guardian*, 9 June: 6.
Cook, William (1994), *Ha Bloody Ha*, London: Fourth Estate.
Cook, William (2001), *The Comedy Store: The Club that Changed British Comedy*, London: Little, Brown.
Coveney, Michael (1983), 'Mad Pookie 2/ Drill Hall', *Financial Times*, 19 January 1983: 21.
Craig, Tony (1975), 'Squatters' Rights?' *Daily Express*, 15 October: 10.
Crick, Olly (2018), interview with Oliver Double, by telephone, 2 March.
Critchley, Simon (2002), *On Humour: Thinking in Action*, London: Routledge.
Crompton, Colin (1979), 'USA Comics on Strike!', *The Stage*, 17 May: 3.
Cunningham, John (1983), 'Game for a laugh', *The Guardian*, 12 October: 18.
Cushman, Robert (1983), 'Good Wood', *The Observer*, 6 November: 33.
*Daily Express* (1979), 'THESE EVIL BASTARDS', 28 August: 1.
*Daily Express* (1981), 'Opinion: A leader for whom?', 22 July: 8.
*Daily Mail* (1975), 'The great squatter scandal', 18 July: 18–19.
*Daily Mail* (1979), 'Premier: Now it's war on terrorists', 28 August: 3.
*Daily Mail* (1981), 'Red Ken faces revolt', 15 October: 2.
Davies, Tristan and Hilly Janes (1985), 'Comics who stand up for themselves', *The Times*, 16 November: 11.
Davis, Kim (1991), 'The funny business', *City Limits*, 5–12 September: 16–17.
Day, Kevin (2018), interview with Oliver Double, by telephone, 11 May.
De la Tour, Andy (1982), '"Alternative" comics breaking new ground', *The Stage*, 7 January: 8.
De la Tour, Andy (2013), *Stand Up or Die*, London: Oberon Books.
De la Tour, Andy (2016), interview with Oliver Double, National Theatre, 10 February.
De la Tour, Andy (2018), interview with Oliver Double, by telephone, 25 January.
Delaney, Sean (1980), 'A political comedian', *An Phoblacht/ Republican News*, 16 February: NP.
Dembina, Ivor (2018), interview with Oliver Double, Waterloo, 2 February.
Denselow, Robin (1981), 'The Comic Strip', *The Guardian*, 18 September: 10.
Dexter, Felix (1990), interview with Oliver Double, University of Sheffield, 18 January.
Double, Oliver (1997), *Stand-Up! On Being a Comedian*, London: Methuen.
Double, Oliver (2012), *Britain Had Talent: How Variety Theatre Worked*, Basingstoke: Palgrave Macmillan.
Double, Oliver (2014), *Getting the Joke: The Inner Workings of Stand-Up Comedy* (2nd edn), London: Bloomsbury.
Douglas, Mary (1999), *Implicit Meanings* (2nd edition), London: Routledge.

## References

Dowie, John (1990), *Why I Stopped Being a Stand Up* [unpublished script].
Dowie, John (2018a), interview with Oliver Double, London NW1, 8 February.
Dowie, John (2018b), *The Freewheeling John Dowie*, London: Unbound.
Dudanski, Richard (2013), *Squat City Rocks*, London: Richard Dudanski.
Duffin, Claire and Josie Ensor (2013), 'Heard the one about Labour from a BBC comic? You probably won't', *The Sunday Telegraph*, 17 March: 17.
Dunkley, Chris (1980), 'The fatuous faces of freedom', *Financial Times*, 12 November: 17.
Eclair, Jenny (2018), interview with Oliver Double, by telephone, 21 March.
Elton, Ben (1987), *Motormouth* [LP], UK: Mercury.
Elton, Ben (1988), *Motorvation* [LP], UK: Mercury.
Elton, Ben (2018) interview with Oliver Double, London WC2E, 2 February.
Eugenecheese (2014), *Podomovski (Andrew Bailey) & John Hegley* [online video] Available at: https://www.youtube.com/watch?v=G2OpYQi_LXE (accessed 16 March 2018).
Fairhall, David (1980), '£5 billion Trident deal is agreed', *The Guardian*, 16 July: 1.
Fisher, John (1973), *Funny Way to Be a Hero*, London: Frederick Muller.
Flag, Bob (2015), *Drumshtick*, UK: Bob Evans Flag.
French, Dawn (2008), *Dear Fatty*, London: Arrow Books.
Friedman, Sam (2014), *Comedy and Distinction*, Abingdon: Routledge.
*Fundamental Frolics* (1981) [LP], UK: BBC Records.
Gibson, Ellie (2016), interview with Oliver Double, Crofton Park, 16 May.
Gill, Liz (1979), 'Maggie's grief for a hero', *Daily Express*, 31 March: 2–3.
Grahame, Peter (2018), interview with Oliver Double, by telephone, 12 September.
Green, James (1988), 'In the pink, but not in the blue', *The Stage*, 17 November: 6.
Greer, Germaine (1991), *The Female Eunuch*, London: Paladin.
Gribbin, Steve (2018), interview with Oliver Double, by telephone, 12 June.
Griffiths, Trevor ([1975] 1979), *Comedians*, London: Faber and Faber.
Grimchops (2009), *Old French & Saunders Sketch* [online video] Available at: https://www.youtube.com/watch?v=8li4LSAtsCM&t=214s (Accessed 16 March 2018).
*Guardian, The* (1980a), 'Cinemas', 3 May: 7.
*Guardian, The* (1980b), 'Entertainments Guide', June 27: 22.
*Guardian, The* (1980c), 'Bomb PC wants to get back to work', 22 May: 3.
Guttridge, Peter (1990), 'Les's laughter code', *Radio Times*, 9–15 June 1990: 18.
Hamilton, Ian (1981), 'The Comic Strip', *London Review of Books*, 3 September: 20.
Hampson, Chris (1979), 'My great grief – by the Queen', *Daily Mirror*, 28 August: 3.
Hannan, Tony (2009), *On Behalf of the Committee*, Leeds: Scratching Shed Publishing.
Hardee, Malcolm (with John Fleming) (1996), *I Stole Freddie Mercury's Birthday Cake*, London: Fourth Estate.
Hardy, Jeremy (with Kit Hollerbach) (1989), interview with Oliver Double, Sheffield, 29 April.
Hardy, Jeremy (2018), interview with Oliver Double, by telephone, 15 March.
Harrison, John and John Passmore (1979), 'Murder at the House', *Daily Mail*, 31 March: 1–2.

# References

Harron, Mary (1981a), 'Welsh volleys', *The Guardian*, 20 November: 11.
Harron, Mary (1981b), 'Rock', *The Guardian*, 27 November: 11.
Harron, Mary (1983), 'Rock', *The Guardian*, 11 February: 15.
Hay, Malcolm (1987), 'Living in London: Cabaret', *Time Out London Student Guide 1987–88*: 80.
Hay, Malcolm (1989), 'Standing orders', *Time Out*, 11–18 January: 21.
Hebert, Hugh (1979), 'A brake on nuclear traffic', *The Guardian*, 9 July: 13.
Hegley, John (1990), *Glad to Wear Glasses*, London: Andre Deutsch.
Hegley, John (1997), *The Family Pack*, London: Methuen.
Hegley, John (2016), interview with Oliver Double, University of Kent, 24 November 2016.
Heilpern, John (1979), 'Big Yin's Wee Tour', *The Observer*, 15 April: 34.
Hepple, Peter (1969), 'Nightbeat', *The Stage*, 17 July: 7.
Hepple, Peter (1971), 'Nightbeat', *The Stage*, 2 December: 5.
Hepple, Peter (1979), 'Comics' showcase', *The Stage*, 7 June: 4.
Hepple, Peter (1981), 'Alternative and unfunny', *The Stage*, 19 November: 7.
Hepple, Peter (1983), 'Ideal chance for window shopping on the Fringe', *The Stage*, 8 September: 32.
Hepple, Peter (1993), 'Comedy: The laughter business', *The Stage*, 23 September: 11–12.
Hill, Derrick and George Lochhead (1979), 'Stars on Sunday', *Daily Express*, 30 April: 4–5.
HistComPod (2017a), *A History of Comedy in Several Objects* [podcast], episode 20, 'Tony Allen compères the Comedy Store'.
HistComPod (2017b), *A History of Comedy in Several Objects* [podcast], episode 16, 'Bruce Dessau and the Comic Strip review'.
HistComPod (2017c), *A History of Comedy in Several Objects* [podcast], episode 11, 'Pit Stop Tour 1985'.
HistComPod (2017d), *A History of Comedy in Several Objects* [podcast], episode 12, 'Josie Long's Sketchpad'.
Hoggart, Simon (1992), 'Simon Hoggart', *The Observer*, 26 April: 20.
Holland, Charlie (2018), interview with Oliver Double, by telephone, 20 March.
Hughes-Hallett, Lucy (1980), 'The Other Comedians', *NOW!*, 19 December: 74–5.
Humphries, Patrick (1981), 'Have you heard the one about . . . The Comic Strip', *Melody Maker*, 17 October: 19.
Hurst, Mark (2018), interview with Oliver Double, by telephone, 2 March.
Ince, Robin (2014), 'Hey Man, it's only show business. Now light my cigar and take out the cat litter' [blog], 5 May, https://robinince.wordpress.com/2014/05/05/hey-man-its-only-show-business-now-light-my-cigar-and-take-out-the-cat-litter/ (accessed 30 June 2017).
Irwin, Ken (1972), *Laugh with the Comedians*, London: Wolfe Publishing/Independent Television Books.
Itzin, Catherine (1980), *Stages in the Revolution*, London: Methuen.
Jacobson, Howard (1997), *Seriously Funny: From the Ridiculous to the Sublime*, London: Viking.
Joans, John Paul (1968), 'Comedy in Clubs', *The Stage*, 17 October: 28.

# References

Jonze, Tim (2007) 'Laugh? I nearly DIY'd', *The Guardian* (*The Guide* section), 4 August: 4.
Kettle, James (2009), 'From boom to bust: It's no joke for Jongleurs', *The Guardian*, 17 November, https://www.theguardian.com/stage/2009/nov/17/jongleurs-comedy-clubs-standup (accessed 22 November 2018).
Kilgarriff, Michael (1979), *Make 'Em Roar: A Comedian's Handbook*, London: Samuel French.
Koestler, Arthur (1970), *The Act of Creation (Revised Danube Edition)*, London: Pan.
Kohn, Marek (1981), 'Comic cuts', *The Face*, November: 44–45.
Kravitz, Peter (1981), 'Alternative cabaret: Comic business', *On the Fringe*, 20 August: viii.
Laing, Dave (2015), *One Chord Wonders*, Oakland, CA: PM Press.
Lecoat, Jenny (1990), interview with Oliver Double, Sheffield City Hall, 21 April.
Lecoat, Jenny (2018), interview with Oliver Double, by telephone, 14 February.
Lee, Stewart (2010), *How I Escaped My Certain Fate*, London: Faber and Faber.
Lee, Stewart (2012), 'Stewart Lee: the slow death of the Edinburgh Fringe', *The Guardian*, 30 July, https://www.theguardian.com/culture/2012/jul/30/stewart-lee-slow-death-edinburgh-fringe (accessed 31 July 2017).
Lee, Stewart (2015), 'Stewart Lee: I am finding it very, very hard to be funny ...', *The Big Issue*, 5 August, https://www.bigissue.com/interviews/stewart-lee-i-finding-hard-funny/ (accessed 30 June 2017).
*Let the Children Play* (1984) [LP], UK: Panic Records.
Lewis, Jack (1979), 'Your man ... Is he really a clown?', *Daily Mirror*, 2 May: 6.
Liddle, Rod (2016), 'Light four candles to mark the death of Tory comedy', *The Sunday Times*, 3 April: 21.
Lidington, Tony (1987), 'New terms for old turns: The rise of alternative cabaret', *New Theatre Quarterly*, 3(10): 107–99.
*Live at Jongleurs* (1987) [LP] UK: Spartan Records.
Logan, Brian (2002), 'Show me the money', *The Guardian*, 26 August, https://www.theguardian.com/culture/2002/aug/26/edinburghfestival2002.edinburghfestival (accessed 31 July 2017).
Logan, Brian (2013), 'Where are all the right-wing comedians when you need them?', *The Guardian*, 12 March, https://www.theguardian.com/stage/2013/mar/12/where-are-right-wing-comedians-radio-4 (accessed 18 December 2018).
Lovett, Norman (2016), *Norman Lovett – Pyjamarama – Standup 1983* [online video], https://www.youtube.com/watch?v=Rk5zaJS3x2M (accessed 6 April 2018)
Lovett, Norman (2018), interview with Oliver Double, London W1B, 8 February.
Mackie, Lindsay (1974), 'Scot of the anarchic', *The Guardian*, 23 November: 8.
Marriott, RB (1963), 'Farewell to Max Miller', *The Stage*, 16 May: 6.
Mayall, Rik and Ade Edmondson (1998), *Live at the Comic Strip* [cassette], UK: Comedy Club.
McCoid, Bill (1989), 'Stand up and be heckled', *The Stage*, 8 June: 6.
McConville, Brigid and John Shearlaw (1984), *The Slanguage of Sex*, London: Macdonald.

# References

McErlane, Maria [AKA Maria Callous] (2018), interview with Oliver Double, by telephone, 25 May.
Medhurst, Andy (2007), *A National Joke: Popular Comedy and English Cultural Identities*, Abingdon: Routledge.
Melly, George (2008), *Revolt into Style: The Pop Arts*, London: Faber & Faber.
Melville, Pauline (2018), interview with Oliver Double, London N5, 23 April.
Merton, Paul (2014), *Only When I Laugh*, London: Ebury Press.
Merton, Paul (2018), interview with Oliver Double, by telephone, 22 May.
michtyme3 (2006a) *Kevin Turvey live stand up for Nicaragua 1983* [online video], https://www.youtube.com/watch?v=IoMH5BOolSE (accessed 16 March 2018).
michtyme 3 (2006b), *Alexei Sayle on OTT 1982* [online video], https://www.youtube.com/watch?v=SKgSe6ermkY (accessed 4 October 2018).
Midwinter, Eric (1979), *Make 'Em Laugh*, London: George Allen & Unwin.
Miller, Max (1998), *There'll Never Be Another* [CD] UK: Castle Communications.
*Monty Python's Flying Circus* (1972), 'The All-England Summarize Proust Competition', BBC1, 16 November.
Morley-Priestman, Anne (1980), 'Equity AGM – Day Two: Plight of floorshow dancers discussed; Redgrave Israel motion defeated', *The Stage*, 3 April: 5.
Muldoon, Roland (2010), interview with Oliver Double, Barbican Centre, London, 10 September.
Muldoon, Roland (2013), *Taking on the Empire: How We Saved the Hackney Empire for Popular Theatre*, Bridport: Just Press.
Muldoon, Roland (2018), interview with Oliver Double, by telephone, 18 June.
Murray, Chris (1990), 'Punch Line', *What's On*, 11 July: NP.
Myers, Kathy (1986), 'Can Beer + Sexism Survive Ben Elton?', *City Limits*, 17–24 April: 12–15.
Myerson, Jeremy (1979a), 'Comedy Store: Showcase for new comics', *The Stage*, 12 April: 3.
Myerson, Jeremy (1979b), 'Comedy Store search for bigger premises', *The Stage*, 6 December: 3.
Nichols, Peter (1985a), 'Cabaret', *Time Out*, 16–22 May: 38.
Nichols, Peter (1985b), 'Cabaret', *Time Out*, 3–9 January: 31.
Norman, Neil (1981), 'Survival of the funniest', *The Face*, February: 12–13.
Norris, Joe (2018), interview with Oliver Double, by telephone, 14 March.
North, Richard (1980), 'Have you heard the one about . . . ?', *Observer Magazine*, 23 March: 26–28.
*Observer, The* (1982), 'Sayings of the week', 18 April: 8.
O'Kelly, Lisa (1985), 'The moment for change', *The Times*, 9 April: 8.
Okin, Earl (2017), in conversation with Oliver Double, Gulbenkian, Canterbury, 2 February.
Orwell, George (1965), *Decline of the English Murder*, Harmondsworth: Penguin.
Padden, Bernard (2017), interview with Oliver Double, Royal Exchange, Manchester, 16 June.
PawsOfTheSphinx (2015) *Jim Barclay: Wonder Wally* [online video], https://www.youtube.com/watch?v=PCHbv8-1Lyc&t=1s (accessed 15 March 2018).

# References

Peters, Lloyd (2013), 'The roots of alternative comedy? – The alternative story of 20th Century Coyote and Eighties Comedy', *Comedy Studies*, 4 (1): 5–21.
Petty, Moira (1980a), 'After the success of the Comedy Store showcase – Now – Magic Store to start in West End', *The Stage*, 1 May: 3.
Petty, Moira (1980b), 'Comic Strip goes ahead after row', *The Stage*, 25 September: 3.
Petty, Moira (1981a), 'How about some alternative material?', *The Stage*, 24 September: 8.
Petty, Moira (1981b), 'Counting the cost of new wave comedy ... Comedy cabaret in collapse', *The Stage*, 17 December: 5.
Petty, Moira (1981c), 'Comedy replaces strip shows at Gargoyle Club', *The Stage*, 12 November: 4.
Petty, Moira (1981d), 'Sales ban hits award-winning Alexei Sayle', *The Stage*, 22 October: 3.
Petty, Moira (1982), 'Cabaret cocktail fizzes into life', *The Stage*, 21 January: 5.
Petty, Moira (1983), 'Londoners face £30,000 bill for peace cabaret', *The Stage*, 27 January: 4.
Philips, Michael (1984), 'Racist acts and racist humor', *Canadian Journal of Philosophy*, 14(1): 75–96.
Pile, Stephen (1980), 'Atticus in Edinburgh', *The Sunday Times*, 24 August: 24.
Pile, Stephen (1983), 'Oh *that* Rik Mayall', *Sunday Times Magazine*, 20 March: 31–4.
Planer, Nigel (with Roberta Green) (2018), interview with Oliver Double, London SE1, 3 May 2018.
Porter, Robert (1983), '"Thatcher-matazz!"', *Daily Mail*, 6 June: 9.
*Punch* (1979), 'Discoed to Death? .. Bored to Tears?' [advertisement], 13 June: 1060.
Quantick, David (1984), 'Swingeing London', *NME*, 24 March: 49.
Quirk, Sophie (2016), 'Preaching to the converted? How political comedy matters', *Humor*, 29(2): 243–60.
Quirk, Sophie (2018), *The Politics of British Stand-Up Comedy*, Basingstoke: Palgrave Macmillan.
Rayner, Jay (1989), 'Cracks in the cabaret Clubs', *The Observer* (Section 5: Observer in London), 16 April: 18–19.
Revell, Nick (2017), interview with Oliver Double, London EC1, 23 November.
Rodgers, Peter (1982), 'Banks also fall victim to invasion', *The Guardian*, 6 April: 19.
Rosen, Nick (1983), 'Being beastly to the bourgeoisie', *The Guardian*, 6 August: 8.
Rosengard, Peter (2017), interview with Oliver Double, Claridge's, London, 27 April.
Rough Theatre (1977), *Rough Theatre Plays*, London: Open Head Press.
Rouse, Rose (1984), 'Girls on Top', *The Face*, April: 38–9.
Rush, Pat (1984), 'Cast New Variety', *The Stage*, 5 January: 5.
Sadowitz, Jerry (1988), *The Total Abuse Show* [VHS], UK: Virgin.
Sahl, Mort (1958), *At Sunset* [LP], USA: Fantasy.
Sahl, Mort (1959), *1960 or Look Forward in Anger* [LP], USA: Verve Records.
Sahl, Mort (1976), *Heartland*, New York: Harcourt Brace Jovanovich.
Sarler, Carol (1987), 'Comedy Story', *London Daily News*, 27 February: 32–3.
Sarler, Carol (1989), 'Standing up to be counted', *Festival Guardian*, 29 July: 7.
*Saturday Live: The Best of Series Two* (2008) [DVD], UK: Granada Ventures.
Saunders, Jennifer (2014), *Bonkers*, London: Penguin.

# References

Savage, Jon (1997), *Time Travel*, London: Vintage.
Savage, Jon (2009), *The England's Dreaming Tapes*, London: Faber & Faber.
Saville, Ian (2018), interview with Oliver Double, by telephone, 2 March.
Sayle, Alexei (ND), *The Alexei Sayle Pirate Video* [VHS], UK: Springtime/ Videospace.
Sayle, Alexei (1982), *Cak!* [LP], UK: Springtime Records.
Sayle, Alexei (1983), *Live at Theatre Royal, Nottingham* [bootleg audio cassette, BSUCA].
Sayle, Alexei and Oscar Zarate (1987), *Geoffrey the Tube Train and the Fat Comedian*, London: Methuen.
Sayle, Alexei (1998), *Live at the Comic Strip* [audio cassette], UK: The Comedy Club.
Sayle, Alexei (2003), interview with Oliver Double, 21 November.
Sayle, Alexei (2013), 'Alexei Sayle: "I'm still full of hate"', *The Guardian*, 22 January, https://www.theguardian.com/stage/2013/jan/22/alexei-sayle-still-full-hate (accessed 18 December 2018).
Sayle, Alexei (2015), *Talking Comedy* (live interview with Oliver Double), Assembly Rooms, Edinburgh, 20 August.
Sayle, Alexei (2016), *Thatcher Stole My Trousers*, London: Bloomsbury Circus.
Sayle, Alexei (with Linda Sayle) (2017), interview with Oliver Double, London WC1, 23 November.
Sayle, Alexei (2019), interview with Oliver Double, by telephone, 7 March.
Schaffer, Gavin (2016), 'Fighting Thatcher with comedy: What to do when there is no alternative', *Journal of British Studies*, 55 (2): 374–97.
Shearman, Colin (1985), 'Weed that pulls you up', *The Guardian*, 31 May: 13.
Short, Robert (1980), *Dada & Surrealism*, London: Octopus.
Silverton, Pete (1980), 'Hello John, Got a New Motor?', *Sounds*, 27 December: 14 [BSUCA].
Smith, Arthur (2009), *My Name is Daphne Fairfax*, London: Arrow Books.
smorodina (2009), *Kevin McAleer on Friday Night Live* [online video], https://www.youtube.com/watch?v=9FMjCB5-xw8&t=1s (accessed 16 March 2018).
*South Bank Show, The* [TV] (1993), ITV, 5 December.
Spencer, Charles (1981), 'Humour', *New Standard*, 31 March, NP [BSUCA].
*Stage, The* (1968), 'Waitresses/ Personality Girls' [advertisement], 19 December: 18.
*Stage, The* (1976), 'More plays in performance', 23 September: 37.
*Stage, The* (1978), 'Current production', 31 August: 12.
*Stage, The* (1979a), 'Comedians Wanted', [advertisement], 29 March: 22.
*Stage, The* (1979b), 'The Comedy Store', [advertisement], 17 May: 43.
*Stage, The* (1979c), 'The Comedy Store', [advertisement], 24 May: 29.
*Stage, The* (1979d), 'Comedy Store off to a great start – New home for US-style showcase?' 31 May: 3.
*Stage, The* (1980a), 'Threepenny Theatre', 6 March: 13.
*Stage, The* (1980b), 'The Comic Strip' [advertisement], 30 October: 30.
*Stage, The* (1980c), 'Production news', 8 May: 28.
*Stage, The* (1981a), 'Only an alternative to the real thing', 24 December: 10.

## References

*Stage, The* (1981b), '. . . Losing out on the Last Laugh', 17 December: 5.
*Stage, The* (1981c), 'A cabaret alternative', 19 March: 3.
*Stage, The* (1981d), 'Comic Strip to play fleapits', 27 August: 4.
*Stage, The* (1982a), 'The Store goes gay', 7 January: 3.
*Stage, The* (1982b), 'Recruitment drive for variety members', 8 April: 3.
*Stage, The* (1982c), 'And now for the new wave variety', 21 January: 3.
*Stage, The* (1982d), 'GLC gives "New Variety" boost', 12 August: 29.
*Stage, The* (1983a), 'Comedy Store set to re-open in Leicester Sq.', 24 February: 5.
*Stage, The* (1983b), 'Performers benefit from new showcase', 3 February: 4.
*Stage, The* (1984), 'Agents and Managements' [small ads], 31 May: 25.
*Stage, The* (1985), 'End of the road?' 17 October:, 3.
*Stage, The* (1988), 'An unfunny alternative', 24 March: 16.
*Stage, The* (1989), 'Store celebrates with Whitbread', 4 May: 3.
*Stage, The* (1990), 'Thompson to ban offensive jokes', 15 February: 3.
Steed, Maggie (2018), interview with Oliver Double, by telephone, 7 February.
Steel, Mark (1996), *It's Not a Runner Bean*, London: Do-Not Press.
Steel, Mark (2018), interview with Oliver Double, by telephone, 2 March.
Stuart, Keith (2014), 'How to survive 100 gigs as a standup: Ellie Gibson's comedy crash course', *The Guardian*, 30 May, https://www.theguardian.com/stage/2014/may/30/standup-ellie-gibson-comedy-crash-course-eddie-izzard (accessed 2 November 2017).
*Sunday Times Magazine* (1981), 'Alexei: Sold out?', 8 November: 9.
Sweeting, Adam (1982), 'Behind the scenes, beside the sea', *Melody Maker*, 27 March: 20–21.
Taylor, Steve (1982a), 'Talking Turvey with Rik Mayall', *The Face*, January: 28–30.
Taylor, Steve (1982b), 'On yer bike, commie', *The Face*, December: 16–19.
Taylor, Steve (1983), 'Spilling the lentils', *The Face*, February: 42–43.
Thatnuttysound (2016), *Fredderick Benson* [online video], https://www.youtube.com/watch?v=v0cq-BS8PKo (accessed 6 April 2018).
*The Comic Strip* (1981), dir. Julien Temple [film], UK: Gladiole Films.
*There Was This Fella . . .* (1971), ITV, 7 December.
Thomas, Mark (2015a), *Linda Smith Lecture*, Gulbenkian Theatre, 12 May.
Thomas, Mark (2015b), *Talking Comedy* (live interview with Oliver Double), Assembly Rooms, Edinburgh, 16 August.
Thomas, Mark (2018), interview with Oliver Double, Gulbenkian Theatre, Canterbury, 5 April.
Thorncroft, Antony (1980), 'The Comic Strip', *Financial Times*, 10 October: 19.
Thorne, Steve (1979), 'One about sex and foreigners please and can you wrap up the bad ones . . . .?', *Performance Magazine*, June: 12.
Tickell, Tom (1979), 'Comedy of errors', *The Guardian*, 21 May: 2.
*Time* (1959), 'NIGHTCLUBS: The Sickniks', 13 July: 42–4.
*Time* (1960), 'Comedians: The Third Campaign', 15 August: 56–60.
*Time Out* (1979a), 'Theatre: Fringe Shows & Events', 30 November–6 December: 91.
*Time Out* (1979b), 'Theatre: Fringe Shows & Events', 7–13 September: 29.
*Times, The* (1981), 'Livingstone says IRA are not criminals or lunatics', 13 October: 1.

## References

TonyGemail (2010), *CAST 1967 – 2005 Pt.3 'Reds Under The Bed' + PIT DRAGON* [online video], https://www.youtube.com/watch?v=TkW40B5MUfM (accessed 4 October 2018).

Towler, James (1970), 'Yorkshire relish', *The Stage*, 6 March: 4.

Trimmer & Jenkins (1981) *Live! From London's Fabulous Comic Strip* [LP], UK: Charisma.

Trueman, Matt (2013), 'Peter Kay sees off Michael McIntyre and John Bishop to top comedy rich list', *The Guardian*, 28 May, https://www.theguardian.com/stage/2013/may/28/peter-kay-tops-comedy-rich-list (accessed 18 December 2018).

VHS Video Vault (2015), *John Hegley on Clive Anderson Talks Back* [online video], https://www.youtube.com/watch?v=edQ90jtp_LU (accessed 23 August 2018).

*Vox* (1993), 'You Thieving Get!' 1 September: 68–9.

Waller, JJ (2016), interview with Oliver Double, Brighton, 19 July.

Ward, Christopher (1975), 'Where ever will these squatters squat next?', *Daily Mirror*, 17 January: 7.

Ward, Don (2018), interview with Oliver Double, London WC2H, 2 February.

Ward, Tony (1984), 'Jim Barcley' [sic], *Coaster*, February: 11 [BSUCA].

Watson, John (1982), 'CPGB (M-L) COMEDY!', *NME*, 18 December: 39.

White, Michael (1981), 'Afghan tour freedom claim by MPs', *The Guardian*, 5 January: 20.

Williams, Ben (2012), 'The original alternative', *Time Out*, 5 January: 56.

Williams, Heathcote (1978), 'Corrugated iron in the soul: The community plays of Rough Theatre', *Theatre Quarterly*, 8(29): 3–6.

Williams, Michael (1984), 'The new stand-up, put-down comics', *The Sunday Times*, 7 October: 39.

Wilmut, Roger and Peter Rosengard (1989), *Didn't You Kill My Mother-in-Law?*, London: Methuen.

Wood, Victoria (1983), *Lucky Bag* [LP], UK: Elecstar.

*Young Ones, The* (1984) [TV], Series 2, episode 2, 'Cash', BBC2, 15 May.

# INDEX

ADC Theatre, Cambridge 100, 132, 138, 142, 150, 151, 163, 177
Albany Empire 29, 66, 179
Allen, Dave 26–7
Allen, Keith 3, 36, 45, 58, 77, 155, 159
  Alternative Cabaret 4, 47
  challenging audiences 155, 158–61
  giving up alternative comedy 162, 191
  influence of 11, 91–2
  playing with form 92, 101, 111–12
  theatre background 11, 29
Allen, Tony 1, 8, 27, 36, 43, 55, 75, 89, 120, 130, 159, 163, 177
  Alternative Cabaret 47–52, 64, 132
  anarchism 6, 11, 34, 47–8, 137–8, 171
  attitude to arts funding 50, 67
  attitude to working men's club comedy 20, 95, 107
  compèring the Comedy Store 142–9
  Edinburgh Fringe 64, 131
  folk comedy 24, 26
  influence of 11, 44–5, 46, 60
  influence of Lenny Bruce on 18, 19, 119
  learning craft 87, 91
  non-sexist non-racist ethos 46, 168–9
  playing with form 96, 107, 155
  squatting 33, 137–8
  television 58, 116–17
  term 'alternative comedy' 5–6
  theatre background 29, 31–2, 34
  worldview 118, 131, 137–8, 165, 174, 175, 179, 186
Alternative Cabaret 36, 55, 59, 64, 107, 122, 155
  commercial success 51–3, 56, 58
  Edinburgh Fringe 52, 177
  Elgin 34, 48–9
  ethos 49–51, 166
  formation 47–8, 191
  Goldsmiths College show 160
  influence of 46, 60, 61

material performed with 100, 120, 132, 135, 153–4, 165
name 4, 6, 7
Alternative Comedy Memorial Society 200
Arts Council 27, 47, 50, 67, 68, 82, 89

Bailey, Andrew 80, 113–16, 126, 201
Barclay, Jim 8, 11, 45, 62, 143, 145, 159, 194
  Alternative Cabaret 48, 49, 50, 52, 64, 142, 160
  audience interaction 150, 151, 162–3
  benefit gigs 179, 180, 181, 185
  *Barclay's Birthday Cabaret* 201–2
  *Four Minutes to Midnight* 77–8
  learning craft 90–1
  'Marxist-Leninist comedian' 163–5, 188
  metajokes 100, 103, 106–7, 108
  persona 129
  politics 46, 171, 172–4, 175, 186
  theatre background 29
Bat, Tim 32, 70, 75, 97
Belt and Braces Roadshow 30, 43
Bergman, Martin 62–3
bisociation 108–9, 110, 120
Bobinska, Monika 134, 158
*Boom Boom Out Go the Lights* 1, 58, 79, 116–17, 159–60, 177
Boulevard Theatre (Raymond Revuebar) 3, 16, 54, 56, 57, 162
Brand, Jo 80, 127–8, 134, 156–7
*Brave New Comedy* 76–7, 78
Brecht, Bertolt 31, 92–4, 104, 116, 124–5, 203
Brown, Arnold 36, 43, 60, 119, 191, 201
  *Brown Blues* 76
  Comic Strip 53, 55, 56, 57, 64
  comic style 132–3
Brown, Roy 'Chubby' 183, 197
Bruce, Lenny 15–16, 18–19, 22, 23, 35, 86, 119, 145, 203

# Index

Callous, Maria *see* McErlane, Maria
Campaign for Nuclear Disarmament (CND) *see* nuclear disarmament
Carrott, Jasper 24, 25, 26, 35, 116, 121
CAST New Variety 62, 77, 135
    audiences at New Variety venues 169
    CAST as a theatre company 29, 68
    factor in the spread of alternative comedy 64, 67–71, 82
    New Variety Cabaret Agency 73, 74
    support for the miners' strike 179, 180–1
Christie, Bridget 198, 201, 202
Clarke, John Cooper 35, 111
Clary, Julian (AKA Joan Collins Fan Club) 65, 80, 119, 129, 136, 137–8
Cocker, Cliff 31
Combo Passé 3, 48, 50
*Comedians* (Trevor Griffiths play) 35–6
*Comedians, The* (TV series) 20, 58
Comedy Cabaret (Boulevard Theatre) 3, 16, 162
Comedy Store, the (London) 73, 88, 165
    Alexei Sayle at 94, 130, 203
    anniversary shows 191, 201
    audience 140, 142–9, 161, 184
    bringing together key performers 43–4, 51
    comparisons with other venues 48, 54, 56, 65, 67, 70, 78
    early years 29, 39–41, 64
    factions emerging from 5, 47, 53, 61
    interest of TV in 58–9, 80
    gong 42, 45, 46, 141, 143–9, 161
    non-sexist non-racist policy 46–9
    opening 4, 6, 27, 37–9, 95, 164, 168
    playing with form at 26, 113, 114, 125–6, 159
    political material at 172–3, 174, 177–8
    post-Gargoyle years 62–3
    pre-alternative performers at 90, 91
    showcase for new talent 41–3, 51
    Tony Allen at 18, 32, 87, 142–9
Comedy Store, the (Los Angeles) 38, 39, 89
Comic Strip, the 3, 30, 64, 78, 91, 184
    character comedy at 122–6, 132
    Comic Strip LP 27, 56, 57
    guest acts at 28, 33, 55–6
    influences on 24
    material performed at 85, 95, 101–2, 103–4, 106, 116, 133
    opening 53–4
    press coverage 5, 7, 32, 47, 92, 131, 155–6, 168
    structure of show 54–5
    success of 56, 57–8, 60–1, 79
    *The Comic Strip Presents . . .* 12, 59, 80
    tour 57
Connolly, Billy 24, 25–6, 35, 78, 116, 121, 132
Connor, John 75, 191
Cook, Peter 23, 167, 182
Cook, William 36, 67, 119, 131, 132, 166
Cornes, Lee 43, 46, 168–9
Cresswell, Addison 73–4, 81, 193
Crick, Olly 70, 97
Critchley, Simon 95, 100, 102, 112, 116, 172, 176
Crown and Castle cabaret 62, 65, 169

Davidson, Jim 20, 152, 183, 197
Dawson, Les 45, 196
Day, Kevin 90, 194–5
de la Tour, Andy 8, 11, 58, 82, 91, 92, 149
    Alternative Cabaret 47, 48, 50, 51, 53
    American influences 16, 18, 19
    Arts Council-funded trip to USA 89–90
    Belt and Braces 30, 43
    Comedy Cabaret 3, 16, 162
    comedy trade union 62–4, 66
    Edinburgh Fringe 52, 75–6, 194
    joke theft 119, 120
    material on Northern Ireland 176–8
    politics 46, 166, 179, 184, 187–8
Dembina, Ivor 71, 72–3, 76, 81, 193
Derek and Clive (Peter Cook and Dudley Moore) 23–4
Dexter, Felix 76, 154, 192
DIY comedy 199, 200, 201
DIY ethos 34–5, 49, 50, 61, 63, 65, 71, 73, 81–2, 193
Douglas, Mary 99, 158
Dowie, John 27–8, 35, 88, 121, 131, 180
Downstairs at the King's Head 97, 193, 199

Earth Exchange 62, 65, 142
Eclair, Jenny 67, 76, 87, 161
Edinburgh Fringe 27, 82, 88, 131, 149, 174, 201
    *Alternative Cabaret* 52, 61, 64, 177

# Index

dominance of comedy at 193-4
factor in spread of alternative comedy 75-6, 82
financial aspects of 194
*Four Minutes to Midnight* 77-8
*Late Night Alternative* 5, 52, 130, 203
Edmondson, Ade 42, 78, 80, 194
  Comic Strip 58, 64
  *The Young Ones* 58, 78
20th Century Coyote 2, 24, 53, 76, 102-4, 106
Enterprise Allowance Scheme 1, 9-10, 67, 81
Elgin, the 5, 48-9, 51, 54, 61, 88, 149
  101ers residency 34
  Alexei Sayle at 92-4
  Andy de la Tour at 120, 177-8
  audience 48, 54, 93-4, 142, 184
  financial aspects 49, 53
  Maggie Steed at 135
  Tony Allen at 19, 171
Elton, Ben 1, 3, 35, 64, 112, 196
  Comedy Store 145-6, 148, 149
  criticism of 2, 81, 158
  Manchester University connections 24, 53
  persona 128
  politics 165-6, 180, 181, 182, 185, 186-7
  *Saturday Live* 80-1, 128
  solo tours 81, 151-2
  Spain, performance at resorts in 82
  *Standup Comedy* 75-6, 194
  stand-up debut 55
  Thatcher material 166-7

Falklands War 10, 165, 174-5, 186, 187
Fanshawe, Simon 76, 136
feminism 45, 64, 135-6, 156-7, 169, 171, 172
Flag, Bob 4, 43, 48, 64
folk comedians 24-6, 28, 35, 116, 121, 132, 134
French and Saunders
  alternative comedy circuit 64
  Comic Strip 55, 56
  material 126-7
  performance 88, 93, 169
  television 59, 80
French, Dawn 56, 59, 126-7, 166

Gibson, Ellie 194, 195, 202
Goldsmiths College 160

Goodman, Paul 43, 64, 143
Grahame, Peter 193, 199
Greater London Council (GLC) 10, 33, 34, 68-9, 176, 187
Greatest Show on Legs, the 5, 29, 65, 75, 143, 201
Gribbin, Steve 65, 67, 161, 202

Hackney Empire 66, 69-70
Half Moon Theatre 29, 68, 184
Hamilton, Ian 54, 155-6, 168
Hardee, Malcolm 5-6, 7, 29, 43, 65, 161
Hardy, Jeremy 195, 201, 202
  audiences, views on 142, 169
  changes in comedy circuit 96, 191-2, 196
  early gigs 73
  influences on 27
  Off the Kerb 74
  persona 128-9
  politics 165, 180, 183, 185, 187, 197-8
Hay, Malcolm 141, 191, 193, 200
heckling 141
  Comedy Store 45, 146-8
  dealing with 149-50, 156, 159, 160-1, 202
  supportive 118
  Tunnel Palladium 65, 162
Hegley, John 32, 88, 91, 198, 201
  Comedy Store 143, 146-7, 148
  persona 128, 133-4
Hemingford Arms 65, 118, 149, 163, 165
Holland, Charlie 96-7
Hurst, Mark (AKA Mark Miwurdz) 26, 33, 35, 70, 74, 169, 180
Hutchins, Roy 169, 180

Idle, Eric 23, 25
Ince, Robin 195, 199-200
Irish Republic Army (IRA) 176, 178
Izzard, Eddie 195, 198

Jackson, Paul 58, 59, 60
Joan Collins Fan Club *see* Clary, Julian
Joans, John Paul 20, 21-2, 36, 60
Jongleurs 65-6, 107-8, 154, 184, 196, 198, 199-200, 201

Kinnie, Kim 43, 90
Kinnock, Neil 181, 182
Koestler, Arthur 108-9

220

# Index

Lecoat, Jenny 33, 65, 75, 80
   audiences, views on 142, 169
   changes in comedy circuit 96, 192
   feminism 135-6, 171
   folk comedy 25
   innovation on comedy circuit 114, 117
   Moving Parts 29
   politics 179, 180, 183
   standards of performance 87, 95
   *Three of a Different Kind* 76
*Late Night Alternative* 52, 75
Lee, Stewart 27, 194, 195, 198, 200, 201
Lidington, Tony 32, 152, 155
Livingstone, Ken 10, 176, 178
Long, Josie 198, 199, 200, 201, 202
Long and the Short of It, the 32, 70, 96, 97, 162
Lovett, Norman 20, 33, 76, 112-13, 116, 201

McAleer, Kevin 113, 116
McErlane, Maria (AKA Maria Callous) 87, 88, 134, 162
McIntyre, Michael 73, 193, 197
McIntyre, Phil 78, 81, 82, 185
Manning, Bernard 20, 21, 22, 23, 99, 180
Mayall, Rik 4, 23, 42, 50, 78, 81, 82
   alternative comedy, views on 7, 21, 47
   benefit gigs 179, 180, 181
   Comic Strip 53, 64, 126
   Edinburgh Fringe 75-6, 194
   Kevin Turvey 121, 124-5
   poet character 58, 123-4, 125, 126
   television work 1, 58, 80
   20th Century Coyote 2, 24, 102-6
Marxism 40, 62, 137, 151, 154, 156, 163-4, 171, 172
Melly, George 37, 60
Melville, Pauline 11, 36, 58, 109, 119, 191, 201
   Alternative Cabaret 4, 50, 51, 52, 64
   audiences 141, 184
   benefit gigs 68, 179, 180, 186, 187
   Edie 120, 122, 123, 153-4, 175
   politics 40, 137, 164, 166, 171, 174-5
   Sadista Sisters 30-1
Merton, Paul 80, 114, 119, 151, 195, 201
   *Brave New Comedy* 76-7
   comedy trade union 63, 64
   influences on 23, 36
   material 95, 107-8, 109

microphone stand, difficulties with 88-9
metacomedy 11, 100, 102, 103, 105-6
Midwinter, Eric 164, 172, 176
Miller, Max 26, 42, 121
miners' strike (1984-5) 9, 179-81, 186, 195, 197
Miwurdz, Mark *see* Hurst, Mark
Monkhouse, Bob 4, 196
Monks, Bill 5, 31
*Monty Python's Flying Circus* 11, 23, 24, 25, 56
Muldoon, Roland 29, 48, 67-71, 81, 168, 180-1

non-sexist no-racist ethos 46, 50, 156, 166, 168, 170
Norris, Joe 74, 162, 202
Northern Ireland 21, 26, 46, 176-8, 187
nuclear disarmament 6-7, 107, 172-4, 175, 179, 187
   Campaign for Nuclear Disarmament (CND) 10, 181, 195

Off the Kerb 64, 73-5, 82, 162, 180, 193, 202
Orwell, George 182, 187
Outer Limits, the 18, 30, 33, 44, 53, 58, 123, 166

Padden, Bernard 45, 136, 142, 180
Pentameters Theatre 88
   audience 149-50, 161
   material performed at 107, 111-12, 116-17, 122, 154, 175
   Outer Limits and 20th Century Coyote show 53
Peters, Lloyd 2, 24
Philips, Michael 183-4
Planer, Nigel 58, 76, 78, 119, 181
   Comic Strip 53-5, 57, 60-1, 64
   influences 18, 23
   Neil 30, 44, 58, 123, 125-6, 201
   Outer Limits 28, 30, 44, 122-3
   *Rank* 29-30, 44
Pranksters 71-3, 74, 114, 193
Pryor, Richard 16, 18, 19
public funding of the arts 49-50, 67-9.
   *See also* Arts Council
punk
   art school influence 111
   audience confrontation 57, 152

# Index

direct links with alternative comedy 33, 34
DIY ethos 34–5, 65, 71, 74, 81, 155
influence on alternative comedy 26, 32–3, 34–5, 191
influence on *The Young Ones* 12, 58
musical form 10, 86

racist jokes 7, 11, 15, 21, 25, 89, 149, 158, 161, 196, 203
Randolph the Remarkable (AKA Philip Herbert) 80, 98–9, 100
Rappaport, David 114, 187
Raymond Revuebar *see* Boulevard Theatre
Revell, Nick 5, 24, 80, 87, 170, 201
  *Brave New Comedy* 76–7
  influences 18–19, 20, 23
  John Revell 143, 146
  politics 171, 185–6
Richardson, Peter 59, 60
  Comic Strip 24, 28, 54, 55, 56, 57, 58, 64
  Outer Limits 44, 53, 122–3
  *Rank* 29–30
Rosengard, Peter 4, 38–41, 42, 43, 44, 46, 59, 140
Rough Theatre 31–2, 34, 51

Sadowitz, Jerry 170
Sahl, Mort 16–18, 21, 22, 132
Sarler, Carol 141, 193
*Saturday Live* (also *Friday Night Live*) 1, 79–81, 98, 113, 114–15, 128, 135–7, 186–7
Saunders, Jennifer 56, 91, 126–7, 169, 194
Saville, Ian 29, 68, 166, 180, 183, 184, 202
Sayle, Alexei 4, 8, 59, 64, 160, 196, 203
  Alternative Cabaret 5, 36, 48, 50, 52, 107
  attitude to arts funding 49–50, 67
  Comedy Store 40, 42–3, 44, 46, 47, 60
  Comic Strip 27, 53–4, 55, 57
  confrontational attitude 95, 112, 129–30, 152, 155–8, 159, 161
  Edinburgh Fringe 52, 76
  influences 18, 23, 25, 26, 35, 90
  persona 121, 129, 130–1
  playing with form 7, 85–6, 91–4, 101–2, 116
  politics 165, 166, 167, 171, 172, 179, 182, 183
  return to stand-up 87, 201, 202
  solo tours 78–9, 81, 82, 184, 185

surrealism 109–10, 111
television 11, 58, 79
*The Alexei Sayle Pirate Video* 15–16
Threepenny Theatre 31, 34, 87, 119
Schaffer, Gavin 2, 25–6, 165, 167–8
Scummy Mummies 194, 202
Shore, Cliff (AKA Cliff Shaw) 42, 43, 64
Skint Video 65, 67, 180, 202
Smith, Arthur 63, 75, 192, 200–1
  Comedy Store, memories of 38, 174
  influences on 20, 23
  politics 167, 169, 182
squatting 6, 33–5, 48, 49, 51, 81, 137–8, 171
Soan, Martin 5–6, 7, 29
*Standup Comedy* (Edinburgh Fringe show) 75–6, 194
Steed, Maggie 48, 59, 87, 135, 136, 159, 179, 180
Steel, Mark 65, 76, 194
  influences 19, 23, 27
  politics 154, 165, 167, 169–70, 179, 182–3, 197, 198
Stephenson, Pamela 56, 143, 148
street theatre 57, 70, 71
  Rough Theatre 31, 51
  street performers in alternative cabaret 32, 35, 63, 64, 68, 70, 199
  street techniques in alternative cabaret 96–8, 99
Strummer, Joe 34, 35, 48
surreal comedy 11, 23, 30, 92, 94, 107–10, 111, 122, 126

Talk of the North 15, 18, 20
Thatcher, Margaret
  Airey Neave murder 176–7
  anti-Thatcher left 141
  election of 9, 11, 37
  ideology 9, 37, 59
  material about 47, 53, 120, 165–7, 168, 170, 173–4, 178
  policies 9–10, 50, 132
Thomas, Mark 73, 90, 96, 139, 161, 198–9
Threepenny Theatre 5, 31, 34, 87, 119
Tickell, Tom 42, 140
Tunnel Palladium 65, 161–2
20th Century Coyote 76
  Comic Strip 53, 58
  material 102–6, 116
  student origins 2, 24

## Index

Waller, JJ 32, 68, 70, 75, 97, 162, 179
Ward, Don 38–41, 44, 45, 46, 63, 113
Wear, Peter 43, 48, 64
White, Michael 56, 59
Williams, Heathcote 31, 33
Williams, Robin 16, 18, 88
Wood, Victoria 27, 28
working men's clubs (WMCs) 40
   alternative comedians performing in 179–80
   comedy performed in 11, 20–2, 60, 121, 132, 134, 197, 199
   influence on alternative comedy 85, 90
   lack of originality 20–1, 24, 26, 99, 109, 116, 119, 120
   negative influence on alternative comedy 18, 28, 35, 86
   parodies of WMC comedy 15–16, 101, 107, 203
   racist comedy 21, 46, 132, 134, 149, 196

*Young Ones, The*
   effect of success 1, 12, 59, 60, 79, 80
   live tour 78
   origin of characters 30, 58, 94, 123

Zephaniah, Benjamin 35, 68, 179, 180, 187

www.ingramcontent.com/pod-product-compliance
Lightning Source LLC
Chambersburg PA
CBHW072231290426
44111CB00012B/2052